The German Novel
in the Twentieth Century

The German Novel
in the Twentieth Century

Beyond Realism

edited by
DAVID MIDGLEY

EDINBURGH UNIVERSITY PRESS
ST. MARTIN'S PRESS NEW YORK

© Edinburgh University Press, 1993
Edinburgh University Press Ltd
22 George Square, Edinburgh

Typeset in Linotron Ehrhardt
by Koinonia Ltd, Bury, and
printed and bound in Great Britain
by The University Press, Cambridge

A CIP record for this book is available from the British Library

ISBN 0 7486 0421 9

First published in the United States of America in 1993

Printed in Great Britain

ISBN 0-312-10062-0

Library of Congress Cataloging-in-Publication Data applied for.

Contents

Notes on Contributors

ANDREA CERVI is a former Fellow of Newnham College, Cambridge. Her doctoral dissertation on the artistic relationship between Rainer Maria Rilke and Jens Peter Jacobsen was completed in 1986.

JOHN GUTHRIE is a Fellow of New Hall, Cambridge. His publications include a study of Annette von Droste-Hülshoff, and another of the dramas of Lenz and Büchner.

DUNCAN LARGE is a Lecturer in the German Department at the University of Swansea. He is currently completing his doctoral dissertation on perspectivism and the novel with reference to Nietzsche, Proust and Musil, and has published several articles in this area.

DAVID MIDGLEY is a Fellow of St John's College, Cambridge, and author of a book on Arnold Zweig. He is currently preparing a book on the post-Expressionist literature of the Weimar Republic.

MICHAEL MINDEN, a Fellow of Jesus College, Cambridge, is the author of a book on Arno Schmidt, and of articles on a range of topics from the German cinema to the *Bildungsroman*.

RITCHIE ROBERTSON, a Fellow of St John's College, Oxford, has published books on Heine and Kafka. He has a specialist knowledge of German Jewish writers, and is an editor of the series *Austrian Studies*.

MARY STEWART, a Fellow of Robinson College, Cambridge, has published numerous articles on late nineteenth-century and post-1945 German narrative fiction. She is currently working on a full study of Uwe Johnson.

ANDREW WEBBER holds a joint College Lectureship at Churchill College and St Catharine's College, Cambridge. His doctoral dissertation on sexuality and identity in the works of Musil and Trakl was published in the Bithell Series of the Institute of Germanic Studies in 1990, and he is currently preparing a book on the *Doppelgänger* motif in German Romantic and post-Romantic writing.

I

Introduction
Theories and Techniques

DAVID MIDGLEY

Novel-writing in the twentieth century is a rich and varied phenomenon, and this is every bit as true of the German-speaking world as it is of other literatures. No single book could hope to give a comprehensive account of developments in the German novel between the publication of Fontane's *Effi Briest* in 1895 and that of Christa Wolf's *Kassandra* in 1983, and this volume does not pretend to do so. What it does do is to introduce the student of German, and of European literature, to some specific texts which may be seen as representative of important developments in the German novel, as well as commanding attention in their own right for the themes and issues they present. Each of the eleven chapters that follow examines the particular relationship between theme and technique which gives the novel in question its individual character. The purpose of this introduction is to map out the broad trends in narrative technique, and in theorising about the novel, establish which are essential to an understanding of how these texts relate to each other historically.

In Chapter 29 of *Effi Briest*, the male protagonist, Baron Innstetten, has killed his opponent in a duel over the love affair which his young wife Effi had unwarily become involved in some six years earlier, and reflects on the event as he travels alone by train to Berlin. In his private thoughts, which are presented to the reader in quotation marks, Innstetten persuades himself of the necessity of the retribution he has just exacted. Guilt must be atoned, he reflects, and to let the matter ride simply because an interval of years has passed would have been weak and half-hearted. The inverted commas are then closed, and we read the following statement: 'Und er richtete sich an dieser Vorstellung auf und wiederholte sich's, daß es gekommen sei, wie's habe kommen müssen.' The latter part of this sentence is reported speech: Innstetten 'repeated to himself that it had come as it had had to come'. The first part contains an ambiguity which is difficult to render in English. The verb *sich aufrichten* has the (primary) physical sense of straightening up, adopting an upright posture; but it is also commonly used in the metaphorical sense of lifting oneself up morally, of raising one's spirits, so to speak. The close connection between the moral attitude implied by the metaphor and the 'body language' expressed in the primary sense of the verb enables the statement to be read as a judgement, if not on the character's moral outlook, then at least on the nature of his personality. When all the other information we are given about Innstetten in the novel is taken into account – particularly his behaviour (in Chapter 27) on discovering the fact of his wife's earlier adultery – it is entirely consistent with the metaphor that Fontane has given us to say that Innstetten 'lacks backbone', that he is someone who needs a firm external code of propriety to confirm him in his sense of moral rectitude.

The point of highlighting this particular moment in Fontane's text here, however, is not to anticipate what Michael Minden is going to say about *Effi Briest* in the chapter that follows this one, but to establish an important truth about Fontane's narrative technique. It is scarcely a hint of psychological judgement that Fontane gives us in the statement quoted above, and even this much indication of an authorial view is rare in his novels. It is more generally characteristic of his manner of story-telling that he merely shows his reader how his characters behave, and allows the characters themselves, whether privately or in open conversation, to reflect on the implications of the situations they find themselves in and on the moral options available to them. When I referred earlier to what we are shown of Innstetten's behaviour in Chapter 27, I had in mind that his reaction on discovering the fact of his wife's adultery is to share this information in conversation with his friend Wüllersdorf – and then to insist that *because* the affair is now public knowledge, the only appropriate response he, Innstetten, can now make is to challenge his rival to a duel. As we read Fontane's text, we hear a narrating voice which is studiously reticent in the expression of any conclusion about what it has to tell, but apparently confident that its empirical observations are unequivocal, that 'the facts' can speak for themselves.

If we present Fontane's novel here as a typical example of 'Realism' in fiction, then we do so in the awareness that any such overarching label for literary practice is something of an artificial construct, and merely an aid to differentiation between one kind of practice and another: in so far as nineteenth-century authors thought of themselves as Realists, they were defining their practice and their world-view in relation to a complex set of historical tensions (Ritchie, 1961). What we are thinking of when we use the term here is a refinement of convention that had come to dominate novel-writing in the late nineteenth century. That convention amounts to a contract between author and reader to the effect that characters will, as far as possible, *only* be revealed through what they do and say. A parallel trend can be observed in the French novel of the same period, and may be summed up in a formulation which is often quoted from Flaubert, namely that the author's relationship to his work should be like that of God to creation, he should be 'everywhere present, but nowhere visible'. The clearest theoretical formulation of this convention that we find in the German context comes from a slightly younger contemporary of Fontane's, Friedrich Spielhagen. It was in a speech to the Goethe Society in 1895, the same year in which *Effi Briest* was published, that Spielhagen spelt out precisely what was to be demanded of a truly 'literary' novel, a *dichterischer Roman*. Like the epics of Homer, it should contain only active personages:

> behind whom the author so completely disappears that he may not utter the least opinion for himself, neither about the way of the world, nor about how he wishes his work as a whole or any particular situation to be interpreted, and least of all about his characters, who should reveal their personality, their intentions, their desires and beliefs through what they do or omit to do, what they say or omit to say, without the assistance of the author. (Spielhagen, 1898, p. 5)

Drawing a comparison between Goethe's *Wahlverwandschaften* and Fontane's *Effi Briest* in a later essay, Spielhagen acknowledges that Fontane comes close to his own ideal, but objects to even the slightest element of authorial description of Innstetten, for example, as an unwarranted 'intrusion' of the author into his text (Spielhagen, 1898, pp. 115–8). In short, Spielhagen represents an extreme example of a prejudice which lingered on in English literary criticism of the 1920s and 1930s in the form of a categorical preference for 'showing' over 'telling'.

Spielhagen's views on novel-writing have long been recognised not only as unduly purist and limiting, but also as distinctly naïve. The demands that he makes of the novel rest on the assumption that the social world that is being depicted can be known in its entirety, and that the simple reporting of characters' words and actions is an adequate expression of the reality of that world. Seen in a historical context, Spielhagen is a late representative of that simplistic scientific faith that is often called positivism – namely, the belief that empirical observation in itself is both an adequate and a reliable means of comprehending the world in which we live. By his insistence on 'objectivity' in the style of narration, Spielhagen in fact limits the range of what is depicted to what can plausibly be experienced by an observer who is himself part of that social world, and thus commits the novel to an extreme form of *subjectivity* (Hellmann, 1957). By comparison, Fontane shows a much subtler awareness of the significance of narrative perspective than Spielhagen, but his own narrative convention nevertheless shares this sense of limitation. If we were to imagine Fontane's narrator as a person in his own right, he would have to be someone moving in the same social circles as his characters and taking part in the same dinner-table conversations. In the subsequent development of novel-writing, particularly in the early part of the twentieth century, two things stand out above all. One is an expansion of the purview of literary expression to encompass aspects of human existence which do not readily find admission to conversations in genteel society. The other is an increasing elaboration of narrative technique, partly to accommodate that greater range of expression, and partly in reflection of a growing awareness of narration itself as something problematic.

A first step beyond the naïve dogmatism of Spielhagen is the recognition that the narrating voice we hear in a work of fiction is something distinct from the person of the author. This insight was articulated in 1910 by Käte Friedemann, in an essay which draws on the fundamental philosophical awareness that any attempt to make a statement about 'the world out there' is necessarily constrained by a subjective point of view. In the context of a work of narrative fiction, the implication is that the sense of a narrating voice belongs to the very medium through which events are communicated: you cannot have a story without the sense that someone is telling it. She expresses the point like this:

> What we are talking about is not author X who, in a more or less disguised form, is committing indiscretions towards himself and others which the historical school of literary criticism never tires of investigating; rather 'the narrator' is that authority which evaluates, feels and observes. He symbolises the perception which is familiar to us since Kant, that we do not comprehend the world as it is in itself, but as it has passed through the medium of a beholding spirit. (Friedemann, 1910, p. 26)

In effect we have already applied Friedemann's insight when discussing the kind of narrator we find in Fontane's novel, and the distinction she makes has provided the basis for much further refinement of critical discussion since her day. It is possible to distinguish further, for example, between a mode of narration which is close to the perspective of a character in the fiction ('figural'), and one that expresses a viewpoint independent of the characters ('authorial'). The terms I have used here in brackets are those of Franz K. Stanzel (1984), who has developed a subtle terminology for the analysis and differentiation of modes of narration.

The theoretical position adopted by Käte Friedemann had grown out of an awareness that techniques of novel-writing had in any case developed beyond those discrete assumptions that were commonplace in the 1890s. In particular, the early works of Thomas Mann had come to fascinate literary scholars because they evoked a rather different sense of contract between author and reader than what we saw in Fontane. Mann's first novel, *Buddenbrooks*, of 1900 already displays much subtle interplay between 'figural' and 'authorial' perspectives, creating a flexible mode of narration which can now evoke sympathy for a character's views and feelings, and now distance the reader from them. In a word, Thomas Mann had developed that complex craft of narrative irony for which he is famous. Here is an illustrative example from *Buddenbrooks*, in which we observe and experience the emotions of young Tony Buddenbrook on encountering her suitor Grünlich:

> Fräulein Buddenbrook had halted as Herr Grünlich began to speak; but her eyes, which she had half closed and which suddenly darkened, did

not raise themselves above the level of Herr Grünlich's chest, and around her mouth there lay the mocking and totally merciless smile with which a young woman measures a man and rejects him .... Her lips moved – what should she reply? Ha! It had to be a remark that would send this Bendix Grünlich reeling once and for all, that would destroy him ... but it had to be an elegant, witty, pertinent remark that would both wound and impress him ...

'The feeling is not mutual!' she said. (Buddenbrooks, Part 3, Chapter 2)

The narrating voice that we hear in this passage is 'authorial', and indeed authoritative; but it is also capable of suggesting great intimacy with the character's self-perceptions. Without abandoning that sense of external perspective indicated by the third-person narration ('what should *she* reply?'), the text simultaneously adopts the 'figural' perspective of the character – her question, her vocabulary, her aspiration, even her expletive ('Ha!'). In this particular instance, the self-evident purpose is to build up a sense of the character's inflated pretensions, of the eloquence with which she would like to express her indignation, only in order to undercut these with the banality of the reply she actually manages to utter; it is a typical example of Thomas Mann's comic technique. But the phenomenon we are looking at here is equally capable of evoking high pathos, as well as bathos, and Mann himself uses it in this way elsewhere in the same novel. It is the phenomenon that has come to be called in German *erlebte Rede*, in order to distinguish it from the traditionally recognised forms of discourse: direct speech (*direkte Rede*) and reported speech (*indirekte Rede*). In English (following the French terminology) it is often referred to as 'indirect free style' or 'free indirect speech'. It is a phenomenon which can be identified to some extent in narrative texts well before the twentieth century, but it comes to have a special significance in novel-writing from the time of Flaubert onwards, as writers look for means to convey the subtler internal workings of their characters' minds. Because it implies a narrative situation in which the reader effectively hears the voices of both character and narrator simultaneously, Roy Pascal (1977), who has conducted the fullest study yet of the phenomenon in its broad European context, gives his book the title *The Dual Voice*.

The sense of an authoritative narrating voice is something which readers of English literature will be accustomed to expect of the Realist novel throughout the nineteenth century, from Jane Austen to Arnold Bennett; and Thomas Mann may fairly be regarded as the subtlest exponent of that Realist tradition writing in German. Indeed, Mann's refinement of the Realist tradition evidently helped to stimulate a further development on the theoretical plane, because a mode of narration that is not only authoritative, but also displays an ironic self-awareness of its own mediating role lies at the heart of the theory of the novel elaborated by Georg Lukács and published in 1920. Lukács approached the form of the novel as a philosophical problem. In various earlier writings, he had interpreted the formal structures of works of literature as the means by which world cultures had expressed their particular sense of a coherent world view (Márkus, 1983). This was an argument which was easier to apply to the relatively self-contained form of the drama as it had appeared in ancient Greece, Renaissance Spain and England, or seventeenth-century France, for example; but it was much more difficult to apply it to something as diverse and loosely-structured as the novel, particularly as it had developed since the eighteenth century. Moreover, the young Lukács had an overwhelming sense that any notion of cultural unity had been increasingly eroded by that progressive fragmentation of social relations brought about by the development of the market economy since the Renaissance. In *The Theory of the Novel* he accomplished two things: firstly, he described the disintegrated condition of modern consciousness by contrast with that of earlier cultures, and secondly he described the novel as the representative literary form of the modern age. The telling of a story from a subjective point of view (or from various points of view) was an inherent feature of the novel – but by cultivating a sense of ironic self-awareness in the telling of the story, the novelist was able to reflect intellectually the fragmentation and subjectivity that characterises modern culture, and thus regain through literary expression a 'concrete totality' of cultural awareness. Drawing on the philosophy of Hegel, who had interpreted the course of history as a progress towards enhanced rational consciousness, Lukás was able to resolve his problem of identifying a literary form that revealed the sociological structure of society in the era of modern capitalism (Lukács, 1971).

It was an ingenious argument, but one which enthroned the Realist novel as the sole literary form capable of adequately expressing the nature of modern society. In a series of debates with other intellectuals and literary writers in the course of the twenties and thirties, it became increasingly apparent that, much as he favoured a radical *political* solution to society's problems, Lukács's premises committed him to a *conservative* model for literary expression in the twentieth century (Schmitt, 1973; Midgley, 1988). Given the importance that he attached to irony in his theory of the novel, we should not be surprised to find him consistently preferring Thomas Mann to more experimental contemporary authors; and he was indeed able to point to a continuing tradition of Realist representation of twentieth-century society in the works of other novelists, including Heinrich Mann and Arnold Zweig, Maxim Gorky and Romain Rolland. What Lukács's theoretical position was unable to accommodate was the variety of innovative approaches to narration which had manifested itself since about 1910, and which he could only view as symptomatic of that drift towards cultural disintegration which, he believed, artistic forms existed to overcome.

The approach of individual novelists to their task has indeed become so diverse in the twentieth century that any attempt to establish a common theoretical framework for their literary practice is bound to invite contradiction (cf. Žmegač, 1983). What we can do is to identify certain trends which allow us to distinguish the cultural climate of Modernism from what had gone before.

David Lodge, in his latest collection of essays, discusses narrative perspective as one way of distinguishing between Realism and Modernism in fiction, developing a technical vocabulary which is derived from the modern French theorist Gérard Genette, and ultimately from Plato. Whereas Realism (as we have noticed in the case of Thomas Mann) entails a delicate balance between authorial utterance (diegesis) and the reflection of observed reality (mimesis), Modernism tends to pursue mimetic methods 'to their limits' (Lodge, 1990, p. 41). This is not a new observation – except that in Lodge's case it enables him to suggest that an important indicator of what we might call 'post-modernism' in narrative fiction is, by contrast, the dominance of diegesis over mimesis. The Spanish writer Ortega y Gasset was already speaking in 1925 of a trend towards 'infrarealism' within Modernist fiction, which had led novelists such as Joyce and Proust to intensify their depiction of reality to the point where they discovered, 'lens in hand, the micro-structure of life' (Ortega y Gasset, 1968, p. 35ff.). Georg Lukács, seeking to extract an 'ideology of modernism' from the works of Kafka, Döblin, Musil, and Joyce, highlighted the loss of perspective that he saw resulting from their fascination with direct, naturalistic representation of the minutiae of personal experience (Lukács, 1963). And more traditional German literary scholarship of the 1950s also sought to account for the 'crisis' that had apparently overcome the conventions of novel-writing in the twentieth century by attributing it to such radicalised naturalism of depiction (Kayser, 1955).

It is certainly true that a refinement of psychological observation can be traced in narrative fiction around 1900, and that this refinement has consequences for the development of narrative technique. This aspect of the development of modern fiction in Europe and America is the subject of a fine study by Dorrit Cohn (1978) with the title *Transparent Minds*. If we read systematically through the stories of the Viennese author Arthur Schnitzler, for example, from 1895 to 1901, then we notice a growing intimacy in the depiction of the mental life of his characters until, in *Leutnant Gustl*, he contrives to reflect the entire action of the story through the perceiving mind of the fictional character himself. Schnitzler's command of narrative perspectives progresses through an increasingly subtle use of *erlebte Rede* until it arrives at a technique which we have come to know as 'interior monologue'. It is a technique which still appears clumsy and limited in 1901, because external occurrences are registered in the text by Gustl asking himself such questions as 'What was that?' and 'What did he say?' But by 1924, in *Fräulein Else*, Schnitzler was able to make use of the reading public's awareness of unconscious motivation, which had grown in the meantime, in order to give an engaging account of a moment of crisis and catastrophe in the life of a young woman. In this development of his narrative technique, Schnitzler was evidently stimulated by the same late nineteenth-century French text which James Joyce mentions as a precedent for his use of interior monologue in the final section of *Ulysses*, Édouard Dujardin's *Les lauriers sont coupés* (Mitchell, 1976, p. 92). We owe the very term 'interior monologue' to the literary scholar Valéry Larbaud, who interviewed Joyce in 1920, elicited from him the information about this text, and subsequently produced an edition of it. It is apparent from Larbaud's foreword to *Les lauriers sont coupés* that he shared with Ortega y Gasset the perception of Modernist developments as derived from the radicalisation of the mimetic approach, thinking of interior monologue as an extension of another kind of late nineteenth-century fiction, the diary-style *récit* (Larbaud, 1925). But to confine the discussion to superficial characteristics of narrative technique in this way is, as David Lodge clearly recognises, to overlook the more profound developments in intellectual culture which underlie literary Modernism, and which Joyce's *Ulysses* epitomises.

An earlier study by David Lodge, *The Modes of Modern Writing* (1977), takes us some distance further towards understanding the shift in ways of perceiving and representing the world that had taken place between the late nineteenth and the early twentieth centuries. Following the literary theorist Roman Jakobson, Lodge presents the stylistic devices of metaphor and metonymy as literary equivalents of particular ways in which the mind structures its awareness of reality. Metonymy, which implies the representation of an object or class of objects by one of its attributes, had been the characteristic structuring device of Realism, where individual characters and events had been taken as typical in a general way of the social world depicted. In Modernism, by contrast, metonymy can still be found at the level of detailed representation, but the manner in which the fiction is structured owes much more to perceived similarities between experiences and objects which logic would ordinarily separate: the characteristic structuring device has become metaphorical. As the discussions of individual texts in his book show, Lodge's terminology contributes much to describing the new mode of perception that characterises the novels of Virginia Woolf, to explaining the associative structure of the narrative in Proust, and to expressing the function of overarching mythical connections (and of much else besides) in *Ulysses*. In the German context, too, it has its applications. But there is a further dimension in the emergence of a distinctive Modernist literature beyond what Lodge has described, and which is perhaps more markedly apparent in the German sphere than elsewhere. That dimension is a radical questioning of the assumptions which underlie the very possibility of narrative representation of reality.

The reasons for this are complex, and relate to a variety of factors in the German intellectual tradition. We have seen how important the Kantian insight into the *mediated* nature of perception was for the theory of narration developed by Käte Friedemann in 1910. In some senses the intellectual roots of German Modernism go back to the late eighteenth century, when the early

Romantics began to respond to the material and aesthetic implications of what Kant had shown about the necessary limitations of human knowledge (cf. Frank, 1989; Bürger, 1988, p. 63f.; Petersen, 1991, p. 32). Amongst the authors discussed in the present volume, Musil, Döblin and Thomas Mann certainly derived important insights from a critical engagement with the writings of Novalis, Friedrich Schlegel, and the philosopher Schelling – but such connections lie beyond our immediate concerns here. If we are looking for a single influence which served to sharpen the intellectual self-awareness of German writers at the turn of the century, then we shall find it in Nietzsche (cf. Petersen, 1991, p. 16ff. and passim). But Nietzsche's works themselves incorporated all the diversity – and the mutual contradiction – of philosophical awareness that had been cultivated in the course of the nineteenth century. He was both an intellectual moderniser and a critic of modernity, now criticising morality and other idealist assumptions in the light of modern scientific findings, now criticising scientific thinking in the light of the integral view of life provided by religion and art. Even among those late fragments of Nietzsche's which were posthumously published under the title *Der Wille zur Macht* (The Will to Power), and falsely represented as a systematisation of his view of life, we find him emphasising that meaning (*Sinn*) is 'necessarily a matter of relationship and perspective', and that it is in the nature of language or any other means of expression 'that it merely expresses relation' (Pütz, 1963, p. 8ff.).

Nietzsche pointed the way for the creative intellects of the early twentieth century to advance, but the course that he showed them was one of critical self-awareness both towards value systems and towards the modes of linguistic expression. Precisely the registering within the text of an epistemological doubt and self-irony – which tends to be thought of in the English-speaking world as a '*post*-modernist' development has been seen as *the* distinguishing feature of European Modernism (Fokkema and Ibsch, 1987, p. 38ff.). Certainly it is the factor which enables us to speak of Thomas Mann as participating in the literary development that we are calling Modernism, at least in such later novels as *Der Zauberberg* (The Magic Mountain) of 1924 and *Doktor Faustus* of 1947. While it is no doubt true that reflexive self-consciousness can be found as a counter-current to the mimetic principle throughout the history of the novel (Dowden, 1986, p. 2), it has quite specific functions to fulfil in specific contexts – as we shall see from the chapters that follow.

We have seen three dominant trends, then, which are said to characterise the broad stream of literary Modernism: the intensification of mimetic representation, the emergence of metaphorical as opposed to metonymic structures of awareness, and a self-conscious, implicitly anti-mimetic moment in the presentation of narrated events. We should not, of course, necessarily expect all three trends to be evident in any one text, but they are subtly interrelated nevertheless. In the early works of Musil and Döblin, for example, we encounter the deliberate radicalisation of mimetic representation in opposition to a traditional, conceptualised narrative psychology, and this has the effect of turning imagery and metaphorical connections into the sustaining structures of the narrative. The later Musil, on the other hand, develops a form of authorial narration which displays all the self-consciousness of one who has witnessed the pursuit of such radical possibilities to their limits; while in Döblin's *Berlin Alexanderplatz* of 1929 we find the paradoxical phenomenon of a text which, through its technique of montage, actually combines radical mimesis with overt indicators of self-conscious narration. Even Kafka, who does not overtly express authorial self-consciousness in his texts – and is therefore peremptorily excluded by Fokkema and Ibsch from their 'Modernist' canon – nevertheless displays a sensitivity towards the way in which language itself structures consciousness which would enable us to speak of an anti-mimetic moment in his writing too, or at least of an evident acknowledgement of the limitations of mimesis. After all, not the least of reasons why Joyce's *Ulysses* is commonly thought of as the epitome of a Modernist novel is the fact that the sheer diversity of styles and 'voices' presented in the text, coupled with the very sparing use of authorial narration, *implies* a highly developed awareness that perception is a function of the medium in which it is expressed (cf. Kenner, 1978).

The most promising theoretical basis for discussing novels to have emerged in recent years is one developed between the world wars by the Russian Mikhail Bakhtin. (Written in isolation and fugitive seclusion at the height of Stalinist repression, the work in question was published for the first time in 1975, and became available in English in 1981.) In Bakhtin's view, what has distinguished the novel – ever since classical antiquity – from more clearly defined literary forms such as tragedy, lyric poetry, or the heroic epic, is its capacity for interaction with the various systems of linguistic communication that prevail in any society at any given time. Not only does it absorb the varieties of diction that occur in official and unofficial, literary and non-literary discourse into a multi-layered or 'polyphonic' composition; by virtue of the potential for parody, allusion and irony that it can command, the novel is endowed with a perennial power to challenge and subvert the orthodoxies of its time. It is also possible for these characteristics to be introduced from time to time into other genres which, in Bakhtin's term, become 'novelised' in their turn. But the novel is for him the genre *par excellence* that is capable of challenging the perceptions of the present and cultivating an openness to the future (Bakhtin, 1981). To say this is to remind ourselves, once again, that individual authors develop individual ways of responding to their sense of contemporary reality; that such a sense of reality is itself mediated through the diverse forms of linguistic utterance; and that individual novels, once published, themselves constitute elements in the perception of reality to which other writers subsequently respond. In a period when assumptions about what literary writing can and should achieve are rapidly shifting, the scope for interaction *between* authors and texts is likely to give rise to a particularly vigorous growth of diversity in the actual practice of novel-writing. That is what we see happening in the German novel of the twentieth century. That is the spirit in which we present our individual texts here.

Robert Musil, in his first novel of 1906, can be seen to be testing the limits of the assumptions upon which the conventions of Realism rest. *Die Verwirrungen des Zöglings Törleß* (Young Törless) explores the heightened sensibilities of adolescence in their heuristic (investigative) as well as their sexual dimension, raising disturbing questions about the nature of identity and the durability of moral values as it does so. The chief insight that Törless himself is able to articulate towards the end of the novel concerns the sense in which the most intimate workings of his mind and body obstinately remain a mystery to him. He has discovered an irreducible vital principle inside himself 'which thinking cannot fathom, a life which cannot express itself in words'. It was the attempt to articulate the intricate play of mental and emotional processes that led Musil into his most intensely experimental phase in the years that immediately followed. The result is a pair of extremely dense prose texts, published in 1911 under the title *Vereinigungen* (Unions), which offer a remarkable illustration of the first two aspects of that transition from Realism to Modernism that we have been discussing. Because the processes that Musil is evoking cannot be expressed directly in words, he has to describe them in terms of the physical or physiological experiences they resemble; and it is to the resulting network of metaphorical images that we have to look for the 'meaning' of what is happening to the character (Midgley, 1991). In these texts we can observe at the minutest level of composition how the pursuit of 'infrarealism', as Ortega y Gasset termed it, could lead to that reordering of perceptual structures in fiction that David Lodge has described.

Rilke's *Aufzeichnungen des Malte Laurids Brigge* (Notebooks of Malte Laurids Brigge) has acquired a certain emblematic status in histories of the German novel because of the direct way in which it poses the problem of grasping the reality of the twentieth-century world by telling stories about it. For a long time after it was published in 1910, the work was neglected by scholars and critics because it did not fit into known categories of literary analysis. It literally takes the form of 'notebooks' in which we are to imagine a young Danish aristocrat recording his impressions of the impersonal modern urban environment he is encountering in Paris, together with a variety of recollections of his personal family background, historical legends, and biblical motifs. The puzzle that this work presents to the critical imagination, then, is one of making sense of the relationships between these seemingly disparate elements. Only with the benefit of historical distance has it become possible to view the *Aufzeichnungen* as a representative literary work of its time, precisely because of the powerful expression it gives to the sense that human culture has lost its coherence, and individual life has been deprived of any unity of meaning. It is the intensity with which Rilke personally experienced this sense of loss, coupled with the vibrance of his poetical utterance, that makes the work a landmark, still, in the development of modern German fiction.

Kafka's works have come to be thought of as epitomising that alienated condition of modern humanity that Rilke was confronting. The great danger in approaching Kafka nowadays, however, is that the sense of sinister and potent mystery that he gives us has become so familiar that we pay too little attention to the precise signals that are contained in the text. The style of narration that Kafka adopted and consciously developed from 1912 onwards is one which appears to concentrate exclusively on the description of what is being done and said by the (male) central character and those around him; but this insistence on scenic representation is also an important clue to a deeper self-consciousness about the expressive potential of the fiction, and indeed of language generally. A major reason why the description of courtrooms and criminal proceedings in *Der Proceß* (The Trial) appears so uncanny to us is not just that we come to recognise it as a metaphor for something else that the central character is undergoing (and which the text itself refuses to translate into any other terms), but that it shows a constant awareness of how words and actions are open to interpretation and misinterpretation. As Ritchie Robertson argues in his chapter on *Der Proceß*, the quality of alienation that Kafka's text conveys is derived in large part from the play that it makes on the conventional expectations of Realism – the expectations that human clothing and behaviour, as well as language, will provide reliable pointers to an objective reality. It is perhaps above all with his radical sensitivity towards the conventions of fictional representation that Kafka makes his special contribution to the development of literary writing.

The human capacity for projecting fantasies in scenic fashion is also at the heart of Hesse's *Steppenwolf* novel of 1927. It cannot be claimed for Hesse, admittedly, that he ever developed that sensitivity about the representational power of language that we find in Kafka: for all that he drew on some of the most advanced psychological thinking of its time, Hesse's story-telling is consistently couched in the comforting conceptual language which more self-critical authors had already rejected before 1914. *Der Steppenwolf* nevertheless remains an envigorating text to read. On the one hand it captures that sense of cultural crisis that was prevalent in Germany after the First World War, when old value systems had collapsed along with the political structures that sustained them. And on the other hand it expresses that awareness of personality as something disunited and disparate, which is an important strand in the Modernist revolt against traditional methods of narrative representation. The chief interest of *Der Steppenwolf* in our present context lies in the fantastic dimension of its plot and imagery, and in the interplay of its symbolic motifs, for these are the means by which it evokes psychic tension and crisis.

In Döblin we meet an author who, like Musil in this respect, had quite deliberately set out to challenge the conventions of psychological narrative in the years before the First World War. Döblin is the most robustly and self-consciously avant-garde of our authors, in the sense that he continually sought to disrupt the power of cliché to mould human understanding, whether he found it in conceptual language, current popular parlance, or the comforting shape of a sequentially-told story. In his speeches and essays he had a great deal to say about the role of the novel in the modern world, but if we look to him for a developed theory of the modern novel we shall be disappointed (cf. Scheunemann, 1978). It was Döblin's purpose, at least during the years 1910–30 (the heyday of the European avant-garde), to be persistently provocative, rather than intellectually consistent. When *Berlin Alexanderplatz* was published in 1929, it inevitably invited comparison with Joyce's *Ulysses*, which had been translated into German shortly beforehand, because both novels evoked the complexity of modern urban life by means of a multiplicity of styles and voices. But while Döblin may well have been inspired by Joyce in certain respects, the montage technique that he develops is related to the positions he adopted in the cultural debates of his day, as well as to antecedents within his own works. He constructs a novel which challenges the very notion of a unifying narrative subject, but he does so for reasons which are culturally specific.

On the face of it, Musil reinstates that unifying subject in his novel *Der Mann ohne Eigenschaften* (The Man Without Qualities), the first volume of which was published in 1930. But the narrating voice that we hear in this work is one that speaks with knowledge and experience about the insights acquired by avant-garde writers and intellectuals since the turn of the century. It knows about the refinement of scientific and technological awareness in its own time, it knows about the extension of these into the domain of human psychology, and it is aware of how the nature of personal identity has become problematic as a result. It knows very well how human experience has become 'unnarratable' by comparison with that of earlier ages. But it can refer to all these things in a jovial fashion, with irony, as problems which are by now familiar to sophisticated readers. (We can measure the distance we have travelled in terms of narrative convention since the time of Fontane and Spielhagen by the observation we find in Book I, Chapter 39 of Musil's novel that no-one nowadays can even be certain that his anger is really *his* anger because so many people appear to know more about it than he does.) Musil's novel is also fully aware of the persistent role of the irrational in determining human affairs. Set in Vienna in the twelve months preceding the outbreak of the First World War, it has great scope for presenting the major political and cultural dilemmas of twentieth century Europe with the benefit of ironic hindsight. The question of an 'experimental' approach to life, on which Duncan Large focuses in his chapter on *Der Mann ohne Eigenschaften*, is a theme which links the manner in which the work is narrated to the problems of morality in the modern world which it explores.

The two works by Musil which we are presenting in this volume may be said, then, to mark the beginning and the culmination of Modernist experimentation as such in German prose fiction. Our remaining four novels are works which confront various aspects of the political convulsions which followed historically, and the combined legacy of National Socialism and Stalinism in the German-speaking world. In doing so, however, they show a heightened self-consciousness about the functioning of narrative communication which is recognisably related to the insights gained by the earlier authors we are discussing.

Modernist culture itself becomes an object of depiction in Thomas Mann's *Doktor Faustus* (1947). The central figure in the novel is a composer, Adrian Leverkühn, whose very name is a pointer to his Nietzschean heritage: it implies living dangerously. With his allusive treatment of the Faust legend in this novel, Thomas Mann creates the scope for multi-layered references to German culture and history, but it is the compositional significance of this legendary material that is of particular interest to our present discussion. In one sense, Faust's pact with the devil clearly provides a metaphorical structuring device of the kind that we have recognised as typical of Modernist works of fiction. By having the fictional composer Leverkühn express his self-perception as an artist in a composition on the subject of Faust, however, Mann contrives to combine a (Realist) reflection of Modernist tendencies with an ironic refraction of them. To complicate the picture further, the ironic awareness of the difficulties of reconstructing reality in narrative form is itself expressed in the adoption of a fictional first-person narrator. It is on the subtle interplay of conventions associated respectively with Realism and Modernism that Ritchie Robertson concentrates especially in his chapter on *Doktor Faustus*.

When Günter Grass spoke, in an essay of 1967, of Döblin as his 'teacher', he had in mind the model of an anti-classical novelist and someone who views the course of history as something inherently absurd. The novel that made him famous, *Die Blechtrommel* (The Tin Drum), published in 1959, bears him out on this score, both in its deployment of linguistic detail and in its narrative technique. Grass, too, chooses the device of a first-person narrator, but one who is characterised by a bizarre eccentricity of viewpoint: Oskar, who tells us on the first page that he is currently an inmate of a mental asylum, and whose instability of perspective is suggested also by the way that he occasionally refers to himself in the third person, claims to have made a conscious decision at the age of 3 to halt his physical growth by falling down a flight of stairs. The effect is to create multiple opportunities for jolting the reader out of complacency about the authority of narrative, about the dependability of 'factual' knowledge about the past, and even about the use of language as a referential system of communication. As a vehicle for the satirical investigation of the moral and political issues associated with National Socialism and its aftermath, this narrative device is not without its problems, as Michael Minden's chapter makes clear. But coupled as it is with inventive allusion to the human capacity for irrational fantasy and psychic projection, the work continues to command attention as a provocative evocation of the Nazi experience.

Uwe Johnson's novel *Mutmaßungen über Jakob* (Suppositions about Jakob), also published in 1959, addresses that other legacy of the Second World War, the division of Germany into East and West, with all the political tensions and uncertainties that that brought into individual lives. In adopting a rigorous technique of montage and multi-perspectival narration, Johnson also shows an affinity with Döblin, but his technique, and some of the idiosyncrasies of his language have grown out of the doubt and secretiveness of an altered and historically distinct situation. If the texture of his novel appears obsessively mysterious to us, then that is because he never loses sight of the fact that interpretation of observed reality is a never-ending process. To read Johnson is to be constantly reminded that the truths about really significant human experiences can only be reconstructed in retrospect, and by dint of relentless struggle.

Christa Wolf, finally, is writing for a world in which the patterns of enmity have become fixed. In *Kassandra* (1983) she explores the echoes of contemporary reality in the mythical representation of war in classical antiquity, in Homer's *Iliad*. Her novel is both a reinterpretation and a parable: it reconstructs the familiar account of the Siege of Troy by placing the female seer Cassandra at the centre of the male-dominated action, and it points up parallels with the great-power rivalries of recent memory in the cycle of threat and counter-threat, armament and rearmament, that characterises the mental habits of the male figures. Here is an attempt, in other words, to provide a counter-mythology for patterns of thinking which continue to dominate political life in our time. And it is another text which self-consciously displays its sense of purpose in its narrative technique: at both beginning and end, a narrating voice draws attention to *its* inventive role in *constructing* this alternative scenario for an imagined history.

As I said in my opening paragraph, this book is not attempting to give a comprehensive account of developments in the twentieth-century German novel. It is, if you like, telling one kind of 'story' about those developments, and it is being necessarily selective about the texts it presents. Professional readers will undoubtedly notice the absence of one author or another. In the early 1930s, for example, Hermann Broch and Elias Canetti were also pursuing their own kind of radical experimentation in the novel; and new and varied kinds of intellectual radicalism can be found after 1945 in the works of Arno Schmidt, say, or Peter Weiß. Equally, the traditions of Realism are upheld and developed by other German authors whose names may well be familiar: Heinrich Mann and Lion Feuchtwanger, Anna Seghers and Arnold Zweig, Heinrich Böll and Martin Walser. (Some works of secondary literature which cover these and other authors are included in our Guide to Further Reading at the end of this volume.) We have chosen texts which we have found, in our experience as university teachers, to appeal readily to English-speaking students, and which demonstrate in one way or another the expressive potential of narrative writing that lies beyond the traditional conventions of Realism. What these novels share is a manifest consciousness of the ways in which the human mind itself structures its sense of reality.

REFERENCES

BAKHTIN, M. M. (1981), *The Dialogic Imagination*, translated by Caryl Emerson and Michael Holquist, Austin: University of Texas Press.

BÜRGER P. AND BÜRGER, C. (1988), *Prosa der Moderne*, Frankfurt: Suhrkamp.

COHN, D. (1978), *Transparent Minds: Narrative Modes for Presenting Consciousness in Fiction*, Princeton: Princeton University Press.

DOWDEN, S. D. (1986), *Sympathy for the Abyss. A Study in the Novel of German Modernism: Kafka, Broch. Musil and Thomas Mann*, Tübingen: Max Niemeyer Verlag.

FOKKEMA, D. and IBSCH, E. (1987), *Modernist Conjectures: A Mainstream in European Literature 1910–1940*, London: Hurst.

FRANK, M. (1989), *Einführung in die frühromantische Ästhetik*, Frankfurt: Suhrkamp.

FRIEDEMANN, K. (1910), *Die Rolle des Erzählers in der Epik* (reprinted Darmstadt: Wissenschaftliche Buchgesellschaft 1965; extracts in Klotz V. (ed.) *Zur Poetik des Romans* (Wege der Forschung, vol. 35), Darmstadt: Wissenschaftliche Buchgesellschaft 1965).

HELLMAN, W. (1957), Objektivität, Subjektivität und Erzählkunst. Zur Romantheorie Friedrich Spielhagens (reprinted in Brinkmann R. (ed.) *Begriffsbestimmung des literarischen Realismus* (Wege der Forschung, vol. 212), Darmstadt: Wissenschaftliche Buchgesellschaft 1969).

KAYSER, W. (1955), *Entstehung und Krise des modernen Romans*, Stuttgart: Metzler.

KENNER, H. (1978), *Joyce's Voices*, London: Faber and Faber.

LARBAUD, V. (1925), Preface to Édouard Dujardin, *Les lauriers sont coupés*, Paris: Albert Messein.

LODGE, D. (1977), *The Modes of Modern Writing: Metaphor. Metonymy and the Typology of Modern Literature*, London: Edward Arnold.

LODGE, D. (1990), *After Bakhtin: Essays on Fiction and Criticism*, London: Routledge.

LUKÁCS, G. (1971), *The Theory of the Novel*, translated by Anna Bostock, London: Merlin Press.

LUKÁS, G. (1963), The Ideology of Modernism, in *The Meaning of Contemporary Realism*, translated by J. and N. Mander, London: Merlin Press.

MÁRCUS, G. (1983), Life and the soul: the young Lukás and the problem of culture, in Heller, A. (ed.) *Lukács Revalued*, Oxford: Blackwell.

MIDGLEY, D. (1988), Communism and the avant-garde: the case of Georg Lukács, in Timms, E. and Collier, P. (eds) *Visions and Blueprint: Avant-Garde Culture and Radical Politics in Early Twentieth-Century Europe*, Manchester: Manchester University Press.

MIDGLEY, D. (1991), Writing against theory: Musil's dialogue with psychoanalysis in the *Vereinigungen*, in Hickman, H. (ed.) *Robert Musil and the Literary Landscape of his Time*, Salford: Department of Modern Languages, Salford University.

MITCHELL, B. (1976), *James Joyce and the German Novel 1922–1933*, Athens, Ohio: Ohio University Press.

ORTEGA Y. GASSETT, J. (1968), *The Dehumanization of Art*, translated by Helene Weyl, Princeton: Princeton University Press.

PASCAL, R. (1977), *The Dual Voice*, Manchester: Manchester University Press.

PETERSEN, J. H. (1991), *Der deutsche Roman der Moderne: Grundlegung–Typologie–Entwicklung*, Stuttgart. Metzler.

PÜTZ, P. (1963), *Kunst und Künstlerexistenz bei Nietzsche und Thomas Mann: Zum Problem des ästhetischen Perspektivismus in der Moderne*, Bonn: Bouvier.

RITCHIE, J. M. (1961), The ambivalence of 'Realism' in German literature 1830–1880, *Orbis Litterarum* XV, 200–7 (reprinted in Brinkmann, R. (ed.) *Begriffsbestimmung des literarischen Realismus* (Wege der Forschung, vol. 212), Darmstadt Wissenschaftliche Buchgesellschaft 1969).

SCHEUNEMANN, D. (1978), *Romankrise: Die Entstehung der modernen Romanpoetik in Deutschland*, Heidelberg: Quelle & Meyer.

SCHMITT, H.-J. (ed.) (1973), *Die Expressionismusdebatte: Materialien zu einer marxistischen Realismuskonzeption*, Frankfurt: Suhrkamp.

SPIELHAGEN, F. (1898), *Neue Beiträge zur Theorie und Technik der Epik und Dramatik*, Leipzig: Staackmann.

STANZEL, F. K. (1984), *A Theory of Narrative*, Cambridge: Cambridge University Press

ŽMEGAČ, V. (1983), Zum Problem der Romantheorie, in Lützeler, P. M. (ed.) *Deutsche Romane des 20. Jahrhunderts: Neue Interpretationen*, Königstein im Taunus: Athenäum.

2

Realism versus Poetry
Theodor Fontane, *Effi Briest*

MICHAEL MINDEN

Vielleicht interessirt es Sie, daß die *wirkliche* Effi übrigens noch lebt, als ausgezeichnete Pflegerin in einer großen Heilanstalt. Innstetten, *in natura*, wird mit Nächstem General werden. Ich habe ihn seine Militärcarrière nur aufgeben lassen, um die wirklichen Personen nicht zu deutlich hervortreten zu lassen.
(Perhaps it might interest you to know that the *real* Effi is still alive, doing excellent work in a large nursing home. Innstetten, *in natura*, is about to become a General. I had him abandon his military career in order not to make the identity of the real characters too obvious. – p. 329)

Fontane's most famous and his first commercially successful novel *Effi Briest* (published in 1894/5) is based on a real story, as he genially explained to a reader in October 1895. The story had taken place about ten years before, attracting considerable attention at the time. It involved a society couple (Armand Léon von Ardenne, a Captain in the Hussars, and his wife), a bohemian third party from amongst their circle of friends, an illicit liaison, the discovery of some letters and a duel in which the third party died. Fontane allowed more time to elapse between the misdemeanour and the fatal outcome, he increased the age difference between husband and wife from five years to a generation, he changed the particular geographical settings of the story (from the Rheinland to Prussia; although Berlin features centrally in both), and, perhaps most significantly, he has his heroine die at the end, in disgrace, but reinstated at her parental home and reconciled with her parents and her misfortune. Else von Ardenne herself died in 1952.

The novel's focus becomes this heroine, of whose life Fontane makes a sort of tragedy. Her charm is her youth and her ordinariness, which Fontane conveys by means of his perfect command of the conversational tones and registers of the day. She is ordinary, but Fontane is in love with her and by definition love transfigures ordinariness. Her marriage to the much older Baron von Innstetten offers her a glorious future in society, but is at the same time a bitter curtailment of her youth. The first few pages of the novel – justly renowned – put these circumstances before the reader with unforgettable clarity: a little girl playing in the garden of her youth is called away from her play to meet a gentleman, of whom she is told – a bombshell registered only with the words 'Effi schwieg und suchte nach einer Antwort' (Effi fell silent, trying to think of what to reply, p. 18) – that he wishes to marry her. The cruelty is not explicit, Effi's parents love her and want the best for her, Effi loves her parents (and wants the best for herself!), Innstetten is old but by no means an old man, and attractive enough to have been the object of Effi's mother's affection and aspirations in the past (a circumstance with some resonance). The cruelty is that much more devastating for being implicit: unspoken, unconscious.

Indeed, the exploitation of implicitness is Fontane's style and strength throughout the novel. He narrates from outside, he tells us what can be seen and heard, he does not tell us what cannot, or what it would be improper to see or hear. He does not dwell on sensation, he creates states and moods, attitudes, complex relationships between socially highly defined people, who are not in the habit of verbalising their deepest feelings. The reader knows that these feelings exist, however, and this is the effect and pleasure of the text. When Effi hears that her husband is going to be transferred to Berlin, and that her affair with Crampas can therefore become a thing of the past, her relief, the reader knows, is overwhelming (having to be deceitful is perhaps a worse brutalisation even of her happy nature than marrying young). But she cannot put her relief into words – she is after all in an interview with her husband, who has just taken great pleasure in telling her that they are going to move to the infinitely more interesting location of Berlin. Effi's response – 'Gott sei Dank!', said as if she were praying – is thus massively overdetermined. It exceeds what is appropriate just enough to make her husband pause and wonder for a moment, but in that excess, in that prayer-like 'thank God', hardly a soliloquy, Fontane concentrates for the reader the full intensity of both Effi's vitality and her torment of conscience to superb literary effect (p. 182).

Effi's ordinariness becomes extraordinary by the operation of the plot, which denies her the life of a Berlin society wife to which her qualities entitle her, and condemns her to an early death. In her, Fontane expresses a range of values related simply to the potential value of all human beings. She is highlighted and set aside from ordinary society by a tragic story. At the same time, Fontane has profound sympathy for the society in which and, to an extent, because of which this tragedy occurs. He knows that human beings cannot live without society, indeed he knows supremely clearly that human beings are social beings. Innstetten is in the end as sad a figure as Effi herself, since he has been driven by a principle of honour in which he no longer believes, but by which he feels bound, to kill a man he does not hate, and to forgo the company of a wife he loves. Fontane does not portray him unsympathetically. The narrative style refrains from passing judgement in almost every case, not out of pusillanimity, but from the knowledge that too hasty judgements travesty the true complexity of human affairs.

Effi Briest justifies its place in a volume about the history of the modern German novel as an example of that nineteenth-century European Realism to which more recent developments in the German novel offer alternatives. It is therefore in the context of realism, rather than in further formulation of the qualities of Fontane's novel, that we need to address the novel. The question of realism has an important part to play both in Fontane's place in German literary history and in his own literary development. In the context of German literature, Fontane is the channel through which social realism at last successfully enters German literary history, after what is often described as the provincialism of the nineteenth century. Realism is also a latecomer in the context of Fontane's development as a writer. He spent most of his life working in different areas and forms of writing, only beginning to produce recognisably realist prose fiction in the late 1870s when he was nearly sixty. It has often been argued that it is only with the development of Berlin, after 1870, as a great European city, that a realism of the nineteenth-century sort was possible in Germany, because as a literary style and product, it needs modern cities. In *Effi Briest*, at any rate, Berlin is certainly the home of the real, in the sense that it is a grey area of compromise between the poetically and morally more easily legible places, Hohen Cremmen (Effi's parental home), and Kessin (the bleak province where she commits adultery and effectively seals her fate).

But what is realism exactly? It would be misleading to proceed as if there were a consensus on this point. There is none, but perhaps one can set out clearly enough the poles between which definitions might range. At one end of the scale there are those who argue that it is a 'perennial mode of literature', at the other, those who emphasise instead, little concerned with timeless literary types, the historical specificity of European Realism. In *On Realism* J. P. Stern presents the case for the 'perennial mode' point of view. Realism in this view is a particular creative arrangement between the subjectivity of the writer and the objective circumstances in which he lives, it 'designates a creative attention to the visible rather than the invisible, an unabating interest in the shapes and relations of the system that works' (Stern, 1973, p. 171). Stern accordingly deals with those writers throughout the ages whose common characteristic has been that for them social reality is 'the one and only bedrock certainty there is', a fact which they do not simply accept as given, but which they 'creatively acknowledge' (Stern, 1971, p. 166). Against that there is the view that realism in that sense is best identified with the revolution of the historical middle class, and that its historical function was 'the systematic undermining and demystification, the secular "decoding" of those preexisting inherited traditional or sacred narrative paradigms which are its initial givens' (Jameson, 1981, p. 152). In this view, it has an important blindspot: 'vision, realism's metaphor of reality and its knowledge, cannot contain the fact of realism, its writing, the activity of its *production*' (Heath, 1986, p. 112). In other words, nineteenth-century European Realism lays an exaggerated claim to 'reality', and therefore, by being a specific style which pretends it is not a style – pretends it is not a paradigm, but reality itself – significantly obscures one aspect of reality to which it is necessarily blind: the conditions in which it comes about, in which it comes to be literature.

The word 'literature' is a keyword here, because those who tend towards the former pole will have a commitment to literature as an institution which, *mutatis mutandis*, retains a distinct identity and value as a cultural reality from age to age, while those tending towards the other pole will want to see literature as just one cultural form caught up in the real struggles of history, and reserve the name realism, as Brecht did, for whatever forms or practices break up (as European Realism once had done) the pre-existing paradigms. Perhaps it is worth noting that the debate does not simply divide along political lines, since although Brecht and the post-structuralists are certainly Marxist-inspired, the most prominent Marxist critic of the first half of the twentieth century, Georg Lukács, was in some ways closer in his position on realism to Stern than to Brecht (cf. Stern, 1973, p. 181; Heath, 1986, p. 105), preferring the guarantee of objectivity that comes with European Realism to the threat of subjectivity, of a 'loss of the world' arising from the formal innovations of Modernism (Jameson, 1977).

We can thus tentatively test Fontane's practice in relation to this range of opinion. For Stern he is certainly an exponent of the perennial mode, indeed an extremely fine one, if not quite equal in rank to the greatest (Stern, 1964), while, in his very lateness as a realist he would seem to risk, from our other point of view, incarceration in the European Realist paradigm, unable to question the world which, in a manner of speaking, he represents so well. In fact, his case seems to be that of one who is pulled by both poles in our scheme: whilst a passionately committed realist in the Stern sense, his texts, despite themselves, push towards issues which, though they imply them, they cannot explore or accommodate within their own aesthetic practices. Let us look at this.

Fontane's realism seems like a triumphant aesthetic synthesis of his earlier disparate work as a writer. He was a prolific journalist and travel-writer; a documentarist, a writer of prose, and at the same time he was a poet and storyteller, a writer of ballads. These two strands in his work then unite, fusing to become the realist style of his later years. An intermediate stage was the historical novel *Vor dem Sturm* (Before the Storm, begun 1864), published 1878). Here, Fontane tried to integrate art and social reality under the heading of history: realistically depicted individuals and milieux are taken up in 'heroic' history in the shape of the wars of national liberation against Napoleon (Bance, 1982, pp. 16–20).

In the figure of Napoleon a particular nineteenth-century aesthetic problem finds a focus, the 'dilemma of the decline of the hero' (Bance, 1982, p. 21). Napoleon is both evidently in a certain sense a modern hero – the only near-contemporary, historical example – and simultaneously not one, not only defeated, but especially from the Prussian point of view politically unacceptable, and largely responsible, through his 'heroic' effects, for bringing Europe into what Hegel called the age of prose, the age of the state, of administration and bureaucratic control, the age in which heroism ceases to be an available topic for literature, and most especially, of course, for realistic literature. In the figure of Napoleon, before our eyes, history swallows heroes.

In response to this problem, and after the only partially successful attempt at blending poetry and prose in the historical novel, Fontane turned towards the condition of *women* in late nineteenth-century Prussia (Bance, 1982, p. 19 and *passim*). In his novels about women, notably *Effi Briest*, Fontane felt able to write about contemporary society and criticise it at the same time. Women, 'without necessarily wishing to assert any conscious opposition to society, argue by their very existence as *Naturkinder* [children of nature] [...] the supremacy of natural justice against the distortions of the man-made variety' (Bance, 1982, p. 31). In this way, Fontane is able to master reality poetically: 'the incidentals of social life' are employed 'as the metre and the rhythm which make the poetry possible', thus mounting 'a successful rearguard action [...] to defend poetic values against the prose of modern circumstances' (Brance, 1982, p. 8). In short, the masculine hero is devalued by the vulgarity of *Gründerzeit* histrionics and the progressive depersonalisation of the modern state, and is thus replaced in Fontane's novels by heroic aspects in feminine behaviour. Effi's acceptance of death at the end of the novel is truly stoic and thus poetic, and she finally achieves 'a stature equivalent to that of the self-validating heroic model who loomed so large in Fontane's romantic imagination' (Bance, 1982, p. 36).

In writing about women characters, then, Fontane found a way of combining realistic representation, a repertoire of the customs, attitudes, languages of the times with poetic values: 'females [...] are the natural standard-bearers of the poetic [... their] very dependence adds to their charm' (Bance, 1982, p. 30). Around this central thematic move, the other aspects of his realism fall into place: the balladesque art is relocated within Fontane's often declared programmatic commitment to reality (he speaks of it as the 'quarry' from which the raw material of art must come). Together, they yield the poetic patterning of the novel – its pervasive use of symbols (like windows or the colour red), of prefiguration and echo (*Effi komm*), its circular structure. Indeed, even qualities we would be less likely to associate with the ballad form, the use of conversation, the art of suggestion, the themes of adultery, guilt and retribution, nevertheless have their origin there. Above all the novels display a sense of formal closure which they derive from the ballad (Leckey, 1979).

The question now arises, notwithstanding the undoubted literary excellence of his texts, are we happy to allow that Fontane had, indeed, arrived at an idiom which was without contradiction both realistic and, as he believed, 'poetic'? Critics of J. P. Stern's persuasion who are well disposed towards Fontane are apt to be of the opinion that this is the case. Critics of the other persuasion are more likely to perceive a contradiction between the poetry and the reality. The question really turns upon the function of women in Fontane's construction of the 'poetic'.

To equate women with the poetic when it is their very social underprivilege which qualifies them for such treatment must at best be an extremely precarious aesthetic enterprise. Here we see very clearly the tug between a view which sees literature as, in some significant sense at least, autonomous, and a view which sees it always involved with and contributing to the processes of reality itself. To redeem Effi Briest poetically for the suffering she undergoes at the hands of society is aesthetically valid if poetry or 'literature;' is a sphere apart from the bedrock hardness of the social, a sphere in which the imagination elaborates fantasies which bear witness to their unrealisability in reality, but by that very acknowledgement assert the rights and values of a 'natural justice' which can by definition *never* hold sway on earth. But if you decide, on the other hand, that the representations of culture are in an important sense involved in the constitution of reality by means of the generation and confirmation of social and psychological attitudes, then to privilege poetry in this way, especially when it nourishes itself upon the oppression of women, is to contribute to that oppression, and to mistake the genuine power of poetry which – if I may hazard a definition of sorts – is to challenge language, to recycle it.

In these terms Fontane's realism, at least in *Effi Briest*, does not seem as perfect a blend of poetry and reality as is sometimes argued. I see it as a hybrid style (Minden, 1981, pp. 876–8). The novel is telling two stories at once. The realistic material has an implication of its own which remains resistant to the poetic plot, thus making this plot not poetic in any sense we – as opposed to Fontane – could happily entertain, but rather sentimental, an evasive recoil, symptomatic of a society lacking the language or stylistic means either fully to recognise or address its own alienation.

The 'poetic' story runs like this: the child Effi is brutalised and trampled on by society, redeemed and then taken away young. The plot confers upon her the rightness of an early death. Her poetically patterned fall suggests that the world is in some absolute sense sensitive to her worth, to her spontaneity and naturalness: she embodies 'natural justice'. The poetic pathos of her death, the symmetrical appropriateness of her return to her pre-marital (which in this context comes to mean pre-social) state is nevertheless respected and held within the field of social consciousness of her father, who alone in the novel – and this he has in common with Fontane himself – understands her *love* and her *fear*. The feminine meaning she embodies comes to itself in the masculine consciousness of Herr von Briest and Fontane himself: their benevolent ironic comprehension replaces the social form of marriage with the social form of 'poetry'.

The other story is one of pure waste. It is not a poetic narrative but a Berlin anecdote, a piece of gossip, of the sort Effi herself loves to hear and pass on, about a lady's indiscretion in keeping certain letters and an interestingly long time gap between an act of adultery and the consequent duel with fatal consequences. Far from being unsuited to life in late nineteenth-century Prussia, Effi Briest is in many ways perfectly suited to it (Minden, 1981, p. 874). She survives, after all, seven years as a respectable married woman in Berlin. In the milieu of realism, in the grey area of Berlin, she has presumably been as fulfilled as, realistically, anyone can expect to be.

It follows from this that her fall and the ruination of her life is the result of an accident. On the realistic level it is pure chance. On the poetic 'balladesque' level, on the other hand, it is symbolically linked to Effi's own childlike recklessness by that of her daughter, who, in running up the stairs too quickly, stumbles, thus indirectly leading to the discovery of the letters which incriminate her mother. Poetic inevitability and pure contingency inhabit the same image. It is really a moot point whether this constitutes a transformation of the contingent world of anecdote into poetry or a piece of transparent artifice, in which poetic logic and dull facticity remain at odds with one another.

The effect of Fontane's mixture of these two determinations, a mix which one might feel justified in questioning from the second view of realism with which we are working, is roughly as follows: the poetic narrative of Effi's fate (based, after all, on a real occurrence, with the poetic closure of early death added to the basic plot) makes a tragic *exception* of what in fact was the general rule – the subordination of women within a marriage system massively weighted against their interests. This – to us – obvious social point is sublimated within poetic transfiguration. The poetic balladesque closure of the novel, thus, preserves the very alienation its realistic plot depicts. Indeed, in its portrayal of Effi it composes a heroine who combines exactly the qualities required of women by society at that time. First of all she is a *Naturkind*, so she is both a child and close to nature. This means, turning these values round, that she is removed from the adult social sphere, which is the domain of men. But she is not just a child of nature: in her very childlike abandon, her love for *das Aparte* (something out of the ordinary) and the frisson of risk, she is *also* erotic. This, after all, is the plot of the novel – she is an adulteress, and although her sexuality is the closely guarded secret of the text, the plot turns on it. Now, while within the plot the tragedy of her tale makes her a point of poetic resistance to the lovelessness of the world she lives in, the novel as a social document offers one more example of an ideal woman for men, childlike, 'natural', and thus unthreatening, but then erotically tinged never-theless. She is 'too good' for society *in* the fiction, but *as a* fiction she is the familiar and necessary blend. In this reading, 'poetry', far from being synonymous with some extra-social sphere, is doing the work of men: keeping women in their place, keeping them natural and childlike but also sexual.

> Beneath the society-novel surface of *Effi Briest* there are [...] mysterious underground forces at work, whose ambivalent nature can only be encompassed by poetic means. Fontane's mature achievement is

measurable in the extent to which these forces and this poetry are presented in and through, and not at the expense of, concrete social realism (Bance, 1982, p. 38).

But what can these mysterious underground forces be other than that very alienation which is (partially at least) a social product, and cannot simply be encompassed by a 'poetry' which is also a social product? This is an alienation which this novel hints at, but can never hold or represent by its own aesthetic procedures.

From very early on, Effi shows evidence of an inarticulate fear, and this fear is further thematised in the figure of the Chinaman, an outsider amongst the outsiders of Kessin, fear of whom is exploited by Innstetten in a semi-conscious need to establish and maintain his ascendancy over his bride (an attitude in turn exploited by Crampas to seduce her). This heavily-signalled dread is surely the gap between her internalised patriarchal worldview and the lived experience it entails. That Briest understands it and Fontane represents it only increases the unopposed dominance of the patriarchal perspective. The sense of the uncanny, the ghost of the Chinaman and his solitary grave, the pervasive alienation of Kessin where nobody actually belongs ('die ganze Stadt besteht aus solchen Fremden, aus Menschen, deren Eltern oder Großeltern noch ganz woanders saßen' (the whole town is populated by such strangers, people whose parents or grandparents lived somewhere completely different: p. 46), all obliquely suggest this inner desolation, but the novel veers away from its own implications and into the familiar nineteenth-century novelistic plot of adultery, a narrative eminently legible and in no way uncanny. Effi thinks she has seen him as a ghost behind her in the mirror: 'Aber sie besann sich rasch. "Ich weiß schon, was es ist; es war nicht der", und sie wies mit dem Finger Nach dem Spukzimmer oben. "Es war was anderes ... mein Gewissen ... Effi, du bist verloren."' (But she soon pulled herself together. 'I know what it is. It's not him', and she pointed at the haunted room upstairs. 'It was something else ... my conscience ... Effi, you are lost.' – p. 169) But she is nothing of the sort, she has *found* her bearings as an adulteress and a novel heroine, vanished as such into a social definition and meaning which affords the reader a safe position from which to read.

There is therefore some force to the contention that the realist Fontane cannot help but bolster on a subliminal level the society which, on a local, and even on quite a fundamental level, he criticises. The very notion of 'poetry' and naturalness he uses to criticise it actually is very much part of it. So too is his reticence and tact, that controlling view from which both the poetry and the criticism are arranged. When we look at the perspective from which Fontane narrates – and it is, as we know, notoriously elusive, ironic, seemingly *outside* the phenomena it sees and shapes – it always in fact finally remains within this the social space it evokes. As we have already suggested, it derives its critical distance from the socially and historically very specific sort of perspective enjoyed by Effi's father, a man who is both outside the city, distinct from the opaque and morally confusing reality of Berlin, but also fully *of* society, by his status as a member of the landed gentry and his possession of a country estate. His situation is the very model of detachment, but it is a *safe* detachment; part of, but not at the mercy of, the forces of society; forces which subjugate the unlanded career diplomat Innstetten and bind Wüllersdorf to his *Hilfskonstruktionen* (the little consolations which make reality liveable).

It does not matter what the message is, since it is always the medium which matters. The more complex, critical, sensitive, touching ironic, subtle, re-signed, thoughtful and quietly metaphysical Fontane–Briest are, the more this discourse will appeal to the society for which it was written, which sees itself validated precisely by the sophistication of the representation to which, so runs the implication, it is equal. Realism as Fontane practises it is never a challenge to received patterns of thought or language, only ever a refinement of them, and thus also a reinforcement of them. This is what is meant when European Realism is sometimes described as a medium of social mediation: society mediates itself to itself, telling itself its own stories, reassuring itself about its own hold on reality.

Fontane's vision does therefore suffer from a blindspot about its own condition of seeing. And yet, perhaps it is the very extreme lateness of his particular form and practice of realism which produces a sort of peripheral awareness of its own endangeredness, notwithstanding the 'poetic' illusion which dominates the centre of the picture. This is not so much, I think, to be seen in the images of the Chinaman or the balladesque symbolism of sacrifice (Bance, 1982, pp. 65–7), or the other inarticulate hints of dread in the novel, but for instance in the very fact that the realistic analysis and the aesthetic resources are somewhat at odds with each other, since this in itself might be held to alienate or begin to subvert the suspect aesthetic closure of the novel as a whole. Fontane certainly felt this himself, seeking for more penetratingly critical form in the plotless *Der Stechlin*, and failing to find form for the radical content of a projected novel about the fourteenth-century proto-communist 'Likedeeler'. Furthermore, it is, as we said, precisely the great strength of his social realism to perceive and convey in his characters exactly how socially constructed they are. The way Fontane handles the arrival of Innstetten to claim Effi's hand in marriage illustrates just how close Fontane comes, within realism, to transcending it in a perspective at once poetic and critical. The gentleman arrives a little early, and Effi is caught still wearing her informal attire. At first her mother wants to hurry her upstairs to change into her formal dress to meet the man she (does not yet know she) is about to marry. But then Effi's mother changes her mind. Effi's mother, we read, in a memorable phrase, was perfectly capable, when the circumstances made it appropriate, to be unconventional ('Frau von Briest aber, die unter Umständen auch unkonventionell sein konnte ...': p. 17). The irony of this tiny *aperçu* is that it hesitates between approval and satire: Frau von Briest's social skill is such that there is space within it for the genuinely spontaneous, versus the spontaneous as simply another conventional move. It would, I think, be to misread Fontane's tone to privilege either of these readings; it is precisely the balance which is the socially effective *pointe*, which the implied reader will savour. But the context of this manipulation of the spontaneous pushes towards a less ambiguous deconstruction of the elaborate idiom within which Fontane works. For what is happening here, and expressed with infinitely more skill and force than I have been able to muster, is that Effi herself is being constructed as precisely that blend of little girl *Naturkind* and erotically attractive subject to which we referred before. Effi is childlike and natural, yes, but *for* Innstetten, just as the novel itself, in its ambivalent and resigned advocacy of the natural and the childlike is a representation *for* the implied social readership, for whom Effi is also dimly passionate, in whom naturalness and desire also mix inscrutably: '[Frau von Briest] warf einen Blick auf das jugendlich reizende Geschöpf, das, noch erhitzt von der Aufregung des Spiels, wie ein Bild frischesten Lebens vor ihr stand' (cast a glance at the youthful and charming creature, who, still glowing from the excitement of play, stood before her like the image of freshness and vitality itself: p. 17).

In the early chapters Effi the child is shown to have internalised the values and attitudes of her parents to such an extent that she can accept her engagement to Innstetten, which shatters her childhood world with appalling suddenness, by means of an array of conditioned responses and formulations in which she evidently believes. To be sure, this too is all part of the ultra-refined portrayal of society that binds Fontane ever more into the closed vision of realism. But yet at one climactic point another passage occurs which makes this state of affairs *itself* visible, not a condition of the text, but its object. In Chapter 33 there is a meeting between Effi after her disgrace and her daughter, at which the child responds to her mother's various suggestions for future meetings with a threefold 'I'd love to come, if I am permitted' (O gewiß, wenn ich darf: p. 274). Effi loses her temper at this evident paternal programming and, having dispatched her servile daughter with something like *Empörung* (a word which means both indignation and rebellion) in her manner, fearing that she will suffocate, she violently loosens her constricting clothing, and delivers a discourse which roundly and irresistibly condemns the condescending nature ('he was always a schoolmaster') and pettiness ('I always felt small next to him, and now I see that he was the one who was small') of her former husband. It is always Fontane's way to express psychological states by means of physical signs, but, as with the contrast between formal and informal dress in the passage just discussed, although less ambiguously, when Effi loosens her dress on this occasion the meaning is unmistakably social (the motif has in fact been anticipated in balladesque manner by the episode involving the actress Tripelli in Chapter 11). Effi's tight dress is decoded by Fontane's text as the metonym of a mean and repressive society, just as clearly as in her annihilating and climactic discourse her former husband is revealed as the representative embodiment, as the very instantiation, of an unforgivably repressive and loveless patriarchal society.

It is certainly no coincidence that this *Empörung* against the suffocation wrought by an excessively rigid and formalistic society should rise to its highest level of self-consciousness at this particular moment. For Effi has just been confronted with the perfect image of her own social behaviour: that of a child repeating like an automation the words of her symbolic father, society itself. What she otherwise internalises, seen now from the outside, appears in its true form as alienation. The father's voice confers identity upon the daughter by separating her from her mother, which is the same as saying from herself. Effi sees clearly: 'Mich ekelt, was ich getan; aber was mich noch mehr ekelt, das ist eure Tugend. Weg mit euch. Ich muß leben, aber ewig wird es ja wohl nicht dauern'. (What I did revolts me, but what revolts me even more, is your idea of morality. It would be better to be rid of the whole lot of you. I have to go on living, but mercifully it will not last forever. – p. 275) For a moment Effi is outside a social reality which otherwise defines her.

Yet here we see perhaps even more clearly than before the constitutional limitations of Fontane's realism, for he cannot, even if he wanted to, explore this insight beyond the moment. *Weg mit euch* would mean getting rid of the convention and commodity of Realism, of Fontane's practice and his public at a stroke. The chapter finishes, in a sense, with Effi's 'realistic', that is empty, meaningless, bitter Berlin death: 'Als Roswitha wiederkam, lag Effi am Boden, das Gesicht abgewandt, wie leblos.' (When Roswitha returned Effi was lying on the ground, her face turned away, as if lifeless. – p. 275) But even as he writes this brilliant scene – the true climax of the book – he must steer his heroine towards the pathos of early death ('mercifully it will not last forever'), towards a conventional poetry, the distinguishing characteristic of which is that it achieves closure, delivers 'nature', and leaves everything exactly as it was. The revolutionary *Empörung* is unsustainable, it is what that archetypal realist, Brecht's Mother Courage, would call 'a short anger', not the long anger through which objective circumstances might be challenged.

In the end, Fontane's skill and achievement are more important than debates about realism. Like everybody else he worked to an extent within, to an extent against the circumstances of his time, and to quantify the degree to which he did the one or the other is ultimately fruitless before the pleasure and the presence of his texts. But he surely does stand at a significant juncture in the history of realism, however you understand it, in that he is the exponent of an artistic form and practice about to mutate, and this lateness shines into and gives resonance to his practice. Freud is at hand to elaborate – with enormous difficulty – a language which can begin to speak about the kinds of deformation which Effi suffers. And aesthetically, Fontane's attempt to write balladesque patterned narrative in the metre and rhythms of social reality was very soon to seem outdated. The 'two stories' of *Effi Briest* (1895) signal the impending desertion of the 'incidentals of social life' by meaning. By the end of Thomas Mann's *Buddenbrooks* (1901) there is no adequate style left to represent the death of Hanno, only a morally neutral reference to the cause of typhoid fever. In much of the German prose of the early twentieth century, from early Heinrich Mann and Hesse to Kafka, these 'incidentals' appear in an uncanny facticity – a heap of junk – where once there had been familiarity and pleasure. The 'poetic' – a very elusive quality – will finally be driven to seek its 'metres and rhythms' elsewhere.

REFERENCES

Quotations for which page references only are given in the text are taken from Theodor Fontane, *Effi Briest*, Munich: Hanser 1974.

BANCE, A. (1982), *Theodor Fontane: The Major Novels*, Cambridge: Cambridge University Press.

JAMESON, F. (1977), *Aesthetics and Politics*, London: New Left Books.

JAMESON, F. (1981), *The Political Unconscious*, London: Methuen.

HEATH, S. (1985), Realism, Modernism and 'Language-Consciousness', in Boyle, N. and Swales, M. (eds), *Realism in European Literature*, Cambridge: Cambridge University Press.

LECKEY, G. R. (1979), *Some Aspects of Balladesque Art and their Relevance for the Novels of Theodor Fontane*, Bern: Peter Lang.

MINDEN, M. R. (1981), 'Effi Briest' and 'die historische Stunde des Takts', *MLR* 76, pp. 871–9.

STERN, J. P. (1964), *Re-interpretations*, Cambridge: Cambridge University Press.

STERN, J. P. (1971), *Idylls and Realities*, London: Methuen.

STERN, J. P. (1973), *On Realism*, London and Boston: Routledge & Kegan Paul.

3

Reality as Pretext
Robert Musil, *Die Verwirrungen des Zöglings Törleß*

ANDREW WEBBER

Robert Musil's *Die Verwirrungen des Zöglings Törleß* (1906) can be said to be the first significant experiment with post-Realist writing in the German novel. It is, as it were, the first and formative chapter in the crisis of the great *Bildungsroman* tradition. The *Bildungsroman*, the novel of 'formation', on the model of Goethe's *Wilhelm Meister*, as a great construction of bourgeois humanist identity, is subsumed in Musil's view by a wider generic definition: 'Der Bildungsroman einer Person, das ist ein Typus des Romans. Der Bildungsroman einer Idee, das ist der Roman schlechtweg.' (The *Bildungsroman* of a person is a type of novel. The *Bildungsroman* of an idea is the novel *per se*. – II, p. 830). And he felt that *Törleß* had been mistaken for a conventional personal *Bildungsroman* when it was properly the novel of an idea. *Törleß* is clearly too limited in its scope to uphold the tradition of the *Bildungsroman* as a model way of constructing a personal identity, according to what Musil called 'die organische Plastizität des Menschen' (the organic plasticity of the individual: II, p. 830). Instead, it abstracts a formative episode from the life-story by way of experimenting with, or, to use Musil's terms, *essaying* the *idea* of identity. It is as it were an adolescent essay on an adolescent essayist (Törleß is described as both *Versuchenden* and *Versuchten* (II, p. 997), experimenting and subjected to experiment). This was what Musil called the *List* (II, p. 996), the narrative ploy, whereby he could analyse the problem of selfhood through the relatively manageable and episodic confusions of puberty. The adolescent trials of the formation of an identity in *Törleß* are a prelude to the more epic essaying of the confused characteristics of a Modernist (non)identity in *Der Mann ohneEigenschaften*. This could be said to be the fundamental idea of which *Törleß* is the *Bildungsroman*.

While the form of the novel is not radically Modernist, Musil deploys a whole repertory of narrative modes and stances in the service of his experimentation: from a conventional third-person account to more ambiguous forms of *erlebte Rede*; from authoritative retrospective commentary to the physical immediacy of the mass abuse of Basini, cast in the present tense (II, p. 130); from omniscient control to the sort of discursive crisis which afflicts Törleß both as speaker and writer.

The turn of the century saw multiple revisions of the currency of identity. For the writers of the *Wiener Moderne* (Viennese Modernism), the *Ich* was pronounced, following the philosopher Mach and the aesthetic theorist Bahr, *unrettbar*, beyond salvation: subverted by the claims of the newly-chartered unconscious, and subject to the sort of *Sprachkrise* (language crisis) which afflicts Hofmannsthal's Chandos and comes to inform the radical philosophical project of Wittgenstein. In the first few years of the century, when *Törleß* was conceived, the theoretical analysis of this existential crisis was staked out by such writers as Mach, Weininger and Freud.

Mach, the subject of Musil's doctoral thesis, undertook an analysis of sensations, focusing on the relationship between the physical and the psychic. He saw the individual less as a monistic, organic entity than a constellation of atomistic elements. Musil's *Beitrag zur Beurteilung der Lehren Machs und Studien zur Technik und Psychotechnik* (Contribution to the Assessment of the Theories of Mach and Technical and Psychotechnical Studies) tests the technical, geometric, and economic models of the psyche set up in Mach's theory. Musil stresses Mach's view of consciousness playing 'die Rolle eines ökonomischen Instruments' (the role of an economic instrument: Musil, 1980, p. 25), but one whereby the machinery of continuous exchange is also liable to break down into non-economic discontinuities. In Weininger's in many ways preposterous, but none the less immensely influential treatise on gender and identity, *Geschlecht und Charakter* (Sex and Character, 1903), sexuality functioned as the symbolic ground for a general philosophy of being. He at once set up an essentialist scheme of gender difference and dismantled the same by asserting a shifting scale of sexual identity between the idealised poles of 'M' and 'W' (male and female). Freud, like Mach, proposed a radical new economics of selfhood, but one defined by the dialectical transactions across the threshold between consciousness and the unconscious. The idea of an *a priori* secure identity is superseded in the new science of psychoanalysis by the problematics of identification; that is, the *Ich* is constructed by means of its accommodations with the other.

The experimental constructions of identity in *Törleß* can usefully be aligned with these different theoretical projects. In Musil's terms, 'Das Ich wird förmlich zerspalten, es gewinnt einen doppelten Boden' (The self is literally split, it takes on a double basis: Musil, 1981, p. 14). Indeed, in its depiction of the divided self, the novel distils and integrates the *fin-de-siècle* crises of language, cognition, gender and psycho-sexuality. Mach gives the cue for an analogy between the physical laws of *Technik* and the inner mechanics and forces of *Psychotechnik*. Weininger constructs the model of confusion in gender identity, and the dialectic opposition between the mother and the prostitute. Freud provides the licence for setting desire centre-stage, experimenting with its excesses and deviations from the perceived norm, and for investing objects, structures and language with erotic symbolism. *Törleß* can be seen as a psycho-technical and psycho-analytic *Bildungsroman*, or narrative formation, of all these ideas.

Of course, the novel of ideas also constructs a fiction of reality. A realist perspective is certainly in play in *Törleß*, which is, in one sense, an autobiographical *roman à clef* of life in a cadet-school (see Corino, 1968). But Musil famously dubbed 'die Realität, die man schildert, stets nur ein Vorwand' (the reality depicted always a mere pretext: II, p. 997) for the real business of narrative. Here, the more or less realistic story is a pretext for subverting received fictions of the formation of character. The institutional and parental *Bildung* of the *Zögling* is as inadequate as that depicted in Wedekind's *Frühlings Erwachen* (Spring Awakening), the psychological representation of character equally stylised or in Musil's terms *konstruiert* (constructed: Musil, 1981, p. 13). In either case the natural processes of growth are cast in images of organic blossoming and fruition, but these are made to submit to the forces of social construction. Both works are pervaded by the principle of role-play which subverts any notion of development as natural.

The *fin-de-siècle* produced a series of such texts of adolescent upheaval, often miscast, as at the beginning of *Törleß*, in autumnal torpor. They represent an epochal sense of rejuvenation only under the sign of crisis: a sexual coming-of-age for European literature, but no straightforward spring awakening. During the Realist hegemony of nineteenth-century fiction, sexuality was effectively closeted, operating beneath, above, or behind the surfaces of the fictional living space. This absent presence is represented paradigmatically by the ghost in the attic and the subversive undercurrents of the *Schloon* in *Effi Briest*, where sexuality is, like the story of the Chinaman, the untold 'other'. This crucially covert area is certainly made more accessible to narration in a post-Realist text like *Törleß*; but the dangers of subterranean channels are still lurking in the shape of Törleß' sensuality: 'wie dunkle unterirdische Gewässer, die nur eines zufälligen Anlasses bedürfen, um durch ihre Mauer zu brechen' (like dark underground waters which only need some chance occasion to break through their walls: II, p. 109). At the same time, the closet is transformed into the highly ambivalent, still covert space of the *Versteck* as 'hidey-hole'. It is a scene for the enactment of repressed fantasies, akin to the *Rumpelkammer* in the *Prügler* chapter of Kafka's *Der Proceß*. Above all, in the age of Freud, both Musil and Kafka represent the Modernist crisis of subjectivity as the co-product of the psyche and the body. The division between psychology and the bodily which was made to obtain in so many Realist fictions, is not simply dispelled here, but becomes the explicit subject of the fictional project. Psyche and body are at once thoroughly bound up with one another in *Törleß* and subject to traumatic divisions.

In a frequently quoted prescription, Musil takes issue with the fundamental principle of narrative mimesis by appropriating for his own devices one of the model figurations of European Realism: Stendhal's aphorism that the record-ing of reality in the novel should be as comprehensive as the view from a travelling carriage along a country road. Musil hijacks the Realist for his own carriage purposes:

> die Darstellung eines Unfertigen, Versuchenden und Versuchten ist natürlich nicht selbst das Problem, sondern bloß Mittel, um zu gestalten oder anzudeuten, was in diesem Unfertigen unfertig ist. Sie und alle Psychologie in der Kunst ist nur der Wagen, in dem man fährt; wenn Sie von den Absichten dieses Dichters nur die Psychologie sehen, haben Sie also die Landschaft im Wagen gesucht.
>
> (The depiction of an unfinished individual, experimenting and experi-mented upon, is of course not the real problem, but simply a means of representing or indicating what is unfinished about him. This and all psychology in art is no more than the carriage in which one travels: if you only see psychology amongst this writer's intentions, then you are trying to find the landscape in the carriage. – II, p. 996f.)

This manifesto for post-Realist narrative practice has served the strategic tendency amongst critics to marginalise the more adolescent and corporeal aspects of the text. Notwithstanding the disclaimer, *Törleß* can only indicate what is unfinished – the idea of identity – by means of the reality of the unfinished eponymous hero. Musil also sees that the abstraction of ideas can only be developed as narrative through the representation of what he calls *Somatik* and *Psychologie* (Musil, 1981, p. 47). Intellectual problems, the sense of epistemological disorientation for the protagonists in the texts of Musil or Kafka, cannot be divorced from the physiological and its traumatic metamor-phoses. It is in this sense that the account of the experiments with Törleß, as both scientist and guinea-pig, are represented by Musil as 'eine Vivificirung intellektueller Zustände' (a vivification of states of mind: Musil, 1981, p. 23). The intellect is embodied – and thus sexualised – in a way that prepares it for what Musil called, following Nietzsche, the analytic activity of vivisection. Reiting's graphic image of the lancet penetrating the brain of Basini is characteristic of this principle; his experiments are of course also of a sadistically sexual nature. Similarly, as Törleß attempts to get the measure of things as creative writer, essayist, philosopher and mathematician, his progress is insistently defined and confined by psycho-sexual demands. The desire to know is always confused with the adolescent imperative of an inherently confused carnal knowledge. Accordingly, the literal and metaphorical language of body and mind are insistently mixed throughout the text. Where Törleß is mentally confused, his confusions are compounded by a coinciding sensual arousal. Thoughts, memories and images are recurrently animated – alluring and threatening bestial violence by turns. They work on Törleß' consciousness by way of tactile attentions: 'Erst ein Gedanke weckte Törleß auf wie die leise Berührung einer warmen Hand.' (Törleß was only awoken by a thought as if by the soft touch of a warm hand. – II, p. 106). Thoughts pulsate with flesh and blood: 'mit seinem ganzen Körper fühlte er, daß hinter ihnen ein Stück seines Lebens poche' (he felt with his entire body that a piece of his life was throbbing behind them: II, p. 79). And a thought only comes to life when its logic is rendered incarnate: 'wie einen Anker, der von ihm aus ins durchblutete, lebendige Fleisch riß' (as if it dropped an anchor to tear into the blood-warm, living flesh: II, p. 137).

What might be called the psychosomatic character of *Törleß* is disposed, much as in Thomas Mann's *Tod in Venedig*, between the *a fortiori* extension into the real of Naturalism and the heightened, mystically intensive forms of Symbolism. Both Mann (1961, pp. 176–80) and Musil claimed, perhaps rather defensively, that the 'perverse' subject matter of these works is in some sense a pretext; that they have less to do with the reality of homosexual desire than with its symbolic potential as 'the other' which threatens bourgeois conventions. Musil insists that *Törleß* is no attempt to rehabilitate the 'vice' which dare not speak its name, nor a piece of modish adolescent psychology: 'das Buch ist nicht naturalistisch. Es gibt nicht Pubertätspsychologie wie viele andere, es ist symbolisch, es illustriert eine Idee.' (The book is not naturalistic. It does not purvey pubescent psychology like so many others; it is symbolic, it illustrates an idea. – Musil, 1981, p. 47). On the one hand *Törleß* naturalises and rationalises the real, on the other it mystifies and symbolises, adumbrating the notorious dialectic between *Ratio* and *Mystik* in *Der Mann ohne Eigenschaften* (Albertsen, 1968). For the natural and the symbolic are indeed engaged in a dialectical interdependence in *Törleß* (not least in the pervasive natural symbolism of plant and animal life, etc.) and the prospect of rationalising narrative development is soon undermined by the resultant confusions.

The first page sets the programme. The motto quoted from the Symbolist writer Maeterlinck gives the cue for a narrative of split vision, focused at once on the mysterious and the empirical sobriety which comes with its articulation: 'Sobald wir etwas aussprechen, entwerten wir es seltsam.' (As soon as we utter something we devalue it strangely. – II, p. 7). The beginning of the narrative proper is very much cast in this sober mode and thus incongruent with Maeterlinck's perspective on the shimmering *Schatz im Finstern* (treasure in the gloom):

Eine kleine Station an der Strecke, welche nach Rußland führt.
(A small station on the line which leads to Russia.)

The novel begins with a sort of narrative arrest. A single, isolated line which sets a scene in the most laconic terms, and above all lacks the tense, and thus the tempo of an operative verb. A perspective is opened up for epic travel, but the narrative is resolutely transfixed in the static scene of a station along the line. And a scene it is, a theatrical setting waiting for action to animate it. Like Fontane's *Irrungen Wirrungen* (A Suitable Match), the dramatic pastiche – there *Kulissen* (theatrical sets), here the puppet theatre, each playing with metaphors of clockwork, each lifted out of an active sense of time – sets the scene for, albeit very different, narratives of role-play through *Irrungen*, *Wirrungen* and *Verwirrungen*.

The first page of *Törleß* plays with a model of narrative linearity in open space, a storyline which might be set on track as *endlos gerade* (endlessly straight), in parallel with the railway lines. This projection of an endlessly concurrent linearity at the outset in itself suggests the attenuation of what Musil dubs the 'Prinzip der kürzesten und schwersten Linie' (the principle of the shortest and heaviest line: Musil, 1976, p. 217) as opposed to the extensive perspectives of the Naturalist novel. While the testing of the economics of identity would be best served by a reductive economy of line, tending towards the punctuality of what the author calls *Reduktionspunkte* (Musil, 1976, p. 217), the narrative naturally strains against its reduction. The principle of narrative foreshortening introduces a tension between concision and extension in the text. The novel cannot engage microscopic and telescopic perspectives at once without a vertiginous confusion of focus. This is the only reliable result which emerges from Törleß' own diametric experimentation, gravitating from the telescopic attempt to view the infinity of space (II, p. 62) into the microscopic close-up of animal life (II, p. 66) and dust particles (II, p. 71). The bifocal vision, at once long- and short-sighted 'je nach Ferne und Nähe' (according to distance and proximity: II, p. 139), is transferred to the narrative perspective. The principle of the shortest narrative line is borne out only for the short duration of the truncated opening sentence. As the second sentence stretches the narrative line out, it also closes in to describe other lines in more compound descriptive forms – the lines which run parallel to the rails: 'der dunkle, von dem Abdampfe in den Boden gebrannte Strich' (the dark strip scorched into the earth by the exhaust steam: II, p. 7).

Having cast it into infinity and underscored it, the narrative then proceeds to undo the projection of teleological security by cross-cutting with another geometrical principle altogether: the *Verwirrungen* prescribed in the title. As the action is arrested from the start in a station, so it will dilate into a confusion of contrapuntal lines. The word *breit* is used three times on the opening page as the narrative deviates from the trammelled railway line into the various tracks whose demarcation is less certain. The straight line which opens the narrative is turned in the ensuing sentences into an elaborate syntax bound up in its descriptive contortions. This first page bears out fully Musil's insistence on the reciprocal determination of form and content in what he calls the *Gestalt* of literary work: 'es gibt keine Form, die nicht an einem Inhalt, keinen Inhalt, der nicht durch eine Form in Erscheinung träte.' (There is no form which is made manifest without content, no content without form. – II, p. 1218). Elisabeth Stopp has discussed the inseparability of the two dimensions in the novel as a whole (Stopp, 1968). Here, on the opening page, form and content conspire to defer the entry of dramatic action upon the scene, introducing a narrative timetable of delayed arrivals. The intricate preparation of the scene as lifeless and mechanistic displaces the lives it should set in place.

The entry of the group upon the scene is as artificial in its semblance of animation as is the reified station master.

In the course of the novel the paradigm of a straightened, infinitely open perspective is progressively shifted into that of confused enclosure: the mazy, oblique and obscure ways in which the narrative will move on the way to the *Versteck*. The prospect of the narrative as *endlos* must be reread in retrospect. *Endlos* is crucially not just an instance of casual hyperbole meaning infinite. The suffix *los* recurs both on the first page and throughout the text as a marker of vital deficiency (*kraftlos, leblos, ziellos, fruchtlos*, etc.). It signifies a lack of end in the sense of telos or goal. When Musil applied the term *Endlosigkeiten* (II, p. 1468) to Kafka's writing, it was in just this sense of teleological lack. In *Törleß*, much as in Kafka's tortuous fictional spaces, topographical twisting and constraint, the crossing of lines and perspectives, corresponds to the experience of psychic confinement and disorientation. The dark recesses into which post-Realist fictions lead furnish spaces for subliminal fantasies to be played out, but they also arrest the protagonists at the threshold, or immure them in solitary confinement. This projection of psychic disposition into the 'real' space of the fictional world is a first principle of the Modernist departure or derailment from the tracks of mimetic security in the Realist tradition. There was nothing in the fictional contract of the nineteenth century to suggest that the reader might yet be misguided into such obscure and out-of-the-way places as the attic of *Effi Briest*. This is just what happens in *Törleß* when we are led for the first time along the anything but straightforward way to the *Versteck*. The scene refers back to the opening perspective by departing from the corridor 'der sich endlos lang vor dem Lehrsaale dehnte' (which stretched out endlessly in front of the classroom: II, p. 37). But this overt *Gang* is left behind during a passage which delineates every turn and threshold, imitating the topography of the hidden angles by the forms of its own elaborate architecture. The word *Winkel* recurs as a key word for a narrative given to exploring the nooks and crannies and unconventional angles of the 'engen, winkligen Gemächer der Sinnlichkeit' (narrow, angular rooms of sensuality: II, p. 114). Reading time is virtually synchronised with the time taken over negotiating the series of passages to the *Winkel* (II, p. 39) that is the *Versteck*.

The straight and 'endless' line is turned, then, in this 'passage' into angles both oblique and acute. It is worthwhile to pursue in detail the graphics of the line throughout the novel, as it represents a sort of diagrammatic model for the narrative development, and the lines along which the reader has to proceed through it. Like the lines which cross over the first page, Törleß' first deviations are straight enough; the tangent of his iconic infatuation with the prince finds its 'geradlinige Verlängerung' (rectilinear extension: II, p. 12) in the diametrically opposite company of his more brutal peers. But what he lacks is the fundamental *Linie* (II, p. 14) of character. He treks along the determined course of his life – 'auf dieser einen Linie' (on this unchanging line: II, p. 16), and is unable to follow 'diese, zu ihrer Umgebung in Widerspruch stehende, Linie' (this line standing in contradiction to its surroundings: II, p. 16) of the sign which points upwards. This is the line which his imagination will take as he lies later at the base of the wall; but consciousness and eyesight will both fail to pursue the line to its impossible end in infinity. 'Das Unendliche' (II, p. 63) is exposed to Törleß as a mere rhetorical construct, only seeming to contain an idea which is constitutionally beyond enclosure. Like the 'endless' railway lines, the scene represents a physical contradiction in terms: a direct line with no telos.

Such vertiginous, transcendent perspectives recede as Törleß pursues the 'verwirrte Gänge' (confused passages: II, p. 46) of his desire, recurrently finding himself up against the impasse of brick walls or held up at intractable thresholds. The line is graphically twisted and redrawn as his character is robbed of its 'feste Linien' (stable lines: II, p. 79). The opening prospect of lines running in perfect and open parallel to the horizon is crossed as they converge towards *Verwirrung*. Thus, the power of words to fix experience rationally is subverted, as life and reason, hitherto concurrent, 'als liefen sie parallel und mit der gleichen Geschwindigkeit nebeneinander her' (as if they ran parallel and at the same speed alongside one another), enter into confusion: 'sie schlossen sich verwirrend eng aneinander' (they drew in confusingly close to each other: II, p. 64).

This closing together of the lines parallels another mutation of the line into a figure of separation as *Scheidelinie*. The partition is cast as an inner horizon which recedes before the desire for understanding:

Zwischen den Ereignissen und seinem Ich, ja zwischen seinen eigenen Gefühlen und irgendeinem innersten Ich, das nach ihrem Verständnis begehrte, blieb immer eine Scheidelinie, die wie ein Horizont vor seinem Verlangen zurückwich.

(Between events and his self, indeed between his own feelings and some most inner self, which desired understanding of them, there always remained a border line, which receded before his desire like a horizon. – II, p. 25)

The word *Begehrte* is operative here as a marker of the confusion between desire and the quest for knowledge in the novel. Sexual desire is represented on the same model of an elusive excess – 'Dieses übrige des Begehrens' (This remainder of desire: II, p. 109) – which is always beyond the partitive line of the threshold, always beyond the reach of transgression for the hidebound protagonist. Törleß' experience is continuously liminal in this sense, defined by a sense of boundary, a *Scheidelinie*. The line of separation is an unsatisfactory stand-in for any real object, given that Törleß has 'kein rechtes Ziel' (no true goal: II, p. 97).

The principle of partition is typographically represented in the text of *Törleß* by the lines of dashes which intersect the episodes of the novel. Musil borrows the device from the narrative conventions of such Naturalist writers as Holz and Schlaf, but puts it very much to his own use. The lines delineate thresholds in the sequence of narrative scenes, but are significantly broken. The demarcation is an intermittent one which has as much to do with representing an absence or ellipsis in the narrative – its intermittence – as with drawing sequential lines between the scenes. This is another version of the graphic dismantling of the opening lines, setting out a sort of foreclosure of the story. From the very start the novel is caught up in a dialectic between the closed and open, line and space, substantial being and empty interstices.

On one level these lacunae are frequently equivalent to the breaks between the sections of Kafka's *Die Verwandlung* (The Metamorphosis), corresponding to the protagonist's loss of consciousness. Indeed, the comparison is no idle one, given that the narrative disposition of the two works is so similar. In either case the apparent security of a third-person narrative stance is subtly undermined by effects of *erlebte Rede*, diverting the narrative into the confused consciousness of the protagonist. The reader is at once apart from and involved or enclosed in the traumatic mutations, confusions and incarcerations of the beetle and the *Zögling* respectively. Where their consciousness fails – as when Törleß' awareness 'erlosch. —' (was extinguished. —: II, p. 92) – so does the continuity of the reader's experience of the text.

In the case of *Törleß*, *erlebte Rede* typically arises precisely at times of confusion, where the steady articulation of the third-person narrative line is broken up into the diction of a less assured, more subjective voice. This is marked in the text by the insertion of more broken lines: lines of text punctuated by series of dashes or the dotted lines of ellipsis. Thus, when Törleß is aroused by the view into the houses of the village-women, the narrative takes on the form of his limited awareness that his sensuality 'mit … mit einer Beschmutzung an dem Kot der Höfe … zusammenhängen müsse … Nein, nein; … er fühlte jetzt nur mehr das feurige Netz vor den Augen; die Worte sagten es nicht' (must be connected … with … with being dirtied by the muck of the yards … No, no; … he now only felt the fiery net before his eyes; the words did not say it. – II, p. 18). Both the eye and the articulation of thoughts are bound up in a net as the narrative perspective is captured in Törleß' own, with its 'Versagen der Worte' (failure of words: II, p. 65).

Similarly, when Beineberg describes to Törleß the scene of Reiting's abuse of Basini, the narrative is broken up into the spasmodic rhythms of Törleß' orgiastic vision:

> er sah … Er sah hinter seinen geschlossenen Augen wie mit einem Schlage ein tolles Wirbeln von Vorgängen, … Menschen; Menschen in einer grellen Beleuchtung, mit hellen Lichtern und beweglichen, tief eingegrabenen Schatten; Gesichter, … ein Gesicht; ein Lächeln, … einen Augenaufschlag, … ein Zittern der Haut
>
> (he saw … He saw behind his closed eyes as if by lightning a crazy whirl of events, … people; people illuminated harshly, with bright lights and mobile, deeply engraved shadows; faces, … a face; a smile, … an opening of eyes, … a shivering of the skin – II, p. 55).

But the vision is both immediate and absent. The text transcribes the orgy, but necessarily in terms of images, while Törleß experiences it 'ohne zu sehen, ohne Vorstellungen, ohne Bilder' (without seeing, without ideas, without images: II, p. 55). And the vision is resolutely subliminal – below the threshold of the words given in the text, however intensely telegraphic these may appear to be. He sees the people so clearly 'daß er von ihrer Eindringlichkeit tausendfach durchbohrt wurde, aber, als ob sie an einer Schwelle Halt machten, die sie nicht überschreiten konnten, wichen sie zurück, sobald er nach Worten suchte, um ihrer Herr zu werden' (that he was run through thousand times by their piercing intensity, but, as if halting at a threshold which they could not cross, they drew back, as soon as he sought words to master them with: II, p. 55). The narrative aligned with Törleß' personal perspective, is unable to assert authority over the unseen vision: the transgressive fantasy cannot transgress the threshold of articulate thought.

The punctuation of the narrative line with dots and dashes represents precisely its convergence with the resistant threshold. They mark typographically what the walls, nets and thresholds, which are encountered both on the physical and the metaphorical level through the course of the novel, mark topographically: both the opening up and the closing off of subliminal experience. Musil is essaying here the possibility of a less punctual syntax which might be more appropriate to such experience:

> Solange man in Sätzen mit Endpunkt denkt – lassen sich gewisse Dinge nicht sagen – höchstens vage fühlen. Andererseits wäre es möglich, daß gewisse unendliche Perspektiven, die heute noch an der Schwelle des Unbewußten liegen, dann deutlich und verständlich werden.
> (As long as one thinks in sentences with full stops – certain things cannot be said – at best vaguely felt. On the other hand, it is possible that certain infinite perspectives, which today still lie at the threshold of the unconscious, may yet become clear and comprehensible. – Musil, 1981, p. 53).

In *Törleß*, though, such perspectives are elusive, at best present by omission. The paradigm is given in the line of dashes (conventionally omitted from recent editions) which curiously interrupts the scene between Törleß and Basini in the *Versteck*. Basini recounts the scenes of his affair with Reiting but with a key narrative omission:

> ' ... Dann ist er sogar zärtlich gegen mich.'

> –

> 'Und nachher schlägt er mich meistens ...'
> 'Wonach?!! ... Ach so!'

> ('... Then he's even affectionate towards me.'

> –

> 'And afterwards he usually beats me ...'
> 'After what? ... Oh, I see!' – II, p. 101)

The line represents a break both in Basini's and the master narrative – the editing out of the sexual act. The line of the censor's cut, as it were, also represents the resistance of the listener to that which he may subliminally desire to hear. The sado-masochistic fantasy, and Törleß' involvement in it, is both continuous and discontinuous, open and closed, told and untold.

The development of the *Bildungsroman* is informed by this dialectic play between continuity and discontinuity. Törleß comes to perceive the interplay of similarity and difference, of 'Ähnlichkeiten und unüberbrückbare Unähnlichkeiten zugleich' (similarities and unbridgeable dissimilarities at one and the same time: II, p. 61). On the one hand, the obscure architecture of his *Verwirrungen* appears resolutely closed off from the intact 'durchsichtigen und festen Bau von Glas und Eisen' (transparent and secure structure of glass and iron: II, p. 46) of his childhood world. On the other, the two designs for living threaten to collapse as 'ihre Grenzen heimlich und nahe und jeden Augenblick überschreitbar aneinanderstoßen' (their boundaries converged, secretly and closely and liable to be crossed at any moment: II, pp. 46–7). As Törleß can transgress from one structure to the other, so he comes to assert identity between inhabitants of the domestic order and the other. The mother and the prostitute are assimilated in elaborate ways, with the desire of the son as the link: 'durch ihn hindurch verkettete die beiden ein Zusammenhang' (through him there ran a connection which linked the two of them: II, p. 33). At the same time Törleß' own identity shifts into that of both abusers and abused in the fantasy world of the *Versteck*. He is unable properly to distinguish his *psychologisches Problem* from Beineberg's *Phantastereien* (II, p. 61), his submissions from Basini's (so that he is threatened by the same 'scharfe Spitze' (sharp point: II, p. 46) as Reiting threatens to penetrate Basini's brain with), or his experience from that of Reiting: 'als ob das Schicksal Reitings ihn selbst beträfe' (as if Reiting's fate was his own: II, p. 57). And yet the confusions serve less to construe identity between self and other than to introduce difference into the sense of self.

Törleß' more or less involuntary involvement in the rituals of abuse corresponds at its limit to the mass psychology of political brutality in which Reiting takes such pleasure (II, p. 115). Much like Thomas Mann's *Mario und der Zauberer*, the novel may be read on one level as a political allegory, with the class as 'ein kleiner Staat für sich' (a small state in itself: II, p. 41) and Reiting and Beineberg its charismatic, fascistic leaders. Musil was later to apply just such a reading in the retrospective light of brutal, historical reality: 'Die Triebgrundlagen des Dritten Reiches habe ich bereits im *Törleß* vorweggenommen.' (I already anticipated the fundamental drives of the Third Reich in *Törleß*. – Minder, 1962, p. 84) The subversion of humanist notions of selfhood in the modern novel thus has ideological and political as well as philosophical and aesthetic implications.

The boundary lines between self and other are no more intact than the lines which the subject pursues towards its intellectual and sexual *Bildung*. In the pursuit of objects which are offline, neither desire nor the desire to know can any longer be adequately represented as straight. Lines of thought find more adequate, because more ambivalent, metaphors in the 'winkelzügigsten Kombinationen' (most evasive combinations: II, p. 41) or in the chains of Törleß' imagination. The 'Ketten der Gedanken' (chains of thoughts: II, p. 65) in fact serve to restrain the intellect, as it pursues the resistant remainder – the 'hartnäckiger Rest' (II, p. 65) which always passes its understanding. Meanwhile desire, under cover of the *Versteck* and driven by its constitutional excessiveness, deviates from the straight and narrow. As such it takes on a new graphic line, that of the undercover 'Gänge eines Wurms' (passages of a worm: II, p. 43). The winding ways and body of the worm become the emblem of Törleß' *Verwirrungen*. Such a winding line connects two of the novel's key scenes. And the word 'scene' is operative here given one of Musil's central narrative principles: 'Maxime aus *Törleß*: Wenn man etwas erzählt, immer eine Szene erzählen, die das illustriert.' (Maxim from *Törleß*: When one narrates something, one should always narrate a scene which illustrates it. – Musil 1976, p. 227). The novel which starts with a theatrical scene-setting in a station develops into something akin to the *Stationendrama* pioneered by Strindberg and espoused by the dramatists of German Expressionism. The scenes of Törleß' early times at the academy are described as 'gleichgültige Stationen wie die Stundenziffern eines Uhrblattes' (indifferent stations like the numbers on the face of a clock: II, p. 8), marking time in the manner of the clock-figures on the opening page. The experience of time has only this mechanical continuity, while 'die Stunden seines Lebens fielen ohne innerlichen Zusammenhang auseinander' (the hours of his life fell apart with no inner connection: II, p. 14). When the action of the novel becomes more properly active, it does in fact take the form of a series of dramatic stations. The analogy is furnished by the 'Kulissen' (scenery) stored in the attic space around the *Versteck*, and by the explicit casting of the hypnosis scene as *wie im Theater* or the duping of the teachers as 'eine wohlverabredete Komödie, von Reiting glänzend inszeniert' (a well planned comedy, brilliantly produced by Reiting: II, p. 133). But the drama collapses into the 'groteskes Schauspiel' (grotesque spectacle: II, p. 66) of the sordid scenes in the *Versteck*, an incoherent burlesque, lacking dramatic meaning. And Törleß' role is not simply as witness to the spectacle. From the start he lacks a character: 'Es schien damals, daß er überhaupt keinen Charakter hatte' (It appeared at that time that he had no character at all: II, p. 13) and so can only play a repertory of parts under duress: 'wie ein Schauspieler dazu des Zwanges einer Rolle Bedarf' (like an actor requiring the compulsion of a role: II, p. 13). He beholds the scenes and is beheld by turns, vicariously involved as both spectator and actor in the fantasies they represent.

The first scene to consider is that of Basini's beating by Beineberg and Reiting. In fact, the scene is an absent one, absent, that is, from the field of light which is projected into the darkness of the *Versteck*. Törleß the viewer, or voyeur, takes up the vacant scene, putting himself on exhibition. And the light is metaphorically cast as a beholding eye: '"Ist das nicht wie ein Auge?" sagte er und wies auf den über den Boden fließenden Lichtschein.' ('Is that not like an eye?' he said and pointed at the light spilling over the floor. – II, p. 71) On show only to himself – 'Dabei beobachtete er sich selbst' (Meanwhile he observed himself) – and this 'eye', Törleß goes through the motions of Basini's abuse and is aroused by his enactment of the overheard fantasy. When Basini returns to the 'leeren Rahmen' (empty frame: II, p. 72) of the beam of light, he carries the graphic mark of desire's deviation from the straight and narrow: 'nur über Oberlippe, Mund und Kinn zeichneten langsame Blutstropfen einen roten, wie ein Wurm sich windenden Weg' (except that over his upper lip, mouth, and chin slow drops of blood traced a red path, twisting like a worm: II, p. 72). Törleß too, by his participation in the scene, has turned off from the rectilinear path, wending his way like Basini, who is described by his tormentor Beineberg as a *Wurm*, (II, p. 56); or indeed like Beineberg himself, who speaks in *Windungen*, 'wie ein Weg ohne Ende' (like a path without an end: II, p. 62), and whose body moves in 'sich windende Bewegungen' (twisting movements: II, p. 21) which carry an ambivalent erotic charge for Törleß.

The winding worm is also the graphic symbol of desire in another projected scene, that of Törleß' dream. The dream is prefigured by a waking vision of the familiar line winding through a rectilinear frame of light; a curtain cord hangs 'in häßlichen Windungen herunter, während ihr Schatten auf dem Boden wie ein Wurm durch das helle Viereck kroch' (in ugly twists, while its shadow on the floor crept like a worm through the bright rectangle: II, p. 84). This wormy line is then taken up in the dream in the figure of the 'Bandwurm' (endless sentence/tapeworm), which I have analysed in detail elsewhere (Webber, 1990). Like a classic Freudian portmanteau, the *Bandwurm* condenses the idea of winding discourse or lines of thought and the deviations of desire. The concrete metaphor – both body and idea – encodes the involvement of Törleß' intellectual and sexual confusions. After the dream the projection of the 'worm' remains as a fearful chained beast. Like the nets, partitions and thresholds elsewhere, here it is bars which represent the familiar double bind between the opening up and closing off of the subliminal.

As Törleß beholds the ambivalent figure, he is made to think of his infantile desire to be a girl. The worm thus also comes to stand for a deviation from the straightened polarity of gender which yields confused sensual pleasure to Törleß. But the fantasy of being the other is as ambivalent as is the emblematic worm. The desire focuses on the idea of an inviolate inner *Versteck*, the haunt of worms, slugs and snakes elsewhere in the narrative (e.g. in the *Verstecke* of the *Winkel*: II, p. 66) at the base of the wall in the park). But the *Versteck* is as much a place of incarceration as a secure hidey-hole. It corresponds to the subsequent casting of Törleß' sensuality as 'eine höchste, versteckteste Mauer' (a most high and hidden wall: II, p. 87). The wall provides a hide from the inquiry of others, but one that is itself *versteckt*. Walls recur as images of exclusion in *Törleß,* akin, that is, to the more abstract figure of the *Scheidelinie.* Here, the wall serves to represent Törleß' sensuality as a monumental partition denying all access. The door-less Törleß – to appropriate the pun coined by Freij in his *Türlosigkeit study* – is always already shut out, standing as here 'vor einem verschlossenen Tore' (before a locked door: II, p. 87).

At the end of the novel Törleß abandons himself to the condition of 'Wortlosigkeit' (wordlessness: II, p. 140), accepting that words will not open doors on the elusive other. This, in its turn, leads the novel into an ending which is in fact a departure for another station along the line of development. The conditions of *Tor/Türlosigkeit* and *Wortlosigkeit* had earlier combined to exclude Törleß from himself; when he sought to find his way back to himself, silence held watch 'vor allen Toren' (before all the gates), so that he renounced the quest for words which might gain access: 'Da suchte Törleß kein Wort mehr.' (Then Törleß looked for no more words: II, p. 108.) Both *Türlosigkeit* and *Wortlosigkeit* are concomitant with the principle of narrative *Endlosigkeit* which Musil enshrines in this his first narrative essay: 'Meine Geschichten waren alle endlos.' (My stories were all endless. – II, p. 839). Of course, Törleß uses words even in his wordlessness, but words which say 'nothing', are crucially unable or unwilling to express the real ends of his desire:

'Was willst du, mein Kind?'
'Nichts, Mama, ich dachte nur eben etwas.'
('What do you want, my child?'/ 'Nothing, Mama, I just had a thought.'
– II, p. 140)

The only conclusion that is given is a suitably essayistic one, as Törleß tests his mother's perfume, to an uncertain end. The 'endless' story thus rejoins at its end the ambiguous *Endlosigkeit* of its opening trajectory. It is both open-ended and resolutely closed to the reader's knowledge. It thereby tests a prototype not only for the unfinishable narrative of *Der Mann ohne Eigenschaften,* but for so many of the endlessly open and yet closed-off novels of German literature after Realism.

REFERENCES

References to Robert Musil, *Gesammelte Werke* (2 vols), edited by A. Frisé, Reinbek bei Hamburg: Rowohlt 1978, are given by volume and page number only in the text. (The paperback edition in nine volumes has identical pagination, with vols 1–5 corresponding to *GW I,* and volumes 6–9 corresponding to *GW* II.)

ALBERTSEN, E. (1968), *Ratio und 'Mystik' im Werk Robert Musils,* Munich: Nymphenberger Verlagshandlung.
CORINO, K. (1968), Törleß ignotus: Zu den biographischen Hintergründen von Robert Musils Roman *Die Verwirrungen des Zöglings Törleß, Text und Kritik* 21/22, pp. 18–25.
FREIJ, L.W., (1972), *'Türlosigkeit': Robert Musils 'Törleß' in Mikroanalysen, mit Ausblicken auf andere Texte,* Stockholm: University of Stockholm.

MANN, T., (1961), *Briefe 1889–1936*, Frankfurt am Main: Fischer.

MINDER, R., (1962), *Kultur und Literatur in Deutschland und Frankreich*, Frankfurt am Main: Insel.

MUSIL, R., (1976), *Tagebücher*, ed A. Frisé, vol. 1, Reinbek bei Hamburg: Rowohlt.

MUSIL, R., (1979), *Young Törless*, translated by E. Kaiser and E. Wilkins, London: Granada.

MUSIL, R., (1980), *Beitrag zurBeurteilung der Lehren Machs und Studien zur Technik und Psychotechnik*, Reinbek bei Hamburg: Rowohlt.

MUSIL, R., (1981), *Briefe 1901–1942*, eds A. Frisé and M. G. Hall, vol. 1, Reinbek bei Hamburg: Rowohlt.

STOPP, E., (1968), Musil's *Törleß:* Content and form, *MLR* 63, pp. 94–118.

WEBBER, A. J. (1990), *Sexuality and the Sense of Self in the Works of Georg Trakl and Robert Musil*, London: Modern Humanities Research Association/Institute of Germanic Studies.

4

The Composition of Reality
Rainer Maria Rilke,
Die Aufzeichnungen des Malte Laurids Brigge

ANDREA CERVI

Although published only twelve years after Fontane's last novel, Rilke's *Aufzeichnungen des Malte Laurids Brigge* (Notebooks of Malte Laurids Brigge) breaks radically with the nineteenth-century Realist tradition in which Fontane's work was so firmly rooted. Although not recognised as such by Rilke's contemporaries, it has retrospectively been acknowledged as a seminal text in the development of the German novel, indeed of the European novel, inviting comparisons with the work of Proust and Kafka, Musil and Sartre. Certainly the novel represents Rilke's most radical position in the course of his own artistic development. It is no coincidence that the idea of 'das Äußerste' (the extreme) occurs in various contexts within the novel, but, significantly, the novel makes no conscious claim to be innovatory, arising rather from the author's inner, spiritual *need* to formulate a response to the age as manifested in, and symbolised by, the urban experience. It is in this sense that he speaks, in a letter, of Malte's *Aufzeichnungen* as being constructed out of the 'Vokabeln seiner Not' (vocabulary of his need).

Begun in 1904 in Rome, the novel's composition spanned six years until its publication in 1910, with the most intensive phase of the writing being concentrated in 1908–9. Here it is perhaps useful to remind ourselves that this was Rilke's one and only novel, and that these same years produced the two books of the *Neue Gedichte* (New Poems), the positive, optimistic counterpart, as it were, to the *Aufzeichnungen*. (I shall return later in this chapter to this question of 'positives' and 'negatives'.)

Let us look first of all, then, at the structure and layout of the novel as it first presents itself to the reader. Most crucial, of course, is the fact that it is written in the manner of a diary, the notebooks of the protagonist. By means of this strategy, Rilke already begins to liberate himself from the constraints of traditional novel writing. Whereas novels cannot avoid having beginnings and endings, however abrupt and however ambiguous they may be, the diary form accommodates hesitations and retractions, introspection and retrospection, inconsistency and irresolution, to a degree which even the conventional first-person narrative would resist. This very presentation of the text as 'diary' ensures that there can be no question of a 'story', while the fact that Rilke in the event avoids even the word 'Tagebuch' (diary), opting instead for 'Aufzeichnungen' (notes), serves to emphasise the provisional, unfinished, incomplete nature of the content. Indeed, the opening gives the impression of a page torn at random from a diary – only after approximately six pages of text is Paris incidentally mentioned, and in fact it would be wrong to presume that even the first-person voice of Malte himself bestows any real authority or guarantees any ultimate authenticity: the authenticity with which the novel is concerned is of a different order entirely.

As a collection of notes, the novel is therefore of necessity – that is, of circumstantial and artistic necessity – episodic. As a result, the reader is more conscious of a circularity in the text, a kaleidoscopic, accumulative vision, rather than any linear sequence. The traumatic groundposts of the city, death, childhood and love are thus significant throughout for lending structure to the text as much as for their metaphoric import. Indeed, throughout much of the middle section of the novel, the first-person narrative *persona* almost disappears from view, becoming absorbed in its own narrative preoccupations. This is not least a consequence of the complex time structure of the text, the diary form allowing various arbitrary jumps forward in time, just as it allows reflection and retrospection. Nor is it surprising, given the episodic nature of the text, that the order in which such episodes appear in the novel bears no relation to the order of their composition during the six years of its genesis.

If we follow the erratic indications of date, we can discern that Malte's diary appears to be written within the space of little more than six months: the opening passage is dated 11 September; there follow references to the winter months, and the latest episodes talk of spring, but also still of cold weather. In practice, one is scarcely aware of any detailed chronology. Many passages draw us firmly back into the present with adverbs such as *nun, jetzt, diese Nacht*, and the unobtrusive transitions between the episodes allow for the assimilation of past recollection into present experience as it unfolds.

Paris provides the central setting and focus of the novel, and indeed the topography of the city can be recreated in some detail. The protagonist, Malte Laurids Brigge, is the scion of an old aristocratic Danish family, and so Copenhagen, together with the country homes of Malte's two grandfathers, is the scene of recollection of his childhood experience, and thus the focus also for a second temporal level of the narrative. Finally, Malte's reflections on various historical legendary figures from the past give occasion for episodes set in Moscow, Petersburg, Avignon and Burgundy. The immediate present of the Paris experience is coloured by Malte's sensibilities which at times constitute no less than a persecution mania; the childhood recollections are shadowed by *Angst* and intimations of death; while the historical past (probably the least successful element of the triadic structure) provides models for the alienated solitude of the poet Malte – this, at times, dangerously reinforcing his subjectivity.

Rather than a linear narrative, then, it is an associative and contrastive technique which binds the text, supported by the recurrent theme of relation. The relation of Self/Other is fundamental to Malte's perceptions of Paris and urban life; the theme of love which dominates the final pages of the novel explores the relation of Self/Other on a personal plane, widening the perspective to consider also divine love and man's love of God. The theme of death, meanwhile, which strikes the ground-note for the first part of the novel, deals with the division of Self from the world, but also with the relation which Rilke would like to see us establish between our existence and our own death.

Malte, the solitary poet wandering the streets of Paris, experiences acutely the spiritual loneliness which haunted Rilke throughout his life, and at various points in the text Malte's longing for the security of a settled life amid familiar possessions finds expression. The figure of Malte is based in part on the Norwegian poet Sigbjørn Obstfelder who spent a similarly wretched period in the alienating city environment of Paris and whose posthumous papers Rilke read and reviewed in 1903 – but this background information does not imply any detailed or constructive parallells between the two. Baudelaire's presence is if anything more powerful in the spirit of Malte's quest for authentic experience amid the soulless, materialistic horror of the city. The narrative *persona* is invaded by impressions of his physical surroundings, and this bombardment of impressions represents both an inspiration and a threat; in the early stages of the novel, it is above all a real threat to Malte's sanity. (It is significant, too, that Malte finds himself in a foreign city: unlike Kafka's Prague or Joyce's Dublin, Malte's/Rilke's Paris does not represent for its author a peculiar blend of alienation and nostalgia: here, the alien horror is unmitigated. On the other hand, it has to be said that Paris was for a time 'home' to Rilke as no other city every became, so that this point may be seen to have more relevance for Malte than for Rilke.) Since Baudelaire, and especially around the turn of the century, many European poets fluctuated between seeing themselves as poor wretches suffering with the poor, and affecting an air of aloof, aristocratic detachment. Malte sees himself always as the onlooker, the exception, even something of a pariah. An aristocrat of the spirit, he does not appear to feel pity in response to the suffering and squalor he witnesses in the city – or at least he does not express any. He is thus fundamentally in a situation of confrontation, experiencing the world and all that is in it as an 'opposite' (*ein Gegenüber*). For Malte, the *essence* of experience is made inaccessible by what he thinks of as the 'Vorwände der Natur, welche immer bemüht ist, von ihren tiefsten Geheimnissen die Aufmerksamkeit der Menschen abzulenken' (pretexts of Nature, which is always concerned to divert the attention of people from its innermost secrets: p. 23).

Rilke's own experience was no less shocking, no less devastating than Malte's, and many passages, especially in the earlier pages of the novel, are based very closely on letters written from Paris during the first years of his work on the novel. A key letter is the one written to Lou Andreas-Salomé (this one in fact from Worpswede) on 18 July 1903, and the following extract illustrates how Rilke uses his experience to construct a kind of inner landscape from which he will then in turn cast his text.

> O es haben tausend Hände gebaut an meiner Angst und sie ist aus einem entlegenen Dorf eine Stadt geworden, eine große Stadt, in der Unsägliches geschieht ... O was ist das für eine Welt. Stücke, Stücke von Menschen, Theile von Thieren. Überreste von gewesenen Dingen und alles noch bewegt, wie in einem unheimlichen Winde durcheinandertreibend [...]. Und alle diese Menschen, Männer und Frauen, die in irgend einem Übergang sind, vielleicht vom Wahnsinn zur Heilung, vielleicht auch auf den Irrsinn zu [...]. Hätte ich die Ängste, die ich so erlebte, *machen* können, hätte ich Dinge bilden können aus ihnen, [...]. Im Bestreben, sie zu formen, wurde ich schöpferisch an ihnen selbst; statt sie zu Dingen meines Willens zu machen, gab ich ihnen nur ein eigenes Leben, das sie wider mich kehrten und mit dem sie mich verfolgten weit in die Nacht hinein. Hätte ich es besser gehabt, [...] vielleicht hätte ich es doch gekonnt: Dinge machen aus Angst.
>
> (Oh, a thousand hands built this Angst of mine, and from a remote village it has become a city, a great city, in which unspeakable things happen. Oh, what kind of world is this. Fragments, fragments of people, parts of animals, scraps of things that have been, and everything still in motion, as if blown in to disarray by a fearful wind. And all these people, men and women, who are in some kind of transition, perhaps from madness to healing, perhaps towards madness. If I could have fashioned those fears which I experienced, if I could have formed things out of them. In the effort to form them, I became responsible for their creation; instead of making them objects of my will, I only gave them a life of their own, which they turned against me, and with which they pursued me far into the night. If I had been more fortunate, perhaps I could have done it after all: fashioned things out of fear. – *Materialien*, pp. 23–30)

The description of the 'fragments of people', 'scraps of things that have been', and so on, relates to the beggars of the Paris streets who in the novel are termed by Malte 'the discarded ones' – a distinction he emphasises: 'They are remains, shells of people, whom fate has spat out' (p. 40). Despite the alienating horror of such observations, Rilke is able to interiorise them sufficiently to think in terms of 'forming things', the technique which he was concurrently employing with such rigour in the *Neue Gedichte*. Here, as in the poems, his attention is captured above all by animate and inanimate embodiments of a state of transition or *Übergang*. This accords with Rilke's fundamental view of this world as a *Zwischenland* or 'space between', i.e. between birth and death, and of human beings as the 'Fahrenden' (travellers) of the Fifth Duino Elegy, or the 'Treibenden' (drifting ones) of the *Sonnets to Orpheus* (I, XXII). Within the context of the novel, this consciousness of transition underlines above all the sheer multiformity of experience, its openness – perhaps more accurately, its exposure – to an almost limitless number of interpretations.

Within such multiformity, what Malte 'sees' determines the very substance of the *Aufzeichnungen*. The act of 'Schauen' (looking) acquires here, as indeed already in Rilke's early poetry, especially the *Buch der Bilder* (Book of Images) and *Neue Gedichte*, a special dimension and intensity, and verbs of seeing such as 'einsehen' (to realise), 'erkennen' (to recognise) as well as 'sehen' (to see) provide continual pointers, a recurrent leitmotif even to Malte's confrontation with reality. Already on the third page of the novel, Malte identifies this discipline:

> Ich lerne sehen. Ich weiß nicht, woran es liegt, es geht alles tiefer in mich ein und bleibt nicht an der Stelle stehen, an dem es sonst immer zu Ende war. Ich habe ein Inneres, von dem ich nicht wußte. Alles geht jetzt dorthin. Ich weiß nicht, was dort geschieht.
>
> (I am learning to see. I don't know why it is, everything is penetrating more deeply into me and does not stop at the point where it always used to cease to be. I have an inner core of which I knew nothing. Everything reaches it, I don't know what happens there. – p. 9)

The process of observing and then committing to paper his impressions functions as a kind of exorcism, helping Malte to preserve his sanity. At the same time, however, that 'inner core of which he knew nothing', which previously had been spared such impressions of external reality, is now mercilessly invaded, so that the very boundaries of Malte's consciousness are continually being eroded. The hypersensitive narrative *persona* becomes, in effect, as much object as subject; his inner world breaks out into the outer world, while the objects of the outer world impinge ever more deeply on his innermost self.

It is clear that we have now left far behind the social and historical realities which still underpinned the novels of Fontane and his contemporaries. What Rilke has to communicate can in no way be communicated through conversation, through the social interaction of characters, nor yet by means of the author's confiding in his reader. Nor, for Rilke, does that distinction between 'showing' and 'telling' apply, by which Spielhagen set such store (cf. above, p. 3). With Rilke we have moved to a different order of objectivity, indeed in this text we are presented not so much with the penetration of the protagonist's intimate thoughts and reactions by the author, but rather with their spontaneous explosion. While the *Neue Gedichte* aimed to contain and transcend disruptive and disjunctive experiences, the text of the

Aufzeichnungen positively embraces the plurality and diffuseness of urban reality. Yet this is, in the manner of Kafka, a controlled, 'silent' explosion: verbal coherence serves to intensify the horror of what is described. This horror is above all the horror of contingency, of the shapeless, inconsistent arbitrariness and 'inhumanity' of human existence. It is the horror of a nauseous and viscous reality such as Sartre's Roquentin confronts, nearly thirty years later in *La Nausée*. One of the most striking examples is probably Malte's extended description of the half-demolished houses – 'houses, which were no longer there' (p. 45). What is exposed to view is their *Innenseite* or 'inside' (it has been claimed that all of Rilke's work turns to a greater or lesser extent on the interplay and relation between 'inside' and 'outside'), but Malte sees beyond the remnants of their physical structure to the 'sinewy life' which had been lived out inside them. And the horror of this, for Malte, *das Schreckliche* is the shock of recognition: 'Ich erkenne das alles hier, und darum geht es so ohne weiteres in mich ein: es ist zu Hause in mir' (I recognise all of this here, and that's why it enters my being so easily: it is at home within me. – p. 47) For Malte, as for Rilke, the challenge is to overcome contingency by means of such uncompromising representation, but since such a disruptive, discontinuous reality can allow of no perceivable beginnings and endings, there must always remain an underlying tension between paradigmatic form and contingent reality.

This problem is exemplified by the difficulty Malte experiences in coming to terms with a reality which is so alien, so demanding, so devastating, that it subjects him to continual change, in his inner self as much as in the outer world. Soon after his arrival in Paris he addresses the problem:

> Ich habe heute einen Brief geschrieben, dabei ist es mir aufgefallen, daß ich erst drei Wochen hier bin. Drei Wochen anderswo, auf dem Lande zum Beispiel, das konnte sein wie ein Tag, hier sind es Jahre. Ich will auch keinen Brief mehr schreiben. Wozu soll ich jemandem sagen, daß ich mich verändere? Wenn ich mich verändere, bleibe ich ja doch nicht der, der ich war, und bin ich etwas anderes als bisher, so ist klar, daß ich keine Bekannten habe. Und an fremde Leute, an Leute, die mich nicht kennen, kann ich unmöglich schreiben.

> (Today I wrote a letter, it struck me then that I have been here only three weeks. Three weeks anywhere else, in the country for example, could seem like a day, here it seems like years. I do not want to write any more letters. Why should I tell anyone that I have changed? If I have changed, I am surely no longer the person I was, and if I am different from before, then it follows that I have no acquaintances. And I cannot possibly write to strange people, to people who do not know me. – p. 9)

Later in the novel this fear is extended more especially to the fear of death and the transition or change that it represents. Malte writes:

> Aber ich fürchte mich, ich fürchte mich namenlos vor dieser Veränderung. Ich bin ja noch gar nicht in dieser Welt eingewohnt

gewesen, die mir gut scheint. Was soll ich in einer anderen? Ich würde
so gerne unter den Bedeutungen bleiben, die mir lieb geworden sind ...
(Yet I am afraid. I am indescribably afraid of this change. After all, I
have by no means settled yet in this world, which seems to me a good
one. What should I do in any other? I would so much like to stay with
the meanings to which I have become attached. – pp. 51–2)

Here we see clearly how fear of the unknown can be so strong as
temporarily even to blur the memory of Malte's alienating experience,
leading him here to persuade himself that the world he has known is 'good',
but the reader is scarcely persuaded, since this comes only three or four
pages after the recognition that the horror he perceives is 'at home within
him'. That it is anything but a 'good world' is made abundantly clear; for
this is a world in which even the superficially harmless becomes threatening,
where a tiny thread on a blanket or the button of a nightshirt can take on
menacing proportions (p. 62), or in which the sounds of the night traffic
invade and attack his consciousness: 'Elektrische Bahnen rasen läutend
durch meine Stube. Automobile gehen über mich hin.' (Electric tramcars
race noisily through my room. Motor cars run over me. – p. 8) It has
frequently been observed that this passage on the second page of the text
might stand independently as a prose poem, or indeed as the scenario of an
Expressionist film. It is a world, in short, in which Malte faces the dual
challenge of making sense of such a multiplicity of experiences and of
attempting to reconstruct his own identity through narrative.

This attempt could not be launched under more unfavourable conditions,
as a central passage of the *Aufzeichnungen* illustrates particularly well:

Die Existenz des Entsetzlichen in jedem Bestandteil der Luft. Du
atmest es ein mit Durchsichtigem; in dir aber schlägt es sich nieder,
wird hart, nimmt spitze, geometrische Formen an zwischen den
Organen; denn alles, was sich an Qual und Grauen begeben hat auf den
Richtplätzen, in den Folterstuben, den Tollhäusern, den Operations-
sälen, unter den Brückenbögen im Nachherbst: alles das ist von einer
zähen Unvergänglichkeit, alles das besteht auf sich und hängt,
eifersüchtig auf alles Seiende, an einer schrecklichen Wirklichkeit. Die
Menschen möchten vieles davon vergessen dürfen: ihr Schlaf feilt sanft
über solche Furchen im Gehirn, aber Träume drängen ihn ab und
ziehen die Zeichnungen nach. Und sie wachen auf und keuchen und
lassen einer Kerze Schein sich auflösen in der Finsternis und trinken,
wie gezuckertes Wasser, die halbhelle Beruhigung. Aber, ach, auf
welcher Kante hält sich diese Sicherheit. Nur eine geringste Wendung,
und schon wieder steht der Blick über Bekanntes und Freundliches
hinaus, und der eben noch so tröstliche Kontur wird deutlicher als ein
Rand von Grauen. Hüte dich vor dem Licht, das dem Raum hohler
macht; sieh dich nicht um, ob nicht vielleicht ein Schatten hinter
deinem Aufsitzen aufsteht wie dein Herr.

(The existence of the horror in every particle of the air. You breathe
it in invisibly; but it settles within you, hardens, assumes sharp,
geometric forms between the organs; for all the agony and horror that
has occurred at the places of execution, in the torture chambers, the
lunatic asylums, the operating theatres, under the bridge arches in the
late autumn: all of that is of a tenacious immortality, all of that insists
on its own being and, jealous of all being, clings to a terrible reality.
Human beings would like to be allowed to forget much of this; their
sleep gently smooths over such furrows in the brain, but dreams drive
it away and drown the markings again. And they awake and cough
and let the light of a candle dissolve in the darkness and drink it, as if
it were sugared water, the reassurance of the half-light. But, oh, how
this security hovers on the brink. The slightest turn, and once more
the view over familiar, friendly things has passed and that contour
that was just now comforting becomes clearer than an outline of
horror. Beware of the light which makes the space more hollow; don't
look round to see whether perhaps, behind you as you sit, a shadow
has raised itself like your master. – pp. 71–2)

This passage highlights very clearly certain characteristic features of Rilke's
style in the *Aufzeichnungen* which, in turn, tell us much about the nature of
the reality which the text seeks to communicate. The invisible becomes
concrete ('assumes sharp, geometric forms') and in the confrontation with
reality there is an acute consciousness of the very angle of approach: what
assumes great clarity is the *contour*, rather than the substance, of what is
familiar. It is not least, however, the last sentence of the above extract that
reflects another important dimension of Rilke's narrative, which has been
termed 'hypothetical narrative' (Ryan, 1971). The light is not to be feared
because it illuminates some actual horror, but because it creates a hollow
space which *potentially* could harbour some horrifying reality. In the same
way the 'reality' which Rilke's text mediates represents in many ways a
potential dimension, as much as an actual, measurable one. It is a reality
which is at every moment reaching beyond the objective, palpable evidence
of the external world, a reality which at best is in the *process* of composition
and is thus, in a most specific sense, integral to the composition of the text
itself.

   In the lines following the above passage, the motif of hollow space is
extended further to convey graphically the full extent of Malte's sense of
exposure, and it is on this level that the otherwise apparently disparate worlds
of the Parisian present and Malte's childhood in Denmark are brought
together. As a child, in the dining-room of his grandfather's house, Malte
experienced a comparable feeling of being 'like an empty space', 'dissolved'
(p. 27), while his existential trauma in front of the mirror is perhaps the most
vivid and memorable illustration of this sense of 'loss of self' (pp. 101–2).

Throughout the text, the reader is presented with the notion of reality as something from which protection must be sought, and something which, when confronted, must be 'survived' *überstanden*. Malte concludes his description of the crowded scene in the *crèmerie* with the admission: 'but now it is over; I have survived it' (p. 49). The fear is real and not to be shirked, a notion which is made explicit very early in the text: 'Something must be done about fear once you have it' (p. 11). In this regard Rilke shares with contemporaries such as Hugo von Hofmannsthal and Kafka (to name but two) what we have come to recognise as a fundamental preoccupation and dilemma of twentieth-century writers. The spiritual need to reconstruct human identity in the face of the cataclysmic external realities of modern existence is coupled with the resultant acute difficulty of sustaining the art of narrative construction to write, to erect an interface of language between the vulnerable individual and a threatening reality is accompanied by the painful realisation that even creativity does not provide a cure or a guarantee of protection. Much of Rilke's late poetry, and in particular the *Duino Elegies*, focuses on the challenge of attempting to utter 'the unutterable' (*das Unsägliche*). Malte quickly comes to the pessimistic conclusion that when people told stories, really told stories, 'must have been before my time' (p. 136). Yet he is also exercised by the thought that perhaps no one has *ever* yet really succeeded in translating reality faithfully into language.

> Ist es möglich, [...] daß man noch nichts Wirkliches und Wichtiges gesehen, erkannt und gesagt hat? Ist es möglich, da man Jahrtausende Zeit gehabt hat, zu schauen, nachzudenken und aufzuzeichnen, und daß man die Jahrtausende hat vegehen lassen wie eine Schulpause, in der man sein Butterbrot ißt und einen Apfel?
>
> Ja, es ist möglich.
>
> (Is it possible that no-one has ever yet seen or recognised or said anything real or important? Is it possible that people have had centuries of time to look, to reflect, and take notes, and that they have let the centuries pass like the recreation at school in which you eat your sandwich and an apple?
>
> Yes, it is possible. – p. 24)

Malte himself perceives the only hope to lie in his (ultimately hypothetical) vision of what he terms 'the age of the new interpretation' (*die Zeit der anderen Auslegung*), a stage at which language might finally take over, become autonomous; the stage at which he, Malte, the poet, 'will be written' and thus guaranteed a new order of identity. A new level of interpretation will apply: 'und es wird kein Wort auf dem anderen bleiben, und jeder Sinn wird wie Wolken sich auflösen und wie Wasser niedergehen.' (And no one word will bear on another, and every meaning will dissipate like vapour and drop like water. – p. 52) For Malte the difference would be of the greatest magnitude:

'Nur ein Schritt, und mein tiefes Elend würde Seligkeit sein. Aber ich kann diesen Schritt nicht tun'. (Only one step and my deep wretchedness would be bliss. But I cannot take that step. – p. 52) It is this very gap between potentiality and actuality that signals Malte's separate identity – separate, that is, from that of his author. For it is, after all, not so much Malte's reflections on his writing, but rather the *Aufzeichnungen* themselves which demonstrate his consciousness.

What is remarkable here is that Rilke is able to describe and reproduce Malte's extreme sensitivity, the extreme subjectivity of his observation, without himself *submitting* to that same external reality to the point where he too would become 'an empty space'. This ability is founded above all in the directness of Rilke's own perspective, his uncompromising 'Schauen' (looking). The importance of such an uncompromising vision is echoed and underlined by the fact that what Malte admires most in the work of Ibsen is the ruthless persistence with which the Norwegian dramatist sought to locate in the external world visual equivalents for what he perceives with his mind's eye: 'unter dem Sichtbaren nach den Äquivalenten suchte für das innen Gesehene' (p. 80). Similarly later in the novel, in the episode where Malte's maternal grandfather, Graf Brahe, dictates his memoirs to young Abelone, he maintains fervently that unless his future readers can 'see' what he describes, they cannot possibly understand his text.

In the very ruthless, deliberately unselective nature of the vision which Rilke advocates, the influence of Cézanne and of Baudelaire is undeniable. In a letter of 19 October 1907 to his wife Clara, Rilke explains how he was confirmed in this approach by the example of Baudelaire. In particular, Baudelaire's poem 'Une Charogne' struck him as having launched a whole development towards objective statement (what Rilke terms *sachliches Sagen* which was then further practised by the painter Cézanne. For the very choice of subject for the poem – a rotting carrion observed in all its most repugnant aspects – serves to highlight how the poet's vision has extended beyond what is seemingly only abhorrent to embrace the essential true Being within. Rilke compares Baudelaire's achievement here to that of Flaubert in 'La Légende de Saint Julien l'Hospitalier', which tells how the saint was prepared to lie down with a leper and share his body warmth with him. And in the novel, Malte's reactions echo precisely those of his creator.

> Erinnerst Du Dich an Baudelaires unglaubliches Gedicht 'Une Charogne'? [...] Es war seine Aufgabe, in diesem Schrecklichen, scheinbar nur Widerwärtigen das Seiende zu sehen, das unter allem Seienden gilt. Auswahl und Ablehnung gibt es nicht. Es kommt mir vor, als wäre das das Entscheidende: ob einer es über sich bringt, sich zu dem Aussätzigen zu legen und ihn zu erwärmen mit der Herzwärme der Liebesnächte, das kann nicht anders als gut ausgehen.

(Do you recall Baudelaire's incredible poem 'Une Charogne'? [...] It was his task to discern in this terrible, seemingly only abhorrent thing the Being which, beneath all that exists, *matters.* There is no selection, no rejection. It seems to me that that is the decisive factor: if someone can bring himself to lie down with the leper and warm him with the warmth of nights of love, it can only end well. – pp. 70-1)

In the letter, Rilke further explains how his insight into Baudelaire's achievement illuminated for him the very significance of the *Aufzeichnungen.* For it is Malte's fate to comprehend the necessity of this kind of uncompromising affirmation of reality, yet ultimately to be incapable of practising it: 'Das Buch von Malte Laurids [...] wird nichts als das Buch dieser Einsicht sein, erwiesen an einem, für den sie zu ungeheuer war.' (The story of Malte Laurids will simply be the story of this insight, illustrated by one for whom it was too overwhelming. – *Materialien,* p. 40)

It is essential, Rilke believes, for any artist (and indeed for us all) to experience intensely this awareness of an ultimate connection or relation between all aspects and manifestations of reality, and to learn in our turn simply to exist, as the earth does, 'not requiring to be held by anything other than the network of influences and forces, in which the stars have their security' (*Materialien,* p. 40). This is, as we have seen, the vital principle underlying the novel's composition. The resultant material is of necessity so disparate that, in the absence of any chronological or causal sequence, the only unifying factor can be Malte's consciousness itself. Rilke was of course only too aware of the lack of an aesthetic unity in the text; in a letter of 11 April 1910 he confessed that it was, 'from an artistic point of view, a faulty unity, but humanly it is possible, and what emerges from behind it is at any rate a blueprint for existence, a shadowy framework of moving forces' (*Materialien,* p. 82).

It is scarcely surprising that the existential doubts and spiritual suffering highlighted in the novel should lead sooner or later to the question of whether any kind of deity can be perceived to preside over such a disordered and alien reality. In a short paragraph towards the end of the novel Malte exposes the full implications of such a possibility.

Mein Gott, fiel es mir mit Ungestüm ein, so *bist* du also. Es gibt Beweise fur deine Existenz. Ich habe sie alle vergessen und habe keinen je verlangt, denn welche ungeheuere Verpflichtung läge in deiner Gewißheit?

(My God, I realised impetuously, this is what you are *like* then. There is evidence of your existence. I have forgotten and I have never asked for any, for what tremendous commitment there would be in the certainty of your existence. – pp. 192–3)

God is used here primarily as an expression for the truth of existence which, as the text tells us, is to be equated with suffering and wretchedness. Yet, even with this Malte remains careful not to make that crucial transition to a position of identification with the 'discarded ones', and by this stage in the text it has become apparent that this is not simply an expression of artistic aloofness, but also, and more pertinently, a way of retaining the objectivity which must be a prerequisite of true *insight*.

Thus it is that the questioning of a divinity becomes inseparably linked to the complex theme of love. Complex because it is developed through a series of disparate, if parallel, passages relating the stories of great lovers of history and literature (notably Héloïse, Sappho, Louise Labé, Gaspara Stampa, and not least, Bettina von Arnim); complex, too, though, because the reader is presented with the challenging notion of *besitzlose Liebe* or 'intransitive love'. The only love, we are told, which is not self-destructive, is a love which demands nothing in return and which does not make any claims to possession of the loved one: 'Geliebtsein heißt aufbrennen. Lieben ist: Leuchten mit unerschöpflichem Öle. Geliebtwerden ist vergehen, Lieben ist dauern.' (To be loved is to be consumed. To love is: to glow with an inexhaustible flame. To be loved is to perish. To love is to survive. – p. 226)

This notion is expounded in the final pages of the novel by means of a radical retelling of the biblical parable of the Prodigal Son. At this point, the figure of Malte recedes into the background (it is his *function* as narrative *persona* which is important) and it is instead the figure of the Prodigal Son which is given prominence. This figure's search for God, his 'lange Liebe zu Gott' is an objectless search ('eine ziellose Arbeit') in itself therefore an intransitive mission; the love of God represents a direction of development, much as it did for Dostoevsky's characters, rather than an action or activity of the soul. Moreover, this intellectual love of God is not the love for a personal 'Thou': rather, God is but yet another name for the abstract concept of the Absolute, Eternal Being ('Das absolut unendlich Seiende'). We are here forcibly reminded of yet another prevalent preoccupation of twentieth-century writers, most notably among them Kafka, namely the emphasis on the quest rather than on the goal. The Prodigal Son's progress in his search for God is fundamentally a quest for the only object of love from which reciprocal love might possibly be bearable. But there is doubt even here. The Prodigal Son has become 'terribly difficult to love' and there is only one who might be able to love him (that is, without 'consuming him'): 'But he was not yet willing' (p. 234).

The negation with which the text appears to end brings us finally back to the question of 'positives' and 'negatives' mentioned earlier, for the novel's conclusion (if one can even use the term) is fraught with uncertainties. Critics are wont to speak of Malte's *Untergang* or downfall, since they cannot with certainty speak of his death: indeed to do so would be absurd, since the final pages are still part of Malte's first-person diary account. Rilke does speak of Malte at least once as *der Untergegangene* (letter of 28 December 1911: *Materialien*, p. 88), but he terms it 'eine eigentümlich dunkle Himmelfahrt in eine vernachlässigte abgelegene Stelle des Himmels' (a strangely dark ascension into a forgotten, remote corner of the heavens). Again and again, in Rilke's own references to the novel we meet these apparently self-contradictory comments which seek to bring together the extreme facets of the text – the unmitigating horror and hopelessness of Malte's present experience in Paris, set against the undeniable, if only intermittent glimpses of a possibility of salvation. In a famous letter of 11 February 1912 to Arthur Hospelt, Rilke persuades his friend that now he must be in a position to understand the novel in 'the ascending mode which is its genuine and decisive one'. To give way, he says, to the temptation of moving in parallel with this text is disastrous; rather, one must be prepared to read it 'against the current' (*Materialien*, p. 99).

But it is in another letter, of 8 November 1915, that we find an interpretation which reinforces the idea of a 'hypothetical reality' and, in doing so, emphasises to what extent Rilke pushes to the limit the definition of 'reality' as it was understood by writers before him. He writes:

> Ich habe schon einmal, vor Jahren, über den Malte jemandem, den dieses Buch erschreckt hatte, zu schreiben versucht, daß ich es selbst manchmal wie eine hohle Form, wie ein Negativ empfände, dessen alle Mulden und Vertiefungen Schmerz sind, Trostlosigkeiten und weheste Einsicht, der Ausguß davon aber, wenn es möglich wäre einen herzustellen (wie bei einer Bronze die positive Figur, die man daraus gewönne), wäre vielleicht Glück, Zustimmung; – genaueste und sicherste Seligkeit.

> (Once, years ago, I wrote of Malte, to someone who had been alarmed by this book, that I myself sometimes experienced it as a hollow mould, like a negative, of which all the troughs and depressions were pain, wretchedness and woeful insights; the cast (of this mould) however, if it were possible to produce one (the positive form one would obtain from it, as with a bronze), would perhaps be joy, assent, the most precise and secure bliss. – *Materialien*, p. 110)

This interpretation emphasises not only the inseparability of form and content, but also the degree to which only the cumulative *process* of reading can distill any clear meaning from such a fragmentary kaleidoscope of meaning. Ultimately, it reminds the reader above all that the 'reality' which he and the text strive to capture is essentially shifting and elusive – not a clearly definable entity, but rather, a rich mosaic which only in interaction with the reader's sensibilities seeks the fulfilment of its composition.

REFERENCES

References given by page number only relate to the Bibliothek Suhrkamp edition of *Die Aufzeichnungen des Malte Laurids Brigge*, Frankfurt 1979 (vol. 343).

FÜLLEBORN, U. (1961), Form und Sinn der Aufzeichnungen des Malte Laurids Brigge: Rilkes Prosabuch und der moderne Roman, in *Unterscheidung und*

Bewahrung: Festschrift für Hermann Kunisch zum 60. Geburtstag, Berlin: de Gruyter (reprinted in *Materialien zu Rainer Maria Rilke, 'Die Aufzeichnungen des Malte Laurids Brigge'*, ed. H. Engelhardt, Frankfurt: Suhrkamp 1974).

GOHEEN, J. (1969), Tempusform und Zeitbegriff in R. M. Rilkes *Die Aufzeichnungen des Malte Laurids Brigge, Wirkendes Wort* 19, pp. 254–67.

Materialien zu Rainer Maria Rilke, 'Die Aufzeichnungen des Malte Laurids Brigge' (1974), ed. H. Engelhardt, Frankfurt: Suhrkamp.

RYAN, J. (1971), 'Hypothetisches Erzählen': Zur Funktion von Phantasie und Einbildung in Rilkes 'Malte Laurids Brigge', *Jahrbuch der deutschen Schillergesellschaft* 15, pp. 341–74 (reprinted in *Materialien zu Rainer Maria Rilke, 'Die Aufzeichnungen des Malte Laurids Brigge'*, ed. H. Engelhardt, Frankfurt: Suhrkamp 1974).

SEGAL, N. (1981), *The Banal Object: Theme and Thematics in Proust, Rilke, Hofmannsthal and Sartre*, London: Institute of Germanic Studies.

STAHL, A. (1979), *Rilke-Kommentar zu den Aufzeichnungen des Malte Laurids Brigge*, Munich: Winkler.

STEFFENSEN, S. (1971), *Die Aufzeichnungen des Malte Laurids Brigge*: Ein Vorläufer des modernen Romans, in *Peripherie und Zentrum: Studien zur österreichischen Literatur*, ed. G. Weiss and K. Zelewitz, Salzburg: Das Bergland-Buch, pp. 311–22.

STEPHENS, A. (1974), *Rilkes Malte Laurids Brigge: Strukturanalyse des erzählerischen Bewußtseins*, Bern and Frankfurt: Lang.

STEPHENS, A. (1975), Essay und Aufzeichnung bei Rainer Maria Rilke, *Jahrbuch für Internationale Germanistik* 7, 1, pp. 88–103.

5

Reading the Clues
Kafka, *Der Proceß*

RITCHIE ROBERTSON

Der Proceß (The Trial) certainly lies beyond Realism; but how far beyond? Its setting forms an extreme contrast to the specific localities and dense descriptions found, for example, in the novels of Fontane. An urban milieu, with blocks of flats, offices, taxis, slums, and a cathedral, is evoked in a decidedly perfunctory way. The operations of the mysterious Court never receive a rational explanation. The laws of Realism are broken when Court officials seem to respond to the protagonist's thoughts; when he finds a sadistic punishment going on in a lumber-room in his offices, and continuing without interruption twenty-four hours later; and by all manner of grotesque and inexplicable incidents. For this reason many commentators have wanted to see Kafka as closely anticipating the mystificatory fiction of Beckett and Robbe-Grillet (Hibberd, 1985; Sandbank, 1989). The tendency of critics to transfer attention from the author's intention to the reader's response has reinforced this approach. It has encouraged the view that Kafka, like later writers, presents a world in which there is no ulterior meaning behind appearances, and that he reduces character and setting to mere counters for use in a game of interpretation, a game whose only outcome can be ever-renewed perplexity (Elm, 1979).

A number of scruples, however, should restrain us from aligning *Der Proceß* with works like *Watt* and *Les Gommes*. Firstly, critics are doubtless correct in saying that *Der Proceß* does not contain any unambiguous message, any secret for the sufficiently persistent reader to extract; but by emphasising this they tend to make the opposite error of trivialising the book. Secondly, such an approach would be anachronistic. There is a great gap in time and literary history separating Kafka, who died in 1924, from a late Modernist like Robbe-Grillet; and Kafka's own literary sympathies lay with Realism rather than with Expressionism (the major German variant of Modernism). The authors he described as his literary blood-relations were all nineteenth-century Realists: Flaubert, Dostoyevsky, Grillparzer and Kleist (Kafka, 1967, p. 460).

In contemporary literature he preferred Realist fiction like Strindberg's novels or Mann's *Tonio Kröger* (Brod and Kafka, 1989, p. 13; Kafka, 1990, p. 547). He found the Expressionists too strident for his taste (Raabe, 1967). Although his fiction has many resemblances to the fantastic narratives of his contemporaries Alfred Kubin and Gustav Meyrink, he showed no interest in these works (Cersowsky, 1983). As a young man Kafka did take some interest in the exotic fiction of the *fin de siècle*, and its influence is clearly visible in his earliest surviving work, the bewildering and seemingly inconsequential *Beschreibung eines Kampfes* (Description of a Struggle) (Anderson, 1992). In the short sketches published in 1912 as *Betrachtung* (Meditation), however, and in some early diary entries, Kafka can be seen practising a concise, nuanced, and sharply detailed mode of writing. The literary breakthrough he achieved with *Das Urteil* (The Judgement) in September 1912 depended on using this mode to embed fantasy in a seemingly Realist setting and in a tautly constructed narrative centring on a dramatic confrontation.

Das Urteil begins by describing its protagonist, Georg Bendemann, sitting at a window, preparing to write to a friend in Russia with the news of his engagement. Nothing is puzzling except his reluctance to tell his friend this news, and his fiancée's reported opinion that someone with such friends ought not to have become engaged. These mild disturbances of the story's Realist surface reveal their importance only later, when Georg's father suddenly and inexplicably turns from a frail old man into a vigorous menacing giant, who denounces Georg's marriage plans, and condemns him to death by drowning – a sentence which Georg dutifully carries out. Much of the story's power comes from Kafka's switch from a Realist mode to one that might be called fantastic or Expressionist. The drably recognisable events of the first part seem continuous and yet incongruous with the second part, in which the father assumes mythic, God-like proportions. In *Die Verwandlung* (The Metamorphosis) Kafka attempts something yet bolder, beginning the story with Gregor Samsa's transformation into an insect and recounting all the subsequent events in minute detail. In order to break the laws of Realism, a writer must first make a show of acknowledging these laws. By doing this, Kafka permits Realism and fantasy to interact in complex ways: the Realist background lends credibility to the fantasy, yet the fantasy exposes the Realism as a flimsy contrivance.

The flimsiness of the Realist setting in *Der Proceß* results in part from the way in which Kafka wrote the novel. Now that the manuscript has been critically edited, it is possible to describe the composition of *Der Proceß* in considerable detail. Kafka began writing it after the dissolution of his engagement to Felice Bauer. The engagement was dissolved in a painful scene in a hotel room in Berlin, when Felice's friends called him to account for his selfish treatment of her. Kafka described it in his diary as a court of justice (*Gerichtshof*: Kafka, 1990, p. 658). Writing the novel was a way of coming to terms with this experience. He started work on *Der Proceß* in early August and seems to have written with comparative ease until the beginning of October, when he took two weeks off work to advance the novel but was less successful than he had hoped. He continued to work on it intermittently until he abandoned it in January 1915.

During the six months of composition, Kafka did not write *Der Proceß* in a linear sequence. Having begun with the chapter about Josef K.'s arrest, he immediately wrote the final chapter, headed simply 'Ende'. This was no doubt a precaution against the tendency of his stories to run away with him. Since he did not plan his narratives in advance, but relied on inspiration, they were liable to develop in unexpected and uncontrollable ways. From the outset, therefore, Kafka intended that Josef K.'s trial should last for a year, that he should be executed on the eve of his thirty-first birthday, and that he should never learn what charges had been laid against him (Pasley, 1990).

The gap between K.'s arrest and his execution was filled in with a number of episodes, each composed as a separate chapter. One can see Kafka trying to divide his novel into units small enough each to be sustained by a separate burst of inspiration. He succeeded in completing some of these chapters, and when he had done so he put the chapter in question into a folder marked with either a title or a summary description of the contents. There were also a number of chapters which he did not succeed in finishing, and which he kept separately. Although these were printed by Max Brod as an appendix to his edition of *Der Proceß*, they were omitted from the English tanslations, and are ignored even by many people who read *Der Proceß* in German. However, Kafka did not discard these chapters: he simply put them aside. What we have, therefore, is a novel which is finished, in the sense that the end is written, but incomplete, in that it includes a number of chapters which break off. They form a kind of penumbra around the main action, indicating further directions in which Kafka might have taken the story. Nor is it altogether clear how Kafka intended to arrange the chapters, complete and incomplete alike. The sequence in Brod's edition accordingly differs from that in the Critical Edition by Malcolm Pasley, and both sequences in turn differ from that proposed by Eric Marson (1975) in his minute and illuminating study of the text. Different sequences are based on different criteria: Pasley follows the indications of time with which many of the chapters begin (e.g. 'In diesem Frühjahr' (that spring), 'An einem der nächsten Abende' (An evening or two later); Marson follows the internal logic of the narrative. These criteria contradict each other, and it would seem that Kafka himself had not made a final decision about the sequence of chapters.

Kafka abandoned the whole novel in January 1915 and never revised what he had written. This accounts for some discrepancies in the text: K.'s Uncle Karl has his name changed to Albert (pp. 118, 131); K. arranges to meet the Italian at the Cathedral at ten (p. 276) and arrives, we are told, punctually at eleven (p. 279). It also helps to account, in part at least, for other curious features of his text. Since he wrote the chapters in isolation from one another, certain details occur once only and with no apparent motivation. They seem to conceal a symbolic meaning, but their meaning is elucidated neither by the immediate context nor by their place in any larger pattern of imagery. Why, for example, are the audience at K.'s preliminary investigation all wearing badges, and why do they have thin beards? Why is Titorelli besieged by young girls, one of whom is deformed? Why does Leni have a web between her fingers? Why do K.'s executioners resemble down-at-heel actors? Such unmotivated details help to create the bewildering and sinister atmosphere of Kafka's fiction. They suggest a meaning which the reader cannot quite grasp. Presumably, however, they result from ideas that occurred to Kafka while writing but were displaced by fresh inspirations instead of being developed. If so, there would seem little point in searching for their latent significance: the meaning they had for Kafka may well be irrecoverable.

Given Kafka's methods of writing, therefore, it would at least be unwise to expect from *Der Proceß* a seamless tissue of words and themes. Nevertheless, the novel is remarkably coherent in its overall design, and one clue to this design is the truncated name of the protagonist, Josef K., which also helps us to begin situating this novel in relation to Realism.

In early Realist literature, the reduction of a proper name to its initial helped to create the 'referential illusion', suggesting that the text referred to a real place or person which it would be indiscreet to identify (Barthes, 1986; Fowler, 1982, Chapter 5). Thus, in Richardson's *Pamela* the heroine's lascivious employer is known throughout as 'Mr B.'; Goethe's Werther meets Prince C. and Fräulein von B. in 'dem traurigen Neste D.' (the dismal hole D.); and Kleist assures us that his *Die Marquise von O ...* is based on a real incident and that he has merely changed its location, and disguised the names of its protagonists, in order to avoid scandal. In nineteenth-century fiction this means of feigning authenticity is largely abandoned. Balzac's Issoudun (*La Rabouilleuse*) and Flaubert's Yonville (*Madame Bovary*) are presented not as specific places which the reader might identify if they were not disguised, but as typical country towns with counterparts in the reader's experience. The novelist's relation to reality has become more abstract, more analytical: Balzac explicitly offers a natural history of society in which individuals are presented as specimens of social types (Demetz, 1968). The concepts of type and typicality are indispensable for analysing nineteenth-century Realism. A familiar though late example is *Buddenbrooks*, where Thomas Mann uses four successive Buddenbrook males to typify their respective generations.

In the twentieth century, however, many Modernist works again present characters and places with abbreviated names, or with no names at all. Josef K. and the unnamed city where he works are contemporary with the anonymous Cashier (*Kassierer*) in Kaiser's play *Von morgens bis mitternachts* (written in 1914), who travels from the town of W. to the city of B. These abbreviations can hardly be disguises: Josef K.'s city bears many resemblances to Kafka's home town of Prague, while Kaiser's W. and B. can easily be identified, for what that is worth, as Weimar and Berlin. The function of the abbreviations is rather to indicate a further step towards abstraction. The nineteenth century's interest in types is giving way to the twentieth century's interest in systems. Kaiser diverts our attention from the specific settings of the Cashier's experiences, and from his individual personality and biography, and directs us to the dehumanising system of commercial exploitation in which he finds himself trapped. Kafka likewise shows less interest in K.'s personality than in the position K. occupies in two systems: the hierarchical structure of his bank, where as managing director he holds a place near the top, and the no less hierarchical court, where as a defendant who is eventually condemned K. seems to slide inexorably downwards towards a degrading death.

Nevertheless, Josef K. is not completely anonymous, and to a limited extent we can still identify him both as a social type and as a type of personality. Kafka tells us not only about his position in the bank, but about his daily routine. His day begins with his breakfast being brought just before eight and ends, after he has worked in the bank until about nine, with a short walk and a visit to the *Stammtisch* in a pub, where he stays in the company of older officials until eleven. Senior colleagues are objects either of his servility (the state prosecutor Hasterer) or his rivalry (the Deputy Director of the bank). It is not difficult to recognise the typical bureaucrat. but we recognise this type from literature rather than from life. Kafka has not troubled to paint a minute or consistent picture of a bureaucrat's way of life. For example, given the position Josef K. has reached and the salary it would command, it is incongruous to find him renting a room in a tenement flat. Instead, Kafka has provided enough details about Josef K. for us to recognise him as belonging to the literary tradition of satire on bureaucrats, in which they are represented as unimaginative, selfish, and obsessed with order. We may think of the registrar Heerbrand in Hoffmann's *Der goldne Topf* (The Golden Pot); of the criticism of bureaucracy as a career delivered by Risach in Stifter's *Der Nachsommer* (Indian Summer); and of the petty official Theobald Maske in Sternheim's *Die Hose* (The Bloomers).

Josef K.'s personality likewise has enough distinctive features to prevent him from being a colourless Everyman figure. He thinks in hierarchical terms, and accordingly treats junior officials at the bank with irritation and disdain. One of the unfinished chapters tells how K. and his *Stammtisch* colleagues delight in humiliating the junior employees who are permitted to attend. In his dealings with other people K. is generally aggressive, calculating and manipulative. This may be illustrated from the episode of his arrest. Near the end of this scene, K. thinks he is gaining an advantage over the Inspector. This belief is manifested in K.'s aggressive manner: he advances menacingly close to the Inspector, and counters the latter's claim to be doing his duty with the bullying words 'Eine dumme Pflicht' (An idiotic duty: p. 26). Meanwhile he is privately congratulating himself on playing with his captors. Then, however, K.'s self-confidence is dented by the revelation that the three people who have been lurking in the room are three junior employees from his bank, and hence that his arrest, which he had thought a matter to be sorted out between him and the Inspector, turns out to have been going on under the eyes of his junior colleagues. K. promptly reproaches himself for his inattention. Indeed, he is so taken aback by this failure in his normal perceptiveness that he fails to notice the departure of the Inspector and the two guards, and when he realises this, he again reproaches himself and resolves to keep a sharper look-out in future. In the rest of the novel, K's self-assurance will gradually be broken down by the Court. His arrogance towards Court officials will eventually give place to a pathetic longing for human contact which he thinks is fulfilled by the Chaplain. The narrative of *Der Proceß* recounts, among other things, the dismantling of a personality.

Like Josef K.'s character, the setting of *Der Proceß* lies beyond but still in sight of Realism. Kafka's descriptions of physical objects hover between metaphor and metonymy. Realist fiction has been said to depend on metonymy, or the contiguity of objects in space: Modernist fiction on metaphor, or the similarity between spatially unrelated objects (Jakobson, 1956; Lodge, 1977). Thus, a Realist novel places its hero in a world of physical detail, like Dickens's London, George Eliot's Middlemarch, and Fontane's Berlin; while a Modernist novel tends to emphasise metaphor and symbolism, even in its title (*The Rainbow, Ulysses, The Magic Mountain, The Sleepwalkers, Steppenwolf*). In Kafka's earlier fiction, such as *Der Proceß*, metonymy shades into metaphor. Everyday objects in his fictional world tend to become symbolic: firstly, because that world is simple, bare, stripped to its essentials, and only those essentials are left to convey meaning; secondly, because the repeated mention of these objects causes them, by accumulation, to take on a more than literal significance. The first time a fictional window is mentioned, it is simply a pane of glass; by the fourth or fifth mention, it has become something more than a window – an item in a chain of imagery. The significance of these images, however, is not obscure or far-fetched.

Windows provide a case in point which is worth examining in more detail. K., in his office, receives a visit from his uncle, who has heard about his lawsuit and urges him to engage an advocate; too tired to argue, K. gazes out of the window and annoys his uncle by his apparent apathy. Raising his arms, K.'s uncle exclaims: 'Du schaust aus dem Fenster' (You're looking out of the window: p. 119). Here staring out of the window is contrasted with attending to one's duties, and is obviously uncharacteristic of K., who at the age of 30 is already managing director of a large bank. In doing so, K. gives way to 'einer angenehmen Mattigkeit' (a pleasant lassitude: p. 119). For him, as for other Kafka characters, window-gazing is initially a relief from the pressures of work. In *Die Verwandlung* Gregor Samsa, after his transformation from a bored commercial traveller into an insect, wistfully recalls how gazing out of the window had formerly given him a sense of freedom. This is a familiar experience; it was especially so to

Kafka. After graduating from Prague with an undistinguished degree in law and spending a year in a lawyer's office, he joined an insurance company, the Assicurazioni Generali, which had its headquarters in Trieste and branches all over the world; and in a letter he expresses the hope, 'selbst auf den Sesseln sehr entfernter Länder einmal zu sitzen, aus den Bureaufenstern Zuckerrohrfelder oder mohammedanische Friedhöfe zu sehn' (to sit on the chairs of very distant countries and see from the office windows fields of sugar-cane or Mohammedan cemeteries: Kafka, 1958, p. 49). It is understandable that in his fiction the window should be the boundary between the world of routine work and that of freedom.

While the bored worker can gaze out of the window, other people can gaze in, and in the early fiction the window is also the means by which the individual's privacy can be exposed to outsiders. K.'s 'arrest' is played out under the eyes of the neighbours across the way, who can follow events from their windows. The Court seems mainly to inhabit rooms without views, or with windows that will not open, or without windows altogether. Another accused person, the merchant Block, sleeps in the house of the Advocate also employed by K.; the room assigned to Block has only enough room for a bed, and instead of a window has only a small opening admitting light from the courtyard outside, which is itself surrounded by high walls. The power of the Court over its victims is conveyed by the increasingly dark and confined spaces which it obliges them to enter. Block's lawsuit has been in progress much longer than K.'s – for over five years – and his room seems to be the ultimate in confined spaces.

The inconvenience of the Court premises is sometimes farcical. When he visits Titorelli's studio, K. finds it to be a miserable garret, no more than two paces across in either direction. The window does not open, making the room intolerably hot, and the view from the window extends no further than the snow-covered roof of the neighbouring house. When a judge comes to have his portrait painted by Titorelli, he enters the studio from the Court offices, through another door which opens on to Titorelli's bed, so that the judge has to climb over the bed, usually when Titorelli is already in it. We hear of yet more fantastic arrangements. The advocates attached to the Court are said to occupy a room with a large hole in the floor, through which their feet can be seen dangling.

Thus Kafka moves from metonymy – the description of K.'s physical surroundings – to metaphor, in which the same surroundings assume symbolic overtones. With the help of these examples, it is possible to distinguish three kinds of space in Kafka's early fiction. At one extreme, there is the open space of the outside world, which can usually only be seen through a window by the bored office worker in a moment snatched from his routine. Then there is the normal interior space of everyday life, consisting of bedrooms, living-rooms and offices. At the other extreme, there is the dark, confined space in which the Court has its premises and where the outside world is visible, if at all, only as a featureless cityscape blurred by snow or rain. K. himself contrasts all three kinds of space when he compares himself favourably with the judge:

> In welcher Stellung befand sich doch K. gegenüber dem Richter, der auf dem Dachboden saß, während er selbst in der Bank ein großes Zimmer mit einem Vorzimmer hatte und durch eine riesige Fensterscheibe auf den belebten Stadtplatz hinuntersehen konnte.
>
> (What a difference there was between K's position and that of the judge, who sat here in this attic whilst K. himself had a big room at the bank with an ante-room and was able to look down through a huge window-pane on to the busy city square! – p. 88)

Another example of Kafka's everyday symbolism is his use of light and darkness. There is a particularly obvious contrast between the lighting of the houses occupied by two of K.'s advisers, Titorelli and the Advocate. Kafka emphasises that the door of Titorelli's studio is 'verhältnismäßig hell beleuchtet' (lit comparatively brightly: p. 190) by a skylight just above it, while the Advocate, who lives at the opposite side of the town, has a gas-jet just above his front door, which sputters but does not provide much light. No private key to Kafka's meaning is required to infer that Titorelli may prove a more enlightening adviser than the Advocate. The symbolism of light and darkness is most abundant in the chapter set in the Cathedral. The weather outside is extremely gloomy, and the Cathedral has scarcely any lighting apart from the candles on the high altar, which go out in the course of the chapter. The atmosphere of gathering gloom is appropriate to the episode in which K. meets the last of his potential helpers, the Chaplain, and fails to pick up the advice implicit in the parable. The following and final chapter contrasts the dark streets through which K. is led by his executioners with the lighted windows in the houses around him, but it also includes an unexpected reference to the moonlight: 'Überall lag der Mondschein mit seiner Natürlichkeit und Ruhe, die keinem anderen Licht gegeben ist' (The moonlight shone on everything with that particular naturalness and peace which no other light has: p. 310). This is unexpected because the light referred to hitherto in the novel has almost always been artificial light, in keeping with the mostly indoor settings. The last chapter provides something new, for his executioners lead K. out of the town to a small quarry on its edge, where they carry out the Court's sentence.

Thus this chapter is set in the first of the three kinds of space distinguished above, the open space visible only through windows, and it is deeply ironic that K. enters this space, with its connotations of freedom, only when he is about to die.

Kafka's treatment of space illustrates a striking feature of *Der Proceß*: the constant need for interpretation. Houses, rooms and streets are not just neutral features of the world, but bearers of metaphorical suggestions to which the reader learns to respond. Interpretation is indeed a central issue in *Der Proceß*. Josef K. tries to interpret the behaviour of the Court; the reader has the harder task of interpreting not only the Court but also Josef K.'s interpretation of it. For a long time the view was current that the reader is helplessly bound to Josef K.'s interpretation of events, with no means of criticising or correcting it. This view was first put forward in a lecture by Friedrich Beissner (1952). Beissner maintains that in Kafka's major fictional writings the narrative viewpoint is always that of the central character. There is no narrator to comment on the action or to provide the reader with information unknown to the protagonist. The reader is always confined to the protagonist's narrow, uncertain viewpoint, and thus shares his perplexity and acquires a feeling of constriction. However, this argument that Kafka practises monoperspectival narration has been severely questioned and needs to be revised (Beissner, 1952; Müller-Seidel, 1986, pp. 91–106).

First, in some of his fiction Kafka does create a narrative standpoint outside the consciousness of the protagonist, though he does so very briefly before adopting the protagonist's viewpoint. Nevertheless, this suffices to separate protagonist and reader by making the latter aware that a possible alternative viewpoint exists. The most obvious example is the opening of *Die Verwandlung*, where the reader is told of Gregor's transformation into an insect, and yet Gregor remains unaware of this and continues to think like a commercial traveller and plan his day's work. Thus the reader is given a standpoint superior to Gregor's, and is able to see that Gregor's perception of his own situation is so fundamentally wrong as to render all his plans absurd. There are also moments in *Der Proceß*, especially towards the end, where the narrative viewpoint departs from that of Josef K.: thus, at the beginning of the final chapter, when K.'s executioners arrive to collect him, we see them outside K.'s door, each inviting the other to enter first. Elsewhere in his fiction Kafka reports the protagonist's thoughts and perceptions in such a manner as to make us question the character's moral standards or his understanding of his situation. One of many examples in *Der Proceß* occurs just after K.'s arrest. The Inspector and the guards are leaving, the three junior officials are going to accompany K. to the bank, and the man who, along with an old couple, has been watching K.'s arrest through his window suddenly appears, All this is mediated through K.'s consciousness, and the interpretations are all his:

Im Vorzimmer öffnete dann Frau Grubach, die gar nicht sehr schuldbewußt aussah, die Wohnungstür and K. sah, wie so oft, auf ihr Schürzenband nieder, das so unnötig tief in ihren mächtigen Leib einschnitt. Unten entschloß sich K., die Uhr in der Hand, ein Automobil zu nehmen, um die schon halbstündige Verspätung nicht unnötig zu vergrößern. Kaminer lief zur Ecke, um den Wagen zu holen, die zwei andern versuchten offensichtlich K. zu zerstreuen, als plötzlich Kullich auf das gegenüberliegende Haustor zeigte, in dem eben der Mann mit dem blonden Sptizbart erschien und im ersten Augenblick ein wenig verlegen darüber, daß er sich jetzt in seiner ganzen Größe zeigte, zur Wand zurücktrat und sich anlehnte. Die Alten waren wohl noch auf der Treppe.

(Then Frau Grubach, looking not in the least guilty, opened the door in the hall, and, as usual, K. found himself gazing down at her apron-strings, which cut into her huge body so unnecessarily deeply. Once outside, K., holding his watch in his hand, decided to take a taxi in order to avoid any further delay – he was already half an hour late. Kaminer ran to the corner to fetch a cab, while the other two were obviously trying to distract K.'s attention; suddenly Kullich pointed to the door of the house opposite, where the big man with the reddish pointed beard had just appeared. A little embarrassed for a moment at revealing himself in his full size, he stepped back to the wall and leaned against it. The old people were presumably still on the stairs. – p. 28.)

K. thinks that Frau Grubach ought to look guilt-stricken and interprets the bearded man's behaviour as resulting from embarrassment. The first of these conclusions seems groundless, and the second to be founded on very insufficient evidence. Nor is there any reason, except K.'s own embarrassment, to suppose that the elderly couple is following the bearded man. It is also unclear why K. should be in the habit of looking at and thinking about his landlady's apron-strings (the word 'so' makes it clear that we are being told his impressions); in the text as a whole, however, he proves to have a fetishistic obsession with women's clothes, evident also from repeated references to Fräulein Bürstner's blouse (pp. 20, 36, 44).

Just after this the narrative perspective momentarily deserts K. as he tells the junior officials not to look at the bearded man, 'ohne zu bemerken, wie auffallend eine solche Redeweise gegenüber selbständigen Männern war' (without realising how other people would be struck by this manner of addressing grown-up men: p. 28). Kafka is drawing the reader's attention explicitly to the absurd inappropriateness of K.'s behaviour. There are several more occasions when the narrative viewpoint moves away from K.'s consciousness, as when we are told what Frau Grubach is thinking (p. 35) or what K.'s unconscious motives are in manhandling a co-defendant: 'K. [...] faßte ihn, unbewußt durch das demütige Wesen des Mannes dazu aufgefordert, beim Arm, als wolle er ihn zum Glauben zwingen' (provoked unconsciously by the man's humble manner, K. grasped him by the arm as if he intended to force him to believe: p. 95). All this provides further evidence against Beissner's thesis that the story is narrated exclusively from K.'s perspective.

Again, there are many occasions when K. responds to his arrest in the hierarchical manner appropriate to his career in the bank. When arrested, he dismisses the guards' talk as 'das Geschwätz dieser niedrigsten Organe' (the chatter of these minions of the lowest rank: p. 15). When he is admonished by the Inspector, we are told: 'K. starrte den Aufseher an. Schulmäßige Lehren bekam er hier von einem vielleicht jüngern Menschen?' (K. stared at the

Inspector. Was he being ticked off like a schoolboy, and by a man perhaps younger than himself? – p. 23) He interprets his lawsuit as a piece of business such as he is used to transacting for the bank: 'Es gab keine Schuld. Der Proceß war nichts anderes, als ein großes Geschäft, wie er es schon oft mit Vorteil für die Bank abgeschlossen hatte, ein Geschäft, innerhalb dessen, wie das die Regel war, verschiedene Gefahren lauerten, die eben abgewehrt werden mußten.' (There was no guilt. The case was merely a big business transaction, such as he had often concluded to the advantage of the bank – a business transaction in which, as invariably happened, there lurked various dangers that had simply to be averted. – p. 168) In such passages we see K. applying to his lawsuit the categories which have served him in his career, instead of attending to remarks and ideas which might have proved valuable had his mind been less closed. And we see, too, how his pompous and inappropriate responses are at first treated satirically: it should not be difficult to understand why Kafka laughed heartily when reading the first chapter of *Der Proceß* aloud to his friends (Brod, 1974, p. 156). Elsewhere, however, the atmosphere of the novel becomes more sombre and K.'s misunderstanding seems increasingly likely to bring dire consequences. This is shown by the desperation with which the Chaplain calls out to him: 'Siehst Du denn nicht zwei Schritte weit?' (Can't you see what is just in front of your nose?. – p. 290)

To call Kafka's narrative method monoperspectival is therefore extremely misleading. His method depends on an uncomfortably close relation between two perspectives. While Kafka does bring us close to the consciousness of the protagonist, with the effect of constriction that Beissner has described, in another way he distances us from that consciousness by intimating to us that the protagonist is an unreliable witness.

Another way in which *Der Proceß* locates itself just beyond Realism is its treatment of pictures and photographs. Both these modes of representation have an uncertain relation to reality. K. shows Leni a snapshot which depicts his girlfriend Elsa just after she has been dancing a reel, with her hands on her hips and her skirt still flying behind her. Thus, despite the supposed faithfulness of the camera, the photograph distorts reality by being unable to represent motion. It is not, however, as unreliable as the photograph in *Das Schloß* which shows a Castle messenger in a horizontal position, either lying on a board or vaulting over a rope (Kafka, 1982, pp. 124–5). Just before showing Leni the photograph, K. has seen a painting of a judge who is apparently on the point of leaping to his feet:

> Es stellte einen Mann im Richtertalar dar; er saß auf einem hohen Tronsessel, dessen Vergoldung vielfach aus dem Bilde hervorstach. Das Ungewöhnliche war, daß dieser Richter nicht in Ruhe und Würde dort saß, sondern den linken Arm fest an Rücken- und Seitenlehne drückte, den rechten Arm aber völlig frei hatte und nur mit der Hand die Seitenlehne umfaßte, als wolle er im nächsten Augenblick mit einer

heftigen und vielleicht empörten Wendung aufspringen um etwas Entscheidendes zu sagen oder gar das Urteil zu verkünden.

(It showed a man in judge's robes; he was sitting on a high throne, the gilding of which stood out from the picture in many places. The unusual thing about it was that this judge was not sitting there in tranquility and dignity, but was pressing his left arm firmly against the back and armrest of the chair, while he had his right arm completely free and was grasping the chair only with his hand, as if he were on the point of leaping up with a violent and perhaps furious gesture in order to say something decisive or even pronounce sentence. – p. 141f)

Leni assures K. that the portrait does not resemble its subject at all. Not only was it painted in his youth, but in reality he is much smaller and sits not on a throne but on a kitchen chair covered with a horse-blanket. Later Titorelli, the Court painter, explains that his paintings are not accurate but follow a fixed set of conventions. Is K. being reproached for his naïve assumption that art must be mimetic? Moreover, Titorelli's painting is executed not in oils, as would be appropriate, but in pastel colours. It seems that on the territory of the Court, artistic conventions are as bewildering as its legal codes.

Paintings are frequently mentioned in Realist texts. Sometimes the characters are defined by their responses to paintings, as in Fontane's *Irrungen Wirrungen* (A Suitable Match), where Botho enjoys modest street scenes, and Leni likes the historical paintings by Benjamin West (Fontane, 1962–4, II, pp. 346, 386). Kafka seems to be employing a similar technique in the odd incident when Titorelli induces K. to buy three landscape paintings that show the sun setting over a heath. Although Titorelli describes them as similar, they are in fact completely identical. What point is K. missing? A likely suggestion is that, as he has just heard about three possible ways of seeking acquittal, and judged all these to be hopeless, the identical pictures represent the identity which all three methods assume in his mind. This is a rather different use of paintings. They are meaningful, but not through what they represent. Since all three pictures purport to show the same landscape, it is hard to believe that any of them is a faithful representation; they seem rather to be stereotyped. It is through their *failure* to represent that the pictures are meaningful. Their meaning is not representational, but symbolic. K. cannot interpret it, because he is still tied to Realist conventions of mimetic interpretation. Only the reader, already distanced from K.'s consciousness, can move beyond Realism and interpret the paintings' symbolic significance.

Another mode of representation used by Kafka is allegory. In saying this, I do not mean to reopen the vexed and probably futile debate about whether his work as a whole can be described as allegorical. I mean simply to point to one passage where Kafka clearly employs allegorical personifications to convey his meaning. In Titorelli's painting of a judge the back of the judge's throne is adorned by an allegorical figure with emblematic properties. It is Justice, holding a pair of scales, and with her eyes blindfolded to show impartiality.

But she is also shown running, with wings on her heels, and Titorelli explains that he was ordered to combine the goddess of Justice with that of Victory. If the goddess passes judgements while running, then, as K. points out, impartiality is impossible. On closer inspection, the figure seems more to resemble the goddess of the Hunt. This gives not only K. but also the reader an insight into the character of the Court. It seems to be hunting accused persons down. Its character is confirmed when the Chaplain explains to K.: 'Das Urteil kommt nicht mit einemmal, das Verfahren geht allmählich ins Urteil über' (The verdict does not come all at once, the proceedings gradually merge into the verdict: p. 289), and by the later aphorism: 'Noch spielen die Jagdhunde im Hof, aber das Wild entgeht ihnen nicht, so sehr es auch schon jetzt durch die Wälder jagt.' (The hunting dogs are still playing in the courtyard, but the quarry will not escape them, no matter how fast it may already be racing through the woods: Kafka, 1953, p. 89.)

The reader of *Der Proceß* has a double task, that of interpreting the Court's behaviour and that of interpreting K.'s reactions to it. This task could be reformulated as that of understanding the various semiotic systems deployed in the novel. Realist fiction represents the world, not by reflecting it, but by inviting the reader to interpret fictional reality in a similar way to extra-literary reality. Realism therefore relies on semiotic systems which are extensions of, or modelled on, those operative in the real world. In social life we learn, usually in a casual and unsystematic way, how to place other people by their appearance, their clothes, their vocabularies, and their accents. We become adept in reading clues, without a conscious grasp of the system that makes our readings possible (Hodge and Kress, 1988; Ginzburg, 1990). The verisimilitude of fiction depends to a great extent on calling these semi-conscious operations into play. Thus, in Fontane's *Der Stechlin*, a character immediately places two new acquaintances as social upstarts by looking at their clothing; and Realism requires that this semiotic code must be immediately intelligible to, and hence shared by, Fontane's readers (Fontane, 1962–4, V, p. 25). Realists often have at their disposal a conscious and systematic version of the knowledge that their readers use casually. Thus nineteenth-century Realism depends crucially on the pseudo-science of physiognomy, formulated by the Swiss clergyman Lavater in his *Physiognomic Fragments*. Physiognomy was a systematic method of reading a person's character by examining not only the face, but also gait, gestures, dress, handwriting and other features; and though few people accepted its claims to scientific status, it decisively affected the European novel by showing novelists how to use a character's external appearance as an index of inner reality (Tytler, 1982). In retrospect, physiog-nomy looks like an anticipation of social semiotics, and Lavater indeed uses the term *Semiotik* to describe it (Lavater, 1775–8, I, p. 52n; Wellbery, 1984). Modern semioticians have studied numerous systems which endow social life with meaning and which vary from one culture to another. One such system is gesture (Bremmer and Roodenburg, 1991). Another is clothing: it is not surprising to find that a skilful Realist of the present day, Alison Lurie, has also written a semiotic study of clothes (Lurie, 1982). Yet another is the control of space. In K's professional world, power is correlated with the amount of space at one's disposal: hence, as we have seen, he contrasts his spacious office with the garret available to the Examining Magistrate. He has to learn that the Court operates a different semiotic system, in which power and space are inversely related, so that the most powerful officials occupy the most confined spaces.

K. tries to interpret the Court by examining various features of those associated with it. He tries, for example, to exercise his physiognomic skill on the clients waiting in the Court corridors, but finds them anomalous in terms of his accustomed semiotics: 'Alle waren vernachlässigt angezogen, trotzdem die meisten nach dem Gesichtsausdruck, der Haltung, der Barttracht und vielen kaum sicherzustellenden kleinen Einzelheiten den höheren Klassen angehörten.' (Their clothes, without exception, looked shoddy, although most of the people there belonged to the upper classes, judging by the expression on their faces, by their manner, by the way their beards were trimmed, and by many small details that were difficult to pin down precisely. – p. 93) This nicely illustrates the difficulty of bringing to consciousness the semiotic systems that one constantly employs: K. cannot quite tell what the details are by which he identifies the social status of the people before him. The clothes of Court employees are described in detail, but their significance is obscure. The guard who enters K.'s bedroom is wearing 'ein anliegendes schwarzes Kleid, das ähnlich den Reiseanzügen mit verschiedenen Falten, Taschen Schnallen, Knöpfen und einem Gürtel versehen war und infolgedessen, ohne daß man sich darüber klar wurde, wozu es dienen sollte, besonders praktisch erschien' (a well-fitting black suit which was like a travelling outfit in that it had various pleats, pockets buckles, buttons, and a belt, and as a result, although one could not quite see what it was for, seemed eminently practical: p. 7). The audience at his first hearing are mostly dressed in long, loose, black coats which K. does not know how to interpret (p. 58). The Court servant is dressed in an ordinary coat (*Civilrock*) with no signs of official status except for two gold buttons which seem to have come from an officer's coat (p. 89); presently K. learns to recognise these gold buttons as the insignia of Court servants (p. 223). This is by no means a fanciful detail, since for most of the nineteenth century Austrian officials were required to wear uniforms which distinguished their ranks and ministries by the design of the embroidery and the colour of the lapels (Heindl, 1991, pp. 241–3). The Information Officer is elegantly dressed, with a grey waistcoat terminating in two sharp points (p. 101), and it is explained that the other employees have clubbed together to provide him with smart clothes with which to make a good impression on clients. Finally, the Whipper who disciplines K.'s two guards is dressed in a curious black leather outfit that leaves his arms and much of his chest bare (p. 109; see Anderson, 1992). Thus, the text keeps inviting the semiotic opera-

tions required in Realist fiction and real life. These attempts at interpretation
are not necessarily pointless: the example of the servants' uniform suggests
that the Court has its own semiotic system, which could be learnt by
experience; but initially they are baffling.

Both in his everyday life and in his dealings with the Court K. is
constantly interpreting signs. Those of daily life are complicated – more so
than the comparatively straightforward sign-systems deployed by Fontane –
but nevertheless intelligible. The fixed grin on the face of K's subordinate
Kaminer is not (as one would normally suppose) a sign of good humour, but
the result of partial facial paralysis. When the Deputy Director invites K. to
spend Sunday on his yacht, this is not a friendly gesture but an attempt at
reconciliation. In both cases the superficial meaning has to be rejected in
favour of a less obvious meaning. In his dealings with the Court, K. is often
on the alert for hidden meanings in looks and gestures. Sometimes he is
baffled, as when the guard Franz looks at him 'mit einem langen
wahrscheinlich bedeutungsvollen, aber unverständlichen Blicke' (a long,
probably significant, but incomprehensible look: p. 13). Sometimes he
acknowledges more than one possible interpretation, as when the Examining
Magistrate moves about in his chair 'in Verlegenheit oder Ungeduld' (either
from embarrassment or impatience: p. 67). Sometimes K. settles for the
obvious interpretation: for example, when the verger in the Cathedral
behaves in a way that K. finds incomprehensible (p. 282); K. considers
obvious interpretations, such as that the verger considers him suspicious or
wants a tip, but does not hit on the non-obvious interpretation, namely that
the verger is guiding him towards the pulpit from which the Chaplain will
address him. More often K. adopts far-fetched interpretations which are not
confirmed by the context. He thinks he sees the Magistrate giving a member
of the audience a sign by means of a look, and launches into a tirade about
the Court's use of secret signs (p. 67). The following passage indicates K.'s
characteristic method of interpretation:

> Es konnte nur ein Zeichen tiefer Demütigung sein oder es mußte
> zumindest so aufgefaßt werden, daß der Untersuchungsrichter nach
> dem Heftchen, wie es auf den Tisch gefallen war, griff, es ein wenig in
> Ordnung zu bringen suchte und es wieder vornahm, um darin zu lesen.
> (It could only have been a sign of deep humiliation, or at least it was
> bound to be taken for this, that the Examining Magistrate reached for
> the notebook where it had fallen on the table, tried to rearrange it a
> little, and held it up again in order to read it. – p. 63f)

This passage is in free indirect discourse, reflecting K.'s thoughts. The second
main clause retracts the first by claiming that even if the Magistrate's
behaviour were not a sign of humiliation, it must be thus interpreted. Why?
To uphold K's self-esteem, even at the cost of misinterpreting his surroundings? There follows, not a description of the Magistrate's behaviour, but an
interpretation of his intentions: he was trying to rearrange the book in order to

read it. If accurate, this interpretation renders unnecessary the further hypothesis that the Magistrate is displaying his humiliation. And it is characteristic of Kafka's procedure that the more far-fetched hypothesis is placed first, then progressively undermined and finally replaced by a perfectly simple and sufficient account of the Magistrate's purposes. This tells us something about K.'s habit of interpreting his surroundings by bold and self-flattering hypotheses which are not confirmed by observation. It also illustrates the interpretative exertions going on throughout the novel. The semiotics of everyday life are complicated enough; those of the Court are still harder to understand, especially as they are mediated through the biased interpretations put forward by K.

In stressing the constant effort of interpretation required both of K. and of the reader, one risks implying that this is a mere disinterested inquiry. For K., however, the interpretation of the Court becomes a matter of life and death, and his relations with the Court always have the character of a power-struggle. Is this because K. always deals with other people in terms of power? Or is he really up against a powerful adversary that is determined to defeat him? We cannot be sure. The guards and the Chaplain assure K. that the Court is an impersonal body with no animus against him (pp 14, 304); yet it has the power to dominate and finally to destroy his life.

A semiotic system which registers power-relations is the system of pronouns. The contrast between the familiar second-person-singular pronoun *du* and the polite form *Sie* can indicate various combinations of power and solidarity (Brown and Gilman, 1960). For the most part people associated with the Court address K. as *Sie*. This establishes a distance between him and them, like the distance separating him from his colleagues at the bank. On two occasions, however, Court officials address him as *Du*. The first occasion is when K. discovers the two guards who arrested him being beaten for misconduct. They call to him: 'Herr! Wir sollen geprügelt werden, weil Du Dich beim Untersuchungsrichter über uns beklagt hast.' (Sir! [or 'Master!'] We're going to be flogged because you complained about us to the Examining Magistrate! – p. 109) There is an odd discrepancy here between the archaic mode of address ('Master') and the familiarity of the pronoun. Just afterwards the guard Willem addresses K. by the pronoun *Ihr*, which in Kafka's day was already archaic as a relatively formal address to a single person. The Whipper always addresses K. as *Du*. Coming from the guards, the familiar pronoun implies a personal appeal; coming from the Whipper, it implies a threat. The second occasion when familiar pronouns are used is the conversation between K. and the Chaplain. Here the familiarity seems reassuring, and K. interprets it as personal friendship; the Chaplain, however, reminds K. that he belongs to the Court, with the implication that the *Du* was appropriate to his office as Chaplain rather than to any affection he may feel for K. Thus K., true to his habit of misinterpretation, seems to have misunderstood the semiotic import of pronouns.

Given that K. is an unreliable narrator, the reader can discern in many of his actions a significance of which K. himself is unaware. He keeps acting in a way that contradicts his intentions. When about to meet the Inspector, he enters the room 'langsamer [...] als er wollte' (more slowly than he intended: p. 8). After his conversation with Fräulein Bürstner, he is firmly resolved to go away (p. 47), but then he stops, returns, and kisses her. He addresses the Magistrate 'schärfer, als er beabsichtigt hatte' (more sharply than he had meant to: p. 62), and raises his voice involuntarily (p. 64). In the lumber-room episode, K. is provoked by Franz's screams into losing self-control and striking him: 'er konnte sich nicht zurückhalten' (he could not stop himself: p. 113). Sometimes he catches himself out in mistakes, as when he thinks he has conceded the guards the right to supervise him (p. 8) and contemplates killing himself (p. 17). All these suggest motives of which K. himself is unaware: his involuntary submission to his guards, for example, might be taken to indicate an unconscious sense of guilt.

Whatever specific interpretations one may favour, an important key to such actions was provided by Freud in *The Psychopathology of Everyday Life* (1901). This book forms part of Freud's project of extending the range of experience that could be interpreted. The year before, with *The Interpretation of Dreams*, he had put forward procedures for interpreting dreams. He now offered procedures for interpreting involuntary actions such as mistakes, slips of the tongue, lapses of memory, and bungled performances. These were all classified as 'parapraxes' (*Fehlleistungen*) and explained by reference to unconscious intentions (Freud, 1901). Although Freud's pretensions to scientific rigour are questionable (Timpanaro, 1974), he greatly extended the range of experience open to interpretation. Like Lavater, who had offered procedures for interpreting physiognomies, Freud performed a breakthrough in semiotics.

By attending to Josef K.'s parapraxes, the reader is in a position to reconstruct his character and the unconscious impulses that bedevil his attempts to deal with the Court. Chief among these are the obsessions with dirt and sex that find expression in some spectacular parapraxes. He ends a conversation with his landlady by picking up her word *rein*: '"Die Reinheit!" rief K. noch durch die Spalte der Tür, "wenn Sie die Pension rein erhalten wollen, müssen Sie zuerst mir kündigen."' ('Clean!' K. cried out through the crack in the door. 'If you want to keep the boarding-house clean, you'll have to start by giving me notice.' – p. 37) After encountering the Whipper and the guards in the lumber-room for a second time, he tells a servant to clean the room out: 'Wir versinken ja im Schmutz' (We're smothered in filth: p. 117). As for his sexual concerns, these are completely explicit in his detailed fantasy of taking the wife of the court servant away from the Magistrate, and covert in his obsession with Fräulein Bürstner's blouse.

In all these ways, Kafka exploits and complicates the semiotic systems used in Realism. Beyond the semiotics of Realism K. has occasional glimpses of another world with its own system of meaning, different from and in some ways antithetical to his everyday reality. The most communicative spokesman for this other world is the Chaplain, who communicates with K. by a non-Realist fictional mode, that of parable. He relates the parable of the door-keeper, which Kafka was to publish separately, under the title 'Vor dem Gesetz' (Before the Law), in his collection *Ein Landarzt: Kleine Erzählungen* (A Country Doctor: Short Stories 1919) (Henel, 1963). He does so in response to K.'s expression of trust, warning him not to mistake the nature of the Court. The story of the door-keeper is evidently supposed to illustrate the mistake K. is making.

The parable is further removed from Realism than any other part of *Der Proceß*. Its setting is simply before the entrance to the Law. Its characters are two figures without names or biographies: the door-keeper and the man from the country. Realistic considerations, like what they ate and where they slept, would be completely irrelevant. If this text can be accepted as revealing the true nature of the Court, then it provides us with an assurance that the Law governing the Court's actions does exist, for the man from the country, just before his death, sees light shining from the entrance to the Law. By its abandonment of Realism, however, the text also implies that the Law cannot be known within the confines of everyday experience.

The parable also makes nakedly obvious the unequal relations of power between Court officials and members of the public. The door-keeper is a primitive-looking figure who remotely recalls the Whipper, and he tells the man bluntly, 'Ich bin mächtig' (I am powerful). Intimidated by the door-keeper's show of power, the man spends his whole life waiting outside the Law for permission to enter, only to learn, as he dies, that this entrance was intended for him all along; the door-keeper is now going to close it. Thus, literally and formally, the parable ends with closure. And yet this closure opens up a range of thematic interpretations which K. and the Chaplain spend a long time discussing. On one possible interpretation, as the Chaplain points out, the actual power-relations could be seen quite differently, since the door-keeper is obliged to stay at his post, whereas the man from the country is free to come and go as he pleases. This would imply that the man surrenders his freedom to the door-keeper. He could have gone away; he could have disbelieved the door-keeper's discouraging account of what lies inside the Law; he could even, perhaps, have disobeyed the door-keeper, who never threatens him physically, and entered the Law for himself. If we try to apply the parable to the story of Josef K., we confront the dizzying possibility that even such an intimidating body as the Court has only the power that its victims voluntarily accord it. It may be that man is free, but is unhappy with freedom and readily surrenders it to an authority. As the Advocate remarks: 'es ist oft besser in Ketten als frei zu sein' (it is often better to be in chains than to be free: p. 258). And perhaps this is what Josef K has done with the Court. When the guards first enter his life, he feels that he is conceding their right to watch him (p. 8). Could he perhaps have disregarded his lawsuit and remained a free man? Or could he, by asking the simple question what he is charged with, have drastically altered his circumstances, and avoided the slow attrition of his energies by the Court?

These questions, like the many others raised in *Der Proceß*, receive no conclusive answer. They suffice to show, however, that interpretation in this novel is no mere game. Recent commentators have favoured the conclusion that the Law is a fiction maintained by its self-appointed representatives and strengthened by its victim's acquiescence (Abraham, 1985). That is one possibility. But we are also invited to consider the more alarming possibility that the Law does constitute an absolute authority. In either case, the Law may be interpreted as malevolent, as impersonal, or even as aimed at K.'s spiritual redemption: there is textual evidence to support all these interpretations, and none can be excluded. Kafka denies the reader any comforting certainty. One such consoling certainty would be precisely the view that the Law is a mere fiction. The reader who adopts this interpretation can look down on K. from the comfortable position of superior enlightenment. Such a reader, however, would not have read *Der Proceß* with much attention. Kafka's narrative technique seems designed to prohibit such an easy response. His text allows the speculation that the Law is merely delusory; but it also, no less compellingly, suggests the more alarming possibility that the Law may be real, and that human life may be going on against the background of a wholly other reality. Everyday life permits only occasional glimpses of this other reality, which inhabits the forgotten corners, the garrets and lumber-rooms, of the familiar world. It can be comprehended, if at all, only in a negative manner, by contrast with Josef K.'s incomprehension of it. It is in this sense that *Der Proceß* is located beyond Realism: in evoking the possible existence of another reality which can be represented only indirectly, by bending and distorting the semiotics of Realism.

REFERENCES

References by page number only are to Franz Kafka, *Der Proceß*, Textband, ed. Malcolm Pasley, Frankfurt: Fischer, 1990. Translations are based on *The Trial*, tr. Douglas Scott and Chris Waller, London: Picador, 1977, modified occasionally.

For an up-to-date survey of Kafka scholarship, see Ludwig Dietz, *Franz Kafka*, Sammlung Metzler 138, 2nd edn., Stuttgart: Metzler, 1990.

ABRAHAM, U. (1985), *Der verhörte Held: Recht und Schuld im Werk Franz Kafkas*, Munich: Fink.

ANDERSON, M. (1992), *Kafka's Clothes*, Oxford: Clarendon Press.

BARTHES, R. (1986), The reality effect, in his *The Rustle of Language*, tr. Richard Howard, Oxford: Blackwell.

BEISSNER, F. (1952), *Der Erzähler Franz Kafka*, Stuttgart: Kohlhammer.

BREMMER, J. and ROODENBURG, H. (eds) (1991), *A Cultural History of Gesture*, Cambridge: Polity.

BROD, M. (1974), *Über Franz Kafka*, Frankfurt: Fischer.

BROD, M. and KAFKA, F. (1989), *Eine Freundschaft: Briefwechsel*, ed. Malcolm Pasley, Frankfurt: Fischer.

BROWN, R., and GILMAN A. (1960), The pronouns of power and solidarity, in T. A. Sebeok (ed.), *Style in Language*, Cambridge, Mass: MIT Press.

CERSOWSKY, P. (1983), *Phantastische Literatur im ersten Viertel des 20. Jahrhunderts*, Munich: Fink.

DEMETZ, P. (1968), Balzac and the zoologists: a concept of the type, in P. Demetz, T. Greene and L. Nelson, Jr (eds), *The Disciplines of Criticism: Essays in Literary Theory, Interpretation, and History*, New Haven and London: Yale University Press.

ELM, T. (1979), *Der Prozeß*, in H. Binder (ed.), *Kafka-Handbuch*, 2 vols., Stuttgart: Kröner.

FONTANE, T. (1962), *Sämtliche Werke: Romane, Erzählungen, Gedichte*, ed. W. Keitel, 6 vols., Munich: Hanser.

FOWLER, A. (1982), *Kinds of Literature: An Introduction to the Theory of Genres and Modes*, Oxford: Clarendon Press.

FREUD, S. (1901), The psychopathology of everyday life, in *The Standard Edition of the Complete Psychological Works of Sigmund Freud*, ed. James Strachey, 24 vols, London: The Hogarth Press, vol. 6.

GINZBURG, C. (1990), Clues: roots of an evidential paradigm, in his *Myths, Emblems, Clues*, tr. John and Anne Tedeschi, London: Hutchinson.

HEINDL, W. (1991), *Gehorsame Rebellen: Bürokratie und Beamte in Österreich 1780 bis 1848*, Vienna: Böhlau.

HENEL, I. (1963), Die Türhüterlegende und ihre Bedeutung für Kafkas *Prozeß*, *Deutsche Vierteljahrsschrift für Literatur- und Geistesgeschichte* 37, pp. 50–70.

HIBBERD, J. L., 'Cet auteur réaliste': Robbe-Grillet's Reading of Kafka, in J. P. Stern and J. J. White (eds), *Paths and Labyrinths: Nine Papers from a Kafka Symposium*, London: Institute of Germanic Studies.

HODGE, R., and KRESS, G. (1988), *Social Semiotics*, Cambridge: Polity.

JAKOBSON, R. (1956), The metaphoric and metonymic poles, in R. Jakobson and M. Halle, *Fundamentals of Language*, The Hague: Mouton.

KAFKA, F. (1953), *Hochzeitsvorbereitungen auf dem Lande und andere Schriften aus dem Nachlaß*, ed. M. Brod, Frankfurt: Fischer.

KAFKA, F. (1958), *Briefe 1902–1924*, ed. M. Brod, Frankfurt: Fischer.

KAFKA, F. (1967), *Briefe an Felice und andere Korrespondenz aus der Verlobungszeit*, ed. E. Heller and J. Born, Frankfurt: Fischer.

KAFKA, F. (1982), *Das Schloß*, ed. Malcolm Pasley, Frankfurt: Fischer .

KAFKA, F. (1990), *Tagebücher*, ed. H. G. Koch, M. Müller and M. Pasley, Frankfurt: Fischer.

LAVATER, J. C. (1775), *Physiognomische Fragmente, zur Beförderung der Menschenkenntniß und Menschenliebe*, 4 vols, Leipzig and Winterthur: bey Weidmanns Erben und Reich.

LODGE, D. (1977), *The Modes of Modern Writing*, London: Arnold.

LURIE, A. (1982), *The Language of Clothes*, London: Heinemann.

MARSON, E. (1975), *Kafka's Trial: The Case against Josef K.*, St Lucia, Queensland: University of Queensland Press.

MÜLLER-SEIDEL, W. (1986), *Die Deportation des Menschen: Kafkas Erzählung 'In der Strafkolonie' im europäischen Kontext*, Stuttgart: Metzler.

PASLEY, M. (1990), *Franz Kafka, 'Der Proceß:' Die Handschrift redet*, Marbacher Magazin 52, Marbach: Deutsche Schillergesellschaft.

RAABE, P. (1967), Franz Kafka und der Expressionismus, *Zeitschrift für deutsche Philologie* 86, pp. 161–75.

SANDBANK, S. (1989), *After Kafka: The Influence of Kafka's Fiction*, Athens, University of Georgia Press.

TIMPANARO, S. (1974), *The Freudian Slip*, tr. Kate Soper, London: New Left Books.

TYLER, G. (1982), *Physiognomy in the European Novel*, Princeton: Princeton University Press.

WELLBERY, D. (1984), *Lessing's Laocoon: Semiotics and Aesthetics in the Age of Reason*, Cambridge: Cambridge University Press.

6

The Refracted Self
Hermann Hesse, *Der Steppenwolf*

MARY E. STEWART

This novel, generally held to be Hesse's finest, first appeared in 1927 and was written over the preceding three years or so, right in the midst of the chaotic period between the two world wars. It was, of course, a time when political and economic life in Germany was in a state of turbulence, when national identity was a major and highly problematic issue, and the novel's core concern is precisely a sense of loss – loss of trust in inherited values and social structures, in concepts of progress, in any secure sense of personal and national identity. It focuses on one man's experience, his sense of being in a world whose current attitudes he cannot share, yet without which he cannot construct his own identity, so it presents a dual sense of deep dislocation: both between the sentient self and social reality, and within the self.

The novel thus asserts itself against the realist tradition, in so far as that is based on the assumption of a shared, stable phenomenal world which can be reliably described in an empirical way, for it is a work which assumes from the very start that the 'reality' its protagonist inhabits is not shared. In a sense it is a text precisely about learning to live with the death of Realism and of the bourgeois society that produced it, with the loss of widely-held values binding society – as also reader and text – together in a common belief that life 'makes sense', that stories can be simply and seamlessly told, that there is a common currency in social morality as in language and an unproblematic exchange mechanism between the two. Hesse's novel draws attention precisely to the discordance of what Realism takes for granted – the notion of a world held in common; it opens up the gaps between individuals, between 'reality' and the attempt to reflect it in words.

Harry Haller, the protagonist, is – significantly – himself a writer, but distanced from his world in a double sense: he is both out of sympathy with the age, and also 'sentimental' in the Schillerian sense: someone who self-consciously reflects on himself and life at an intellectual remove, rather than engaging fully and joyously with it. The novel's concern is not, however, to explore ways in which these gaps might be closed. It does not attempt to show how the individual and his social context, reality and word might be brought somehow 'naïvely' together again, but rather how the very 'unreality' of writing, its detachment from simple referentiality, might be used to evoke a way of existing which makes detachment and distance a positive value. Instead of struggling to write one traditional, coherent story of personality, it writes many unfinished ones; instead of trying to make 'reality' cohere, it admits of diversity and contradiction, but – and this is vital for the particular nature of Hesse's writing – without despair at the limbo of unattainable final meaning or unwilling acceptance of contingency. The uncompleted, unresolved nature of both protagonist and text are ultimately models for a kind of sublime uncommittedness which overcomes the problems of making sense of reality, of somehow differentiating between true and false, real and imaginary, by proliferating them, by allowing everything that is conceivable an equal right to exist. It is thus a novel which would seem to abandon any fixed, objective view of what might constitute reality, and in fact Thomas Mann (1960) saw it as not in any way falling short of Joyce's *Ulysses* or Gide's *Les Faux-Monnayeurs* (The Counterfeiters) in its experimental technique.

As Timms (1990) has shown, the novel must be seen against the background of early twentieth-century psychoanalytic theory. Hesse's own personal life in the years leading up to the writing of *Der Steppenwolf* was, as Michels (1972) reveals, deeply disturbed; an unhappy childhood, difficult relationships with his puritanical parents, his revilement as a pacificist, two broken marriages and recurrent ill-health – all this led him to undergo psychotherapy himself on several occasions, including eventually with Jung. He also undertook systematic study of psychoanalytic writings, reading Freud, Adler and Jung, and finding in their work not only insight into his own traumas, but also new possibilities for literature in the challenge it offered to traditional, bourgeois/realist concepts of character – see the essays *Sprache* (Language), XI; *Künstler und Psychoanalyse* (Artists and Psychoanalysis), X. His family background of missionary work in the Far East also led him to read widely in Eastern culture, which again challenged received Western ideas on the nature of identity (*Lieblingslektüre* (My favourite reading), XI). Yet it was not only this personal interest in new theories which informed his work; many of his essays (e.g. *Die Brüder Karamasow oder der Untergang Europas* (The Brothers Karamazov or the Decline of Europe), XI; *Zarathustras Wiederkehr* (The Return of Zarathustra), X) demonstrate a keen awareness of a broader post-First World War loss of certainties – scientific, political, moral and psychological – which his own personal sense of dislocation in part reflects.

Literature, then, was to probe the unconscious, to break down established categories of thinking about 'reality', about character and action, to express a deeply disharmonious view of the self and the age, and we can see this novel as Hesse's own mid-life autobiography. The parallelism of name and age between author and fictional figure is obvious, and many details are shared:

Hesse also found learning to dance at the age of almost 50 a self-revealing experience. Yet he was not just an analyst. His essays also stress the need for some new kind of totality to embrace the discreteness seemingly opened up by psychoanalysis.

> Alles ist göttlich, weil Gott das All ist. Wir nannten das früher Pantheismus ... die Scheidung von Innen und Außen ist unserm Denken gewohnt, ist ihm aber nicht notwendig. Es gibt die Möglichkeit für unseren Geist, sich hinter die Grenze zurückzuziehen, die wir ihm gezogen haben, ins Jenseits. Jenseits der Gegensatzpaare, aus dem unsere Welt besteht, fangen neue, andere Erkenntnisse an ...
>
> (Everything is divine, because God is everything. We used to call this pantheism ... the distinction between Inner and Outer is part of our thinking but not essential to it. It is possible for our intellect to pass across the limits we have set it, into the Beyond. Beyond the many antitheses of which our world consists other new insights begin. – *Innen und Außen* (Interior and Exterior), IV, p. 378)

Many other texts also express similar ideas (e.g. *Von der Seele* (On the Soul) X; *Eigensinn* (Obstinacy), IX; *Über Jean Paul* (On Jean Paul), XII), and what is important here is the shape of Hesse's thought. It follows earlier writers such as Kleist and Hölderlin in its 'triadic' structure, that is in thinking about the world as somehow faulty, as paradise lost and perhaps regainable, and indeed also reflects the concern of many of Hesse's contemporaries to find some kind of timeless essence to set against the unanchored subjectivity of individual experience: Joyce's 'epiphanies', Thomas Mann's interest in mythology. Yet Hesse stands out amongst them in his apparent confidence in some kind of ultimate or 'higher' truth, and we need to look very closely at how he relates it to his awareness of dislocation and despair in narrative terms, given that language itself must be as suspect as all other traditional values and certainties. In seeking to render some ultimate 'Jenseits' expressible, is Hesse falling back on objective, authoritative narration again, despite the apparent modernity of his concerns and manner of writing?

There is no doubt that Hesse was very aware of the problem of language and its relationship to reality which so preoccupied many of his contemporaries. In the essay *Sprache* (Language, 1917) he laments the 'prosaicness' of language, the gap between available language and potential reality: 'Der Dichter muß für sein Tun dieselbe Sprache benutzen, in der man [...] Geschäfte macht, in der man telegraphiert und Prozesse führt.' (The poet has to use the same language in which business is transacted, telegrams are sent, court cases are conducted.) On the other hand language is unstable:

> Der Dichter kann kein einziges Wort gebrauchen [...] das nicht [...] nach einer andern Seite schielte, das nicht im selben Atemzug mit an fremde, störende, feindliche Vorstellungen erinnerte, das nicht in sich selber Hemmungen und Verkürzungen trüge.

(The poet cannot employ a single word that is not also covertly glancing in another direction, that doesn't at the very same moment recall strange, disturbing, inimical images, that doesn't bear its own constraints and limitations. – XI, p. 92)

There is also a much quoted passage in *Kurgast* (The Convalescent: VII, p. 111), where he talks of wanting a language which could embrace simultaneity like music, instead of functioning merely sequentially, and which would thus be able to reflect the co-existence of multiple discrete elements in human personality. All of this seems very firmly within the framework of literary Modernism; yet there remains the seeming paradox of Hesse's idealistic thinking. How far and by what narrative techniques does Hesse's writing genuinely embody an insight into the fluidity of character and language? How far is he able to integrate this insight narratively with his belief in a 'Jenseits'?

Hesse's first novel to draw on psychoanalytic thought was *Demian* (1919). This deals with the sexual and spiritual development of the young Emil Sinclair through puberty to maturity, tracing his emancipation from the conventional/judgemental moral views of his parental home and his gradual achievement of total personal autonomy. The novel does this by deepening its overtly traditional *Bildungsroman* structure through eclectic symbolism, which is used to mark stages in Sinclair's journey deeper into himself as well as forward in time. It is an interesting but very schematic exercise, overloaded particularly with Jungian motifs which are not successfully integrated into a new narrative mode; it reads in large part as a traditional narrative onto which symbolic figures have been awkwardly grafted. *Der Steppenwolf* is in the most immediate sense a more mature work, firstly in the sense that it deals with an older man in his despairing rather than steadily progressive attempts at self-awareness, and secondly in that it is far less ready to adopt and adapt traditional narrative structures.

Even the title, as Timms points out, already evokes several different possible 'stories' of personality with its Freudian, Nietzschean and jazz-age overtones, its hints of suffering, aggression and sensuality. And indeed it is the endlessly complex nature of self that is at issue here, rather than the self-finding of *Demian*. The protagonist, Harry Haller, is a man approaching 50 who can endure life only because he has promised himself the luxury of suicide at that age. His life is a constant unhappy, restless struggle, without any pattern except that of repeated disjunctures. Having once, it seems, led a fairly conventional academic life, he now pursues a kind of semi-bohemian existence; he is an intellectual who reads voraciously and surrounds himself with books, but whose life-style is disordered and chaotic by bourgeois standards – irregular hours, bouts of drinking, a spasmodic sexual relationship. He has also written anti-establishment pacifist articles, and despises the militarist, jingoistic politics of the age. And yet 'bohemian' does not really define Haller adequately. He is not a 'free spirit'; despite his disaffection with current political trends, he has no time either for the anti-establishment popular culture of the time, the jazz age. His cultural ideals are Goethe and Mozart, but at the same time he cannot throw off a yearning for bourgeois order, cleanliness, decency, and takes lodgings precisely where these conventional and narrow values are embodied. But this paradox sets up a circle of self-disgust within him; he despises that part of himself that is drawn to decency, while yet largely suppressing the latent anti-bourgeois violence within him that threatens at times to disrupt his controlled personality. Thus he remains in some senses a slave to convention, despite his sense of being an outsider. He perceives schisms within society – the disjuncture between Germany's cultural heritage and the superficiality of a materialistic, jingoistic age – and also between himself and society, yet such schisms are also within him. He can be highly intellectual and boorish, leftwing pacifist yet also very bourgeois and prudish, a man at war with himself as much as with the world, whose physical restlessness – he never stays long in one town or lodging – and occasional glimpses of sublimity through music betoken his search for some higher peace. The novel then attempts not only to explore the nature of these schisms, above all the psychological complexity of the individual, but also how they – and the division felt between self and world – might perhaps be healed by transcendent acceptance. This might be achieved firstly by abandoning expectations of coherent, unified being both in terms of society and of personal identity, and secondly by a process of internalising external reality through perceiving it not as hostile, but as part of the potential self.

If Haller's process of radical re-orientation is to carry conviction for the reader, then he/she must also be involved in breaking established modes of thinking and judging. The text must somehow give the reader access to the psychological processes undergone by Haller without simply relating them by means of a traditional narrative voice, for conventional diegesis represents precisely an unquestioned confidence that reality can be readily known, categorised and set down. In fact, from the very start Hesse's text makes it clear to us that all recording is but an approximation, highly partial in both senses of the word. Instead of one authorial voice there are several distinct narrators, stressing the subjective and multiple nature of experienced reality. We are presented with some observations on Haller by the unnamed nephew of his sometime landlady, who simply adopts the role of editor of the papers left by Haller when he moved out, and he is clearly a biassed, unauthoritative narrator. There are hints at a degree of pedantry, of bourgeois certitude in his comments which stress their 'unreliability' or partiality. Indeed, one might say that precisely the confident interpretative assumptions of traditional Realism are ironised here as specifically bourgeois, and Hesse sets against them the first of several differing 'reflections' of Haller, all of which are anything but authoritative. The main body of the text comprises Haller's own writings, but we know nothing of the circumstances of their creation, nor what the 'Editor' may have added or taken out. Included amongst them is the 'Treatise on the Steppenwolf' of mysterious provenance, yet the apparently objective analysis which it represents, and which first puts forward the theoretical notion of endlessly multiple personality, has also a highly questionable status when one looks more closely. In early editions the 'Treatise' was printed on different paper from the rest of the text and still usually appears in distinct font, so it may appear to be 'real' and external to Haller, as the editor's comments are. Yet its place is within his own imaginative record and it is a 'copy' of what he said he received – but in what sense? A literal rendering? A mental image somehow processed?

Even if one then sets aside all these editorial considerations and looks at Haller's own record as a whole, one is still not offered any more security. There is a combination in what these writings record of apparently concrete experience which is referentially grounded – places, streets – and of the hallucinatory, where rules of time and space do not seem to operate. Yet there is no clear transition or dividing line, no steady, progressive movement inward as in *Demian*, and even in the most dream-like sequences the text never loses a foothold in possible 'real' life, in the twenties world of jazz, cafés, dancing. Even the doors of the 'Magic Theatre' are recognizably those of theatrical boxes. This sustained referentiality combined with dream-like uncertainty of focus, what Ziolkowski (1965) calls 'double vision', is a real *tour de force* and fundamental to the meaning of the text, reminiscent in its interplay of musical counterpoint, as we shall see. But what I want to stress at this point is how the text, in its most basic outline structure, refuses to adopt any authoritative narrative position, to tell a simple story. Everything is unstable, multivalent, and to speak of a 'sonata in prose' as Ziolkowski does is potentially misleading, even if he is borrowing such views from Hesse himself: the sonata parallel, although helpful in uncovering some textual quality, is ultimately too firmly structured, too enclosed. What we have here is an unresolved text, there is no clear beginning or end, just a series of reflections, each of untaxable validity, so that it constantly thwarts any attempt by the reader to understand Haller in conventional terms as a self-consistent, continuous subject.

Yet the text does not lack structure or progression; it frustrates conventional expectations of a neat, complete story, but its very fluidity allows us to make new kinds of approach to the problems and progress of its protagonist. The twin terms of 'mirror' (Freedman, 1963) and 'music' (Ziolkowski) might be said to hold together both the process of the novel and its aim. The process is refraction, picturing the multiplicity like light refracted in a sequence of inter-relating mirrors; the aim is to superimpose images, to hold them simultaneously together. Or in musical terms, the process is that of theme and variations, the aim complex harmony. Both motifs – music and mirror - occur frequently in the text, providing initially two kinds of 'syntax' to help hold together the very disparate, and (at first reading) confusing material of the text. It does, in fact, provide us with a whole range of fascinating reflections of (or variations on) Haller, once we realise that the tendency to judge and categorise is not only Haller's problem, but also our own as readers. If we accept the notion of refraction, the blurring of subjective and objective, and cease to look for 'fact', then we can perceive the text not so much as unreliable, but as infinitely rich, encompassing multiple images of Haller even at its most confusing, for ultimately it projects Haller's nature into the outside world, uses it as externalisation of his inner states. This allows a rich insight into the psyche through a variety of striking images, but it is more than literary metaphor; it also opens up the possibility of transcending individuation by denying all separation between self and world, right and wrong, true and untrue. All experience is capable of being perceived as part of the individual, integrable into his being, and everything in the 'outside' world potentially reflects him.

If we take this more positive approach to the fluidity of the text, every stage both offers us some insights and then asks us – by the foregrounding of its own limitations – to question those insights, to probe further and see different reflections, pick up new tones. The 'Editor', as we have seen, makes his limitation of judgement very clear, while reflecting in his respect something of Haller's deep seriousness, as a subject worthy of our interest even if – or because – he clearly eludes conventional understanding. Haller's own opening perception of himself as 'Steppenwolf', as split in two, seems to explain some of the oddities felt by the 'Editor', but it too is self-evidently inadequate, not least because what he records of his own behaviour does not fit with the apparently neat division between the terms used, 'human' and 'wolf', rational and irrational. For example, in the episode where he visits a professor and attacks the wife's cherished image of Goethe (VII, p. 259ff), it is patently the barbaric 'wolf' who is the more perceptive, honest half, yet that 'wolf' or badly-behaved side also seems to attack the anti-bourgeois world of jazz and bars like a prim, disapproving bourgeois moralist. Simple dividedness is not an adequate psychological theory to explain this complexity of behaviour, nor does it help Haller to throw off his bourgeois tendency to be judgemental: it actually reflects it in the simplistic division into 'nice' and 'nasty'. The 'mirror' of the 'Treatise' then provides a very explicit substitute theory – not two poles, but 'unzählbare Polpaare' (countless pairs of polar oppositions), 'Personenknäuel' (bundles of personae) – in order to move right away from the very limited, bourgeois insistence on character as unity, or even simple duality. But even this new, expanded and open-ended theory still represents a kind of categorisation, a stylised form of 'writing' or circumscribing the personality, even if it helps to start releasing Haller (and the reader) from moralistic categorisations. The figures that Haller meets and presents in his own writings take the process of mirroring much further and in different directions, revealing surprising new aspects of his being, including his sensuality. But the nature of the mirroring process also changes again and deepens. What we see are not comments on Haller from outside, but Haller increasingly mirrored in the reality around him, even to the point where it ceases to matter whether the figures he meets are 'real' people he feels an affinity with, or projections of his imagination and need. What does matter is Haller's growing power to react, to project himself into external reality, to use it as mirror and become his own subject – 'write' himself rather than be 'written' by prejudice. Indeed, the 'Magic Theatre' is the test of how far he has achieved this.

How then do Haller's writings mirror his nature and progress? At the simplest level of meaning they record as a story how Haller reaches a point of despairing exhaustion, which perhaps marks a break in his attempt to deny the full extent of his outsiderness. With his defences weakened, he becomes open to new influences and learns to dance to the rhythms of the modern world he so hated, thus starting to overcome his isolation, discovering pleasure where he had least expected it. His learning to dance despite his ailing middle-aged body – means also that he starts to see himself in a new light, discovers unknown potential in himself, including the capacity to overcome his prejudice and see it as just that: pre-judgement which does not indicate cultural superiority so much as fear and self-enclosure, and dependence on external value systems.

This mental opening is then mirrored in an increasing richness of new experience and itself allows other, deeper kinds of mirroring to develop, like musical counterpoint. Patterns begin to emerge which invite a Freudian or Jungian 'mirror' to be held up to Haller's development. A Freudian reading is easily based on the emphasis given to Haller's repressed sexuality, his increasingly rich dream life and the recovery of childhood memories triggered by the figure of Hermine. More satisfying, perhaps, is a Jungian reading of Haller's progress, for it is both closer to Hesse's own experience and allows a fuller exploration of textual detail, as Haller becomes more closely mirrored in and by the world around him. What we can see reflected here is the process whereby the Ego, the centre of consciousness, moves closer to unity with the Self, the totality of psyche. The figures who aid Haller in this can be read both as external to him – as sympathetic friends – but also as projections of aspects of self, with very obvious reference to the Jungian stages of self-development. Clearly the most important is Hermine. Haller himself significantly 'recognizes' her, she reminds him of a boyhood friend and thus functions as a kind of double or twin. He sees her as having qualities he lacks yet also as reflecting parts of himself directly, understanding him intuitively. Her naïve sensuality, her enjoyment of eating for example, complements Haller's intellectuality, but she also clarifies and focuses his sense of being an outsider in her more serious moments, and these two aspects of her relationship to him are constantly interwoven, not separate. At a later stage in the text this interwoven wholeness (as opposed to duality) is made visible; she functions overtly as a kind of ideal self, a hermaphrodite figure, though significantly only when Haller has begun to see and experience the wider range of his potential does *he* see this, as he himself starts to free himself from value judgements and becomes capable of creating a new wholeness in himself. Sexual consummation, the total bonding of their two beings, is held out as the ultimate symbol of Haller's union with his whole potential self.

Clearly Hermine, and the more purely sensual Maria who is in some unspecified way her agent, reflect Jung's concept of the 'anima', the female counterpart of maleness. Together they encompass the four-fold stages of its development through sexuality to wisdom, and fulfil the anima's function as Jung saw it (1964), as mediator between self and Ego, putting Man in tune with his inner riches. Maria's pure sensuality, for instance, helps to release images from the past for Haller (VII, p. 330), which like his rediscovered capacity for dreaming show him, as it were, working vertically downwards in himself with each additional or 'horizontal' new experience to that deeper level where in Jungian terms the collective unconscious begins, where Ego and Self, Self and Universe become one. (In using terms like 'vertical' and 'horizontal' we are, of course, also seeing the text simultaneously as a kind of musical structure again.) It is Maria's 'mirror', for instance, that prepares Haller for the masked ball, enabling him to *enact* his sexuality in dance, 'das Geheimnis vom Untergang der Person in der Menge, von der unio mystica der Freude' (the secret of the individual's submergence in the crowd, of the unio mystica of joy: VII, p. 359f). This is his first intense sense of a possible oneness both with his own despised body, and with the world until now apparently alien and external to him.

The furthest stage of Jungian development is represented by Pablo, the jazz musician. He very obviously recalls some of Jung's symbols of Self – wise man, divine musician, animal spirit of nature (Jung, 1964, p. 196ff). Again bisexual, he is the supreme teacher, both surrendering to life as his physical grace shows, speaking with his body as well as his voice, and yet detached, unconcerned, free. At this point the Jungian mirroring process and the musical images of potential 'harmony' explicitly merge, as Pablo elides into Mozart and also becomes the master of the 'Magic Theatre' with its mirrors.

However, Haller fails to achieve harmony in the Magic Theatre of his own self, he fails to bring all the reflections together in balance by total acceptance. He has certainly made progress; he is able, for example, to acknowledge his own capacity for violence in the section 'Automobile Chase', to see it as not exclusive to the war-mongers he condemns, but also potentially inherent in his own cultural critique of shallow, technology-obsessed modernity. He recovers possible avenues of personal development blocked off by earlier fears, conventional social responses. He can face many, superficially warring aspects of himself in both enacting and observing them in the theatre of his soul, accepting too the fairground-like unserious atmosphere in which self-discovery takes place, which makes no distinction between pleasure and pain. Yet finally Haller proves himself too literal-minded to sustain this self-creative freedom. When he stabs the illusory image of Hermine in Pablo's arms, he shows himself still trapped in a disapproving, excluding mentality, in the judgemental intellectuality and schismatic reactions of the experiential level he was seeking to overcome.

The Jungian 'mirror' helps us perhaps furthest in understanding Haller's psychic journey into himself. Yet the whole text might equally well be interpreted in quite other terms, as our earlier quotation from *Innen und Außen* suggests. There are echoes of German Romanticism there which could apply here too; Haller's movement forwards through time but also downwards into himself recalls, for example, Novalis' *Heinrich von Ofterdingen*, whose shape is also that of a journey of the soul, a movement outwards in space that is also *immer nach Hause*, homewards, into the self. Physical and spiritual landscapes are one. We have already mentioned the Nietzschean associations of the title, the 'Steppenwolf' as predatory beast; the whole text could be seen not only as echoing in a general way Nietzsche's rejection of bourgeois values and celebration of Man's unlived potential for power over himself, but also as quite specifically recalling – in the imagery of the Magic Theatre – his will to treat life as an aesthetic phenomenon. And there are further possibilities for interpretation quite outside any German cultural context. Zen Buddhism, for example – part of Hesse's cultural background – offers a framework, in its concern for the overcoming of all dualisms, the conceptual division of the world into categories. Words and truth are incompatible, because words impose categories whereas truth is 'whole'. The aim of Buddhism is being without thinking, an enlightened state where the borders between what we call self and the rest of the universe are dissolved, perceived – or rather experienced – as mere illusion. This is the true end of dualism, because then there is no system left which has a desire for perception, and the ideal educative process is to break every code, to step further and further outside received images of Self, to widen its scope until it is co-extensive with the universe. One of the procedures used in Buddhist teaching is the 'koan', that is, a kind of logical paradox established in order to break open the systems of logic to which we are addicted so that a kind of spiritual meta-language becomes possible. It is not difficult to see either the general shape of Haller's experience or its specific climax in Zen Buddhist terms. The 'Magic Theatre' defies not only all the boundaries of good taste and our understanding of time and space; it plays, above all, with our notions of self, showing it as both participant and observer, as both unitary and multiple. What better realisation could there be of the 'koan' than this *Jahrmarkt* – fairground – of the soul, moving in its vivid pictures beyond all logic and analysis, announcing clearly the supremacy of being over judging, and thus subverting its own linguistic formulation? Seeing Haller in a Zen Buddhist mirror, we might then say that as he discovers and accepts more and more of his endlessly multiple self, he becomes potentially all experience, becomes the world; or that he ceases to analyse and think, and starts simply to be – a state which can be captured only in the non-logical, metaphorical language of the Magic Theatre, which Haller then alas reduces back to literalness.

The levels of mirroring are many, and we can also see the text not only as Haller's being reflected in the world. If we hold the mirror differently, we see the world reflected in Haller; we can read the whole text not as individual spiritual journey but as socio-historical document, as a critique of German society in the inter-war period, with its reification of established culture (Berman, 1986). In the 'Editor' we see something of the defensive complacency of the bourgeoisie, and in Haller's thoughts and encounters we meet not only some of the jazz-age sub-culture of the twenties, but attitudes like the professor's (VII, p. 265) which show very clearly the deeper spirit of the age. It was an age of tension, of unresolved conflicts, in which concern for national identity masks deeper disorientation. The professor's unabashed militarism, his refusal to acknowledge any German guilt for the First World War is symptomatic, yet almost more worrying is the mix of verbally quite violent bigotry with the pursuit of German 'culture'. No discrepancy is perceived, a love of Goethe co-exists with crude nationalism, and we can thus already see in outline the mentality of the Third Reich, where bourgeois cultural icons are used to reinforce conservative authoritarianism, and there is a direct threat of future war. In a sense the separation between mind and instincts from which Haller suffers at the start of the novel is the wider German situation in microcosm. He, as a highly intelligent, already self-critical and hypersensitive man, is able to learn something of how to relate the different parts of himself together in balance, but there is little indication that Germany's lack of self-awareness is susceptible of improvement, since no sense of self-contradiction is felt. The professor's arcane research is a model of the intellectual attitudes of the period: it represents ultimately an unthinking, conservative belief in history and pseudo-progress. Haller, on the other hand, represents critical self-awareness, rejection of inherited structures of thought and of social organisation.

The body of Hesse's novel thus seems to represent a clear victory of metaphor over metonymy, to use Lodge's (1977) terminology. It is essentially a shifting, shimmering construct, both as real as recent history and as illusory as dream or drug-fantasy, offering us many varied views on the complex issues of identity and self-awareness. But can and does it offer more? Does it manage to give us a glimpse of some higher unity of being beyond all multiplicity, other than through the intimations of Haller's obvious failure? And if it does, does that mean that the text ultimately speaks with an authoritative voice which gainsays the constant stress on the provisional nature of all written accounts and the essential subjectivity of all cognitive approaches?

Haller, as we have seen, fails the test of the 'Magic Theatre'; he is still literalistic, judgemental. But is there hope for him? There remains the model of Art. Mozart's music, explicitly distinguished from Brahms' and Wagner's confusion, is both sublimely complex and *heiter* (serene), unaffected by its distortion in transmission, its contingent butchering on the radio. The immortal artists themselves, Mozart and Goethe, also embody in their lives all oppositions, combine deep seriousness and frivolity, while remaining quite detached from what is made of them and their work in time and space. Their essential quality is humour, the capacity to find pleasure in and yet detachment from every experience. All of this gives us models of that 'higher' self which must become creative in a wider sense than the purely artistic, achieve aesthetic distance from individual aspects of self, see life and personality as the changing but all equally valid and beautiful configurations on a chessboard, to use another image from the text (VII, p. 385). Thus it might be possible for ordinary mortals to 'create' their own lives and identities anew, embracing both self and world in one, accepting all that life offers as of equal value and potentially part of their experience, of themselves. Plurality can thus be harmony, not chaos. Not that Hesse is suggesting the need for Faustian endeavour! It is quite clearly indicated in the figures of Goethe and Mozart, and in the possibility of reading the 'Magic Theatre' as a drug-fantasy, that what he means is not frenzied protean activity but a state of mind, though it is equally true and important that the text shows the world as never ceasing to be physically present, 'real' in that sense. Hesse is not advocating an endless drug-trip either! The world cannot be made to go away; it is a mode of perceiving it that is at issue, and like musical harmony, or role models, or Jungian archetypes, this state of mind is in a sense insubstantial, only image, illusory, and always capable of being fractured by literalmindedness. This brings us right back to the 'Editor', and why he has only a glimpse of something strange, indirectly, through meeting Haller. The editor's mind is pedantic, rule-bound, literal, as we can see from his lengthy attempts to provide fact on the provenance of the notes, and to fix and limit them by cultural explanation. No, he lies beyond redemption, incapable of the aesthetic' state. If Haller reaches it, it will by definition be beyond what can be written, beyond separate images and formulations, for he will have to become those images, become the mirror.

It is quite clear, then, that though Hesse is indeed working with notions of some kind of absolute state of being it is very far from any conventional concept of 'unity of personality', whether literary or psychoanalytical. It goes beyond Freudian recovery of repressed material or libidinous energy. Reintegration through therapy is part of the process, but the final stage seems to break the boundaries of what even early twentieth-century psychoanalysis understood as individual identity. So Hesse cannot from this point of view be accused of inconsistency, of denying the unitary nature of identity whilst sneaking it in again as his goal; what he seems to be visualising in the 'Magic Theatre' is more Jungian than Freudian, more Eastern than Western – a discovery of 'true' self by loss of self, Self and Universe as one.

But is the structure of the text really as Modernist as its concepts seem to be? We have seen that it can be approached in different ways. At one level it might seem very recursive; it does not 'tell a story', its basic plot is in conventional terms absolutely minimal. Instead, it moves by a process of mirroring and 'musical'/thematic variation towards Harmony and Mirroring as its ideal states, but this tendency to self-reflexiveness is not so much frustrating or negative as positive and essential. The novel appears to be suggesting, after all, that help for the modern, discordant, divided self is *in* the self. Our subjectively fragmented world is not to be put back together by some overarching 'final' meaning, whether religious or political, but by embracing its fragmentation. This is made possible for the reader too. We saw how a first approach to the novel leads us further and further into uncertainty; our expectation of a simple story to match the apparent bourgeois conventionality of its opening social setting is utterly frustrated by the ambiguous status of each successive stage of the text. But we also saw how each stage builds on that de-centring of the reader, by offering us new types of insight and asking us simultaneously to question them, allowing ultimately a series of co-existing readings, of alternative but co-extensive texts to be discovered. This uncertain, fluid syntax of reading, with its extraordinary cultural mix, goes beyond what Ziolkowski calls 'dual vision'; it is not merely a formal, stylistic feature, but the precondition of Haller's detachment from narrow 'reality' – and of the reader's detachment from his or her own acquired or inherited models of personality and progress. The textual fluidity replicates Haller's need to live in multiple dimensions at once, and through it, our own reading of reality and any conventional assumptions about how to render it narratively or about our role *as* readers are destabilised; everything is rendered subjective and fluid. Thus our desire to categorise, our residual trust in language as able adequately to fix reality in all its complexity is subverted, and this leads us potentially forward like Haller. In some senses Hesse's text takes us to the very limits of writing and encourages us not to despair, but to live without it, without that desire to circumscribe and 'know' that so diminishes our sense of our own being and our place in the wider world.

It is then true that from one point of view – in moving beyond the need for writing – the text subverts itself in the most modernist, indeed almost post-modernist, manner imaginable; but if we look more closely we may find it less radical than it seems. Despite the obvious narrative instability of the text, it is possible to argue that the reader is not taxed enough, if the goal of unsettling our thinking to the point where we abandon traditional categories, and even thought itself, is serious.

Of course it is true, as we have seen, that each section of the work, whether the 'Editor's' comments or the 'Treatise' is rendered relative, provisional: by its own particular bias in the first case or abstraction in the second. Collectively they emphasise the inadequacy of all attempts to categorise and 'hold' reality in conventional language. Individually, however, these sections do not challenge us so very radically. Each of them addresses us in an easily comprehended, recognisable voice, with the language of bourgeois 'decency' or theoretical analysis or the intimate diary, and despite our ultimate awareness of the macro-text as endlessly relative, as embodying the final inadequacy of language, it is very easy to feel oneself addressed in the moment of reading each part by the all-too-familiar voice of traditional narrative, and to lose sight of the whole. In addition there is some, but not a very marked stylistic difference between the sections. We are all too easily placed as readers in the position of the 'missing' omniscient narrator, as integration point for the text as a whole: that is, we maintain a relatively consistent distance from the text throughout, despite the shifting narrative viewpoint, because we are not constantly forced by stylistic change or linguistic difficulty into reflection *on* the text as we read it. We experience the text in the act of reading almost as diegetic; we do not have an immediate, vivid sense of *multiple* discourse. That stylistic sense of coherence is further reinforced if we look more closely at the apparent breaks in the text, between editor's notes, 'Treatise' and Haller's writings. Although these breaks may indeed be said to decentre us as readers, they are less radical than they at first seem. The various sections do not, for example, really reflect ironically upon each other; there is no such complex or self-questioning relationship between them – they present us rather with a sequence of clearly expanding and deepening insights. Each section neatly picks up threads from the one before, even to the point, for example, of prostitution being mentioned in the 'Treatise', thus anticipating Hermine's key appearance later on. Once one becomes aware of such connections, the earlier impression of 'theme and multiple variations' can begin to seem more like a traditional pattern of plot development.

In other ways too, Hesse's text comes disturbingly close to the kind of traditional narration it seems to want to eschew. If we look at its inclusion of Jungian theory, for example, we might conclude that it is a very avant-garde novel. Yet it in no sense adds to, comments on, *interprets* Jungian theory; we saw above how closely the fictional figures parallel Jung's vision of the developing Self. In fact, that vision – which is admittedly relativised by the existence of other frameworks of interpretation – is handled by Hesse almost *referentially*, as a given and understood entity whose outline needs simply to be reproduced for recognition; that is, he treats it much as a Realist novelist would handle the data of the external world, simply reproducing accepted patterns of connection. Again this means that – at this level at least – the reader is being asked to respond as to a traditional narrative contract, to 'believe' an authoritative narrative voice.

That authoritative voice may be detected elsewhere too. We have seen, it is true, that Hesse replaces traditional realist notions of character unity with a vision of infinitely extensible fluidity; equally, the Immortals do not give us an over-arching source of meaning, so much as glimpses of a state of mind that accepts discontinuity. This does not mean, however, that Hesse abandons all absolutes. The value that he attaches to art in using artists as his 'Immortals' is both obvious and problematic. On the one hand these figures are clearly to be read as indicators of that quasi-Nietzschean 'aesthetic' stance towards life which we are all to aim for. It is their lives which are models for us, not only their works. On the other hand, however, they may seem to suggest a belief that there is a 'Best' in German culture, that Art is the closest we can come to complex Truth embodied. If that is so, then Hesse has indeed reintroduced the possibility of the coherent, authoritative art-form even whilst his own text seems to enact incompleteness. Truth may be fluid, but it is nevertheless accessible to art; the modern novel may seem to be open, unfinishable, but that is precisely where its 'authenticity' lies. Despite all, there is indeed a sense in which Hesse's writing claims the kind of validity – unredeemed by irony – that belongs to the nineteenth rather than the twentieth century.

In his essay *Vom Bücherlesen* (On Reading Books: XI) Hesse differentiates between three types of reader: the one who takes a work literally, the one who follows its symbolic overtones, and the one who uses it as a starting-point for his own ideas and mental flow. This is clearly the reader Hesse himself hopes for, and to a large extent ensures for *Der Steppenwolf* by its focus on self-discovery. Nevertheless, the novel bears some traces, as we have seen, of the authoritative story that it claims not to be able to write: and yet not self-consciously or self-parodyingly so that one might see it perhaps as deliberately attempting just this paradox, like some ultimate Zen koan. For all his stress on humour, it is perhaps precisely that which Hesse lacks as writer, just as his 'liberation' of the non-rational side of Man – all that is 'improper' in bourgeois eyes – remains in illustration actually highly decorous and proper. Even the 'Treatise' has much more to say about misconceptions surrounding the term 'Mensch' than it does about the nature of the 'Wolf'. Ultimately Hesse has not fully achieved that Modernist distance from the norms of Realist writing and its bourgeois readership that his novel seems at first to open up.

REFERENCES

References to the works of Hermann Hesse relate to the *Gesammelte Werke* in twelve volumes, Frankfurt: Suhrkamp, 1970.

BERMAN, R. A. (1986), *The Rise of the Modern German Novel*, Cambridge, Mass. & London: Harvard University Press.

FREEDMAN, R. (1963), *The Lyrical Novel*, Princeton: Princeton University Press.

JUNG. C. G. (1964), *Man and his Symbols*, London: Aldus Books.

LODGE, D. (1977), *The Modes of Modern Writing: Metaphor, Metonymy and the Typology of Modern Literature*, London: Edward Arnold.

MANN, T. (1960), Hermann Hesse zum 70. Geburtstag, in *Gesammelte Werke*, X, Frankfurt: S. Fischer.

MICHELS, V. (ed.) (1972), *Materialien zu Hermann Hesses 'Der Steppenwolf'*, Frankfurt am Main: Suhrkamp.

TIMMS, E. (1990), Hesse's therapeutic fiction, in Collier, P. and Davies, J. (eds), *Modernism and the European Unconscious*, Cambridge & Oxford: Polity Press.

ZIOLKOWSKI, T. (1965), *The Novels of Hermann Hesse: A Study in Theme and Structure*, Princeton: Princeton University Press.

7

The Dynamics of Consciousness
Alfred Döblin, *Berlin Alexanderplatz*

DAVID MIDGLEY

A convict is released from prison. He is resolved to go straight, to lead an upright, honest life. But with the prison gates shut behind him, he is as if paralysed by the prospect of his own freedom: his 'punishment' is only beginning.

This is the concrete human situation with which Döblin presents his reader at the start of *Berlin Alexanderplatz*. But the manner in which that situation is presented lends it a sense of depth and resonance, not so much through the information that it provides about the convict Franz Biberkopf, but rather through the dynamically shifting nature of the narrative technique. What we are told about the person of Biberkopf is very scant at this stage: he has served a four-year sentence, only yesterday he had been digging up potatoes in his prison garb along with all the others, now he is standing outside the gates as if rooted to the spot, watching one tram after another leave for the centre of Berlin. The perspective from which the situation is described is predominantly that of the fictional character – 'yesterday he had ...', 'now he was ...'; we recognise the narrative convention as that of *erlebte Rede*. But the narrating voice that we hear in this instance is one which does not rest content to show, to mimic, to maintain its (potentially ironic) distance towards the character. Within a very few lines we find the flow of psychological empathy disrupted by interjections which strikingly appear in square brackets, and which interrogate the character directly about his emotional responses: 'schrecklich, Franze, warum schrecklich?' and 'Widerwillen, warum Widerwillen' (*why* does this moment appear so terrible, and *why* had the sight of the prison gates filled him with a growing sense of reluctance over the course of the last year?). Once Biberkopf has finally plucked up courage and boarded a tram that will take him into town – with his head involuntarily screwed round in the direction of the prison he has left behind, and anxiety screaming inside him – we find the narrative flow interrupted again by the unmediated presentation of the sounds around him, the cries of newspaper vendors and of the tram conductor. For brief sentences at a time the text moves identifiably into interior monologue as Biberkopf registers unfamiliar impressions in the present tense: 'The police *have* blue uniforms now', '*My brain must be* quite dried out', 'People *have to have* shoes' .... But the narrative mode is constantly fluctuating. The reader cannot be certain whether it is Biberkopf's own voice or another's commanding him to pull himself together, his voice or another's advising him that he will feel better if he mingles with the crowd. The instability of perspective is pointed up by a frequent shifting of subject pronouns between the securely external third person *er*, the impersonal *man* (which could just as well be part of Biberkopf's own idiom as anyone else's), and the intimate second person *du*. The overall effect is a sustained disruption of any inclination on the reader's part to identify the presentation of events with a particular seat of consciousness.

When *Berlin Alexanderplatz* was published in 1929, it was recognised as a radically new and important work, but reviewers were puzzled by its unrestrained mixing of styles and perspectives (*Materialien*, p. 53ff). They tended to interpret it in terms that were familiar to them, seeing the multiplicity of voices in the text primarily as a vivid reflection of the urban milieu in which the central character was moving; and they were quick to compare the novel with James Joyce's *Ulysses*, which had been much discussed in literary circles since its publication in 1922, and had appeared in a German translation in 1927. (The fact that reviewers also claimed to detect the influence of psycho-analysis in *Berlin Alexanderplatz* tells us more about the intellectual climate of the 1920s than about Döblin's actual practice.) Döblin himself published an enthusiastic review of *Ulysses* in 1928, and the complexities of Joyce's work evidently stimulated him to take a more adventurous approach in the presentation of his own material. Another possible stimulus is John Dos Passos' *Manhattan Transfer* of 1925 (Duytschaever, 1975). But Döblin was pursuing his own concerns – both as an author and as a citizen of the Weimar Republic – when he adopted the radicalism of approach that characterises *Berlin Alexanderplatz*. It is a text which challenges ideological as well as narrative orthodoxies, and which explores moral and political issues, as well as demonstrating the aspects of contingency and indeterminacy in modern social identity.

The manuscript evidence for the impact of Joyce's novel on *Berlin Alexanderplatz* is described by Breon Mitchell (1976, pp. 31–50). Döblin had apparently drafted much of Books 1 and 2 before reading *Ulysses*, and then subjected them to extensive reworking, incorporating the mixture of styles, and the interpolations in square brackets, which we have noticed on the opening pages. Later sections of the text also show a greater stylistic complexity and heterogeneity than the earliest portions. At the opening of Book 2, which ostensibly presents Franz Biberkopf's entry into the city of Berlin, Döblin went further and inserted pictorial representations of the various dimensions of urban society, from its gas works to its museums, from its banks and tax offices to its street-cleaning service, followed by passages from a variety of public documents – a planning notice, a hunting permit, the announcement of the retirement of a welfare commissioner – which, if they bear any apparent relation at all to Biberkopf's personal story, do so only as intimations of the official regulation of human affairs which is itself a further ineluctable dimension of civil society. (A 'hunting pass' (*Jagdschein*), it emerges later in the text, is underworld slang for a release from custody.) Döblin quite literally pasted into his manuscript excerpts from newspapers, information leaflets, and reference books, and made continual amendments to the text as fresh points occurred to him (Müller-Salget, 1975, pp. 122–7; Stenzel, 1966). Mitchell points out some elements of newspaper material, public information (e.g. tram routes), and 'scientific style', which suggest that Döblin was emulating Joyce in matters of detail. He also notes that montage as a compositional principle had been at the heart of German discussions of *Ulysses* since 1925 (Mitchell, 1976, p. 100). But what he does not discuss are the compositional implications of the montage technique as Döblin develops it, which arguably point to more substantial underlying affinities between Döblin and Joyce, as well as indicating to what extent Döblin really was his own man.

Döblin's review of *Ulysses* (*Materialien*, pp. 49–52) anticipated what have become some of the commonplaces of Joyce criticism. He noted the adoption of individual styles to suit the expressive purpose of particular episodes: rambling monologue for Molly Bloom's night thoughts (Penelope), punctilious question and answer for Bloom's homecoming (Ithaca), drama mode where the subject matter becomes dramatic (Circe). He recognised the sense in which Joyce exposes the artificiality of narrative invention ('Joyce fühlt die Komik des Fabulierens'), and he stressed the experimental way in which Joyce sounds out the basic elements of narration ('Beklopfen ihrer Grundelemente'). But at the same time his review was a programmatic statement on his own behalf. He commended Joyce's novel to the attention of 'any serious writer' as a text which would expose the shallowness of most contemporary fiction, and which opened up new possibilities for literary writing as an 'odyssey' through the entire range of current empirical experience. When we find him describing Joyce's exactness of observation (in the Ithaca episode) as a 'scientific' style 'without an actual subject'; when he speaks of the expansion of the domain of literature to include the stuff of cinema and newspapers, and the restless discontinuities of city street impressions and modern traffic; when he insists that the heroic dimension of ancient epic has given way to the pervasive influence of economic and political systems, concluding that the contemporary sense of a 'crisis of the novel' merely reflects the fact that the mentalities of literary authors have not yet caught up with events – then we sense that this review is related to a debate about the modernisation of literature in which Döblin had been participating for many a year.

Already before the First World War, as a prominent contributor to the

Expressionist periodical *Der Sturm* (The Storm), Döblin had established himself as one of Germany's most self-consciously avant-garde writers, emphatically challenging the conventional acceptance of the author as an authority. His most important programmatic statements of that time arise out of his personal confrontation with the literary and artistic products of the Italian Futurists, whose paintings were exhibited in Berlin in 1912, and whose manifestoes were published in *Der Sturm*. Döblin wrote enthusiastically about the paintings, welcoming their vibrant dynamism and simultaneity. In particular he admired the 'dancing' quality of Umberto Boccioni's multiple imagery, because it betokened a radical break with the tradition of three dimensional perspective and its implication of a fixed viewpoint (cf. Kobel, 1985, pp. 58–60). When he encountered the literary writing of Filippo Tommaso Marinetti, the leading Futurist, on the other hand, he found that it failed to live up to its avant-garde pretensions, being characterised by tired metaphors and an outmoded aestheticism (AzL, p. 12f). In 1913 Döblin published his own manifesto, a 'Berlin Programme' of literary aims appropriate to the modern age. What he proposed there was the result of a critical engagement, not only with the Futurists, but also with the closeted, introspective, psychological literature which had been prevalent in Germany since the turn of the century, and to which Döblin had himself contributed (Scheunemann, 1978, pp. 89–94). In place of the rationalising categories of popular psychology, he urged his fellow-writers to adopt the technique of precise observation as practised in clinical psychiatry (the discipline in which he had himself been trained), and cultivate the art of 'kinetic fantasy' that was exemplified in the compositional techniques of the cinema. The principle that Rilke had adopted as a matter of existential necessity (see above, pp. 45–58), Döblin pronounced as his precept: 'man erzählt nicht, sondern baut' (we don't narrate, we construct). He called for the breaking of the 'hegemony of the author', and for the 'depersonalisation' of the narrator: 'I am not I, but the street, the lamps, this or that event, nothing more' (AzL, pp. 15–19; Žmegač, 1968). When Döblin makes polemical use of the term 'epic', here and elsewhere, contrasting it with the conventionally known novel of his day, then what he has in mind is this opening up of the text, and of perceptual categories, to events in all their vividness and plasticity, leaving the reader free to fashion his own judgements. In December 1928, shortly before the publication of *Berlin Alexanderplatz* he spoke at Berlin University on the subject of narrative composition ('Der Bau des epischen Werks') and repeated there his arguments in favour of directness of presentation, admitting to a passion for facts and documents because they represented for him the authentic voice of that 'great story-teller' (*Epiker*), nature itself (AzL, p. 113f).

As these programmatic statements suggest, Döblin had also worked through in his own way the implications of multi-perspectival presentation and montage before he began to write *Berlin Alexanderplatz*. In addition to the model of the early cinema (from which the very term 'montage' is derived),

Döblin was familiar with the artistic experimentation of the Berlin Dadaists around 1919, although his explicit approval went rather to Kurt Schwitters, a gentler and subtler artist than the Dadaists, in whose collage technique Döblin again saw a reverent expression of 'nature' (Müller-Salget, 1975, p. 20; Ziolkowski, 1969, p. 108). Among the contemporary references contained in *Berlin Alexanderplatz* is the mention of a sensational new production by Erwin Piscator, who had used new technical facilities to expand the domain of theatrical expression in senses which are consistent with Döblin's use of the term 'epic', and of which he expressly approved (BA, p. 226; AzL, p. 112f). Moreover, Döblin's own earliest attempts at prose fiction of around 1903 reflect a scepticism about the unity of identity which led him to develop techniques for presenting emotional and intellectual conflicts that are already akin to a form of montage. The contrastive juxtaposition of textual fragments that we find in *Berlin Alexanderplatz* has a long heritage within Döblin's own work (Keller, 1980, pp. 43–58; 197–201).

What are the functions of montage in Döblin's novel? For one thing it does convey the special flavour and vibrancy of the city, as the early reviewers recognised. The disparate sequence of texts which we have already noted from the opening of Book 2 continues with a weather forecast, which is in turn interrupted by the description of a tram route. The language of notices regulating public behaviour, again, yields to a fleeting description of someone who risks life and limb by defying such regulation, together with a laconic exchange of comments on the incident between a tram conductor and a policeman. The names of factories and businesses are quoted from the telephone directory of 1928; the streets that converge on the Rosenthaler Platz are described in terms which seem to confer movement and energy upon them; the lives of human bystanders are extrapolated – anticipating, for example, the future career and eventual death of a 14-year-old schoolboy – as if they are merely ephemeral features of a supra-individual being. The section is headed 'Der Rosenthaler Platz unterhält sich' (The Rosenthaler Platz in conversation with itself): it is indeed as if the location has acquired organic properties, of which the ensuing buzz of human conversation in a pub on the square is just another subordinate function. It is through elements such as these, as Walter Benjamin commented in his review of the work (*Materialien*, p. 111), that the city seems to speak through the novel, and the author seems to speak with the voices of the city. Those square brackets we noticed on the opening pages of the novel are deployed elsewhere to introduce a note of vernacular scepticism or an awareness of simultaneous occurrences into the depiction of communal life, breaking up a dialogue with elements of narrative or vice versa. And when they interrupt a series of short news items with the text of a cigarette advertisement that begins 'bitte einen Augenblick' (excuse me a moment), it is as if the advertising pillar that Biberkopf is contemplating has itself sprung to life (BA, p. 186).

In many cases the montage elements also furnish an ironic counterpoint to the actions of characters, particularly those of Biberkopf himself. At the point in Book 1 where Biberkopf experiences sexual failure when visiting a prostitute, the text incorporates a disquisition on the mechanics of sexual potency, snatches of lyrics from a banal operetta, and finally an advertising text for Testifortan, a male hormone treatment (BA, pp. 34–7). At the stage where he tries to earn a living by selling newspapers on the street – without apparent regard for their political orientation – we are presented first with a sequence of visual and aural impressions associated with a newspaper kiosk, and later with passages evidently culled from Nazi publications (BA, p. 85f). When the Nazi connection in turn leads to a breach between Biberkopf and his socialist companions, we find references to rising unemployment, to the Krupp steel consortium cutting the value of pensions, and to limitations imposed upon family benefit, all interpolated into the account of him settling his bill and leaving the pub (BA, p. 99f). At moments of personal rebuff or catastrophe for Biberkopf the reader's attention is withdrawn from his personal experience altogether, and focused instead on observations which serve to place his individual destiny in a broader context. At the end of Book 3 Biberkopf retreats from human company after experiencing deception and humiliation; the opening of Book 4 evokes, not the squalor of the particular room in which he has gone to ground, but the area around it. The incident at the end of Book 5 which, as we subsequently learn, will result in the amputation of Biberkopf's right arm culminates, not in a description of him being run over, but with a pointed contrast, the evocation of a new dawn, a new beginning, and the arrival in Berlin of an international celebrity (BA, p. 232f). At the height of Biberkopf's misfortunes in Book 8 we find interpolated references to Berlin's birth and death statistics and to earthquake victims in Prague (BA, pp. 416, 428). The effect of passages such as these is to relativise the importance of Biberkopf as an individual, reducing him, as Hans-Peter Bayerdörfer (1983, p. 155) aptly puts it, to the status of a 'microbe' in relation to humanity at large.

As we read through the novel, however, we encounter passages which seem to have no specific bearing either on the Biberkopf story or on the life of the city as such. In Books 1 and 2 we find unmediated references to mountains and armies, to scientific theories, and to the vast expanses of time and space through which the sun's rays have travelled (BA, pp. 38–40; 89). In the middle of Book 4 we are given an explicit and extensive description of the operations of the central slaughterhouse in Berlin under a chapter heading drawn from the Bible (Ecclesiastes 3:19); it is followed by a section about the misfortunes of Job. The biblical references proliferate as the story progresses. We are given quotations from the prophet Jeremiah, evocations of the Whore of Babylon from Revelations, the sacrifice of Isaac by his father Abraham, and further motifs from Ecclesiastes chapter 3 suggestive of the eternal patterns in earthly life: 'To every thing there is a season, and a time to every purpose under the heaven ...' (The sources are identified by Hülse, 1965, p. 75f, and Komar,

1983, pp. 39–43). In certain respects it is again possible to read the biblical references as ironic commentaries on Biberkopf's behaviour. The section about Job, for example, is preceded by a brief reminder of how Biberkopf is wallowing in self-pity after becoming the victim of what he sees as a cruel betrayal: Lüders, with whom he had found a kind of partnership as a street vendor, has tricked him of the favours of a seemingly wealthy widow. The most insistent echoes of sentiments drawn from Ecclesiastes are developed in connection with the murder of Mieze, the prostitute who has provided Biberkopf with a sustaining love relationship, at the end of Book 7. Working back from this point in the novel, it is possible to interpret earlier quotations and allusions to some extent as adumbrations of what is to come. The first of many references to Death the Reaper occurs in connection with the figure of Reinhold, the hardened criminal who will murder Mieze when he fails to 'take her away' from Biberkopf (BA, p. 200f). And the echo of Ecclesiastes 3:20, 'all are of the dust, and all turn to dust again', which first appears in the novel at the point where Biberkopf is demonstratively 'cleansing' his living space of the memory of Lüders (BA, p. 126), seems to suggest that there is something in Biberkopf's own behaviour which is going to bring catastrophe on himself and others. But we are here only scratching at the surface of the complex system of interrelated motifs that Döblin has worked into his text.

Otto Keller (1980) has provided the most thorough study to date of the network of thematic associations that runs through *Berlin Alexanderplatz*. The allusion to Hannibal which is recognisable in that early passage about mountains and armies is but one example of references to 'conquerors' down the ages: they include contemporary boxing champions and would-be record-breakers, as well as Julius Caesar, Napoleon, and the ancient Babylonian tyrant Nebuchadnezzar. These elements extend the historical frame of reference and suggest parallels to Biberkopf's attempts to set himself up, assert his identity, and show the world 'what he is made of', which are ironically referred to in the novel (p. 261) as his 'conquests' of Berlin. The specific reference to Babylon is introduced in the course of Biberkopf's early encounter with a pair of Jews, in the form of a quotation from the Book of Jeremiah concerning the need to chastise the Chaldeans, the inhabitants of Babylon, since it has proved impossible to cure them of their iniquities (BA, p. 19). The series of blows that Biberkopf receives is thematically linked to other instances of violence evoked in the text: the slaughterhouse sequence provides graphic images of hammer blows and the wielding of knives and axes which are echoed later in the murder of Mieze and the sacrifice of Isaac, and particularly in the allegorical representation of Biberkopf's ultimate confrontation with Death (swinging an axe rather than a scythe) in the final Book of the novel. The evocation of the Whore of Babylon, too, is related to the theme of Biberkopf's need for chastisement, but we are mistaken if we identify her directly with the city as such, even if the description of her in Revelations might suggest this; she is introduced rather as the 'mother of all abominations' (BA, p. 260), an emblem of deep, archaic, irresolvable forces in human nature (Keller, 1980, p. 170f). There are also countervailing forces in humanity, impulses towards 'helping' and 'healing', which are variously represented in the novel by Mieze, by the Jews of Book 1, and by other figures who stand by Biberkopf in his troubles. The victory of Death over Babylon in Book 9 draws together in pictorial representation the intimations of struggle, destruction, and regeneration which are elaborated in many other recurring motifs in the novel. At the moment of Death's triumph we are reminded that such processes are the stuff of human history: he unfurls his cloak to reveal images of war, revolution and martyrdom. And the Alexanderplatz itself is presented as a symbolic location where processes of demolition and reconstruction take place at the heart of urban society (BA, p. 179f).

Keller is not the first to have noticed that Döblin has reinterpreted the motifs he draws from the Bible, especially the stories of Job and Isaac (cf. Müller-Salget, 1972, pp. 322–4; Reid, 1968, p. 215f). Whereas the Old Testament version commemorates Job for his exemplary faith in God in the face of affliction, Döblin presents him as stricken with shame and self-pity over his sickness and weakness, and presuming to judge God before the tribune of human reason; the fact that Job's healing follows directly upon his surrender of this presumption provides a parallel to the chastisement and reforming of Biberkopf. Döblin's Job, then, participates in the novel's theme of the pride and fall of 'conquerors', while his Isaac becomes an emblem of knowing self-sacrifice, a figure who embraces and overcomes the fear of death (Keller, 1980, pp.155–7, 173). Albrecht Schöne (1963, p. 308f) had recognised the strength of such thematic analogies in the novel, and related them to the theory of 'resonance' in all realms of earthly experience which Döblin expounds in his philosophical treatise *Unser Dasein* (Our Existence) of 1933. It has also long been recognised that the novel is organised in relation to thematic contrasts or antinomies (Schöne, 1963, p. 311; Müller-Salget, 1972, p. 324f). But Keller's detailed exploration of the way in which motifs interconnect also sheds light on a dimension of the novel which others had sensed, but not demonstrated, namely the sense in which individual elements in the montage acquire a dynamic, as it were, energised relationship to each other (cf. Schöne, 1963, p. 315; Müller-Salget, 1972, p. 298). For example, Keller examines the interplay of imagery in two passages which are juxtaposed towards the end of Book 5, at the point where Biberkopf is about to meet with disaster in the course of his involvement with a team of criminals, the Pums gang. The first is a passage from Jeremiah 17:5-8 which directly challenges Biberkopf's characteristic insistence on being 'someone you can depend on':

> Cursed be the man that trusteth in man, and maketh flesh his arm, and whose heart departeth from the Lord. For he shall be like the heath in the desert, and shall not see when good cometh; but shall inhabit the parched places in the wilderness, in a salt land and not inhabited. Blessed is the man that trusteth in the Lord, and whose hope the Lord

is. For he shall be as a tree planted by the waters, and that spreadeth out
her roots by the river ...

The passage which immediately follows shows us the obverse of the implication of fruitfulness in Jeremiah's tree image: it speaks of eery black waters in
the depths of a forest, in which snails and fish lurk, and plants decompose
(BA, p. 215f). The imagery of either passage challenges and relativises that of
the other. To Keller's interpretation of the 'black waters' image it might be
added that there is a link to Biberkopf, not only via the themes contained in
the Jeremiah passage, but also through the characterisation of the pool as
impervious to the threatening storm winds that rage above the forest: the
depths of Biberkopf's mind will be stirred up only by his confrontation with
death in Book 9, in the course of which his consciousness is said to recede to
the level of animals and plants (BA, p. 472f). But the point emerges clearly
nevertheless that the significance of specific images in the text is not fixed, but
takes on a variety of aspects according to the context in which they appear
(Keller, 1980, pp. 160–62, 170).

The mutual relativisation of motifs and thematic associations extends into
all aspects of the novel. When Biberkopf, in his early state of trepidation, finds
refuge in a tenement courtyard, he is told a story which is ostensibly intended
to rouse him from his torpor, but which turns out to illustrate some of the
profound ambivalences in human behaviour. The figure of Zannovich is held
out to him as someone who saw the positive potential available to him in the
cities of Europe and took advantage of it, but the manner in which he did so
involved trickery and deceit; the man who is presented as an example to
emulate turns out to have ended his days in disgrace and squalor – and yet this
is precisely what does arouse Biberkopf to an animated response, a protesta-
tion of shame and outrage (BA, p. 28f). Motifs associated with Biberkopf's
own intentions and behaviour patterns are similarly capable of conveying
ambivalent undercurrents. The 'paradise' motif which suggests his simple
desire to live in peace and harmony with a sexual partner is immediately
trivialised when it first occurs, in the preamble to Book 2, by the juxtaposition
of a childish refrain from Humperdinck's *Hansel and Gretel* (which itself
becomes a recurrent motif). It is subsequently ironised further by association
with the seductive potential of political reaction and racism – 'for there must
be order in paradise' (BA, pp. 85, 99f; cf. Müller-Salget, 1972, p. 307; Reid,
1968, p. 218ff). The memory of the Garden of Eden has its obverse association
in the biblical story of the Fall – which a war invalid can use as an expression
of political resentment (BA, p. 85). Biberkopf himself can evoke the serpent in
a spirit of unthinking recrimination against Lüders, while his own self-image
as a powerful cobra hints again at his own role in the perpetration of evil (cf.
Keller 1980, p. 149f). Echoes of Biberkopf's wartime service are subject to
similar modulation. His singing of Max Schneckenburger's nationalist hymn
of 1840, 'Die Wacht am Rhein' (The Watch on the Rhine), is variously
associated with the reassertion of his manhood, or his response to political

taunts (BA, pp. 34, 96), and generally becomes a marker of his emotional hankering after a security and stability which he has known in former times. The fact that the curious bond of fellowship which repeatedly draws Biberkopf to Reinhold is signalled by lines from the popular Uhland poem 'The Good Comrade' suggests that there is a similar defensive motivation at work there, too. But the military associations can very easily shift to an offensive pattern when Biberkopf takes it upon himself to impose 'order' on Reinhold's unstable relationships with women (cf. Keller, 1980, p. 159ff; Müller-Salget, 1972, p. 313ff). It is the multiple interaction between motifs such as these that becomes the true vehicle for Döblin's 'direct presentation' of his characters' behaviour.

But the examples we have considered so far remain comfortingly close to the sphere of psychological commonplaces, and we know from Döblin's programmatic statements that he wanted literary writing to accomplish more than this. As Keller (1980, p. 218) notes, it is possible to distinguish three anthropological dimensions from which the motifs and montage elements of *Berlin Alexanderplatz* are drawn. These are the modern city, the domain of human historical experience (including the literary and biblical references), and the realm of nature; and in the way that these references are deployed, the conventional divisions of analytical thought themselves become fluid. The description of sunlight falling through a pub window evokes the vast distances it has travelled, the periods of historical and prehistorical time it embraces, and ends with a line from a Christmas carol (BA, p. 89). The dying calf of the slaughterhouse sequence is said to pass through the domains of metaphysics and theology, and beyond that of physiology, until it reaches that of inorganic science, of physics (BA, p. 150). And when the time comes to evoke the transformation of Biberkopf in Book 9, then the boundaries of literary convention are dissolved with the introduction of angels from Hebrew tradition, a modified medieval allegory in the figure of Death itself, and surreal elements which put Biberkopf's soul on intimate terms with animals and the forces of nature.

A particularly revealing passage in this connection, and one which has been much discussed in the secondary literature, is the account of the manslaughter of Ida, the incident for which Biberkopf has served his prison sentence. The section begins with an intricate play of ironic contrasts between the former cement worker, furniture remover and newsvendor Franz Biberkopf on the one hand, and Orestes, a figure likely to be familiar to German readers from Goethe's Iphigenia play rather than directly from ancient Greek tragedy, on the other. On the face of it, the text is urging the great historical difference between their respective situations, which is highlighted once more by down-to-earth interjections in the Berlin vernacular. Here is Orestes pursued by the Furies, cowering at the altar [try finding a church in Berlin that's open at night], cursed by the gods [as if we can know that], having avenged his father by murdering his mother [the one with the unpronounceable name]; and there is Biberkopf, restored to fitness, a denizen of the local gymnasium, swigging beer and schnaps at Henschke's bar as if he hasn't a care in the world. Elsewhere in the novel, too, we find burlesque references to Homer's famous description of the shield of Achilles, to the cuckoldry of Menelaus, or the heroic pretensions of the German classics, notably Kleist's 'Prince of Homburg', as further reminders of apparently antiquated ways of perceiving the world (BA, pp. 266, 144f, 80f). And yet there is something in the text which tends to relativise the emphatic insistence on modern scientific perspectives in its turn. The death of Ida itself is presented to us, pointedly, in terms of a *re*construction of the event. Döblin's choice of the German perfect tense, in preference to the narrative imperfect, emphasises both the definitively past nature of the action and the present-moment perspective of the speaker:

> Franz hat seine Braut erschlagen, Ida, der Nachname tut nichts zur Sache, in der Blüte ihrer Jahre. Dies ist passiert bei einer Auseinandersetzung zwischen Franz und Ida, in der Wohnung ihrer Schwester Minna, wobei zunächst folgende Organe des Weibes leicht beschädigt wurden: die Haut über der Nase am spitzen Teil und in der Mitte, der darunter liegende Knochen mit dem Knorpel, was aber erst im Krankenhaus bemerkt wurde und dann in den Gerichtsakten eine Rolle spielte, ferner die rechte und linke Schulter, die leichte Quetschungen davontrugen mit Blutaustritt.
>
> (Franz killed his fiancée, Ida, the surname is of no consequence, in the bloom of her womanhood. This occurred on the occasion of a dispute between Franz and Ida in the flat of her sister Minna, in the course of which the following parts of the female's anatomy suffered minor injury: the skin over the nose, at the tip and in the middle, the bone and cartilage beneath, which was only noticed in the hospital, however, and subsequently featured in the court records, also the right and left shoulder which suffered slight bruising. – BA, p. 104)

The register selected is that of the sort of dispassionate summary we might expect of a police officer or a pathologist – although we also find an occasional sexual innuendo intruding into it, as well as elements of imaginative psychology in the descriptions of Biberkopf's physical state and Ida's own behaviour at the moment when she was struck with the fatal cream-whisk. We then pass, however, to a disquisition on Newton's laws of mechanics, complete with mathematical equations, which is presented as the modern-day (*zeitgemäß*) way of understanding the action that caused her death, but which is subjected in its turn to explanatory interjections, once more in square brackets, which relate the abstract theory to the specific event – as well as explaining to German readers how to pronounce the name Newton.

Here, too, the various modes in which the event is presented interact, each drawing attention to the provisional and limiting nature of the other. On the one hand it is possible to say that Döblin's characterisation of both Biberkopf and Reinhold is consistent with the latest thinking of criminal psychologists in his day (Ziolkowski, 1969, p. 116ff). On the other hand he has introduced a patently inappropriate scientific theory, Newtonian mechanics, into his evocation of Biberkopf's act of violence. On the one hand the novel contains multiple repudiations of the notion that Biberkopf might be pursued by a 'fate' external to himself. On the other hand it can be shown that there are perfectly serious parallels between the respective plights of Biberkopf and Orestes in the form of a moral need to strike a balance between fear and hubris (Duytschaever, 1979, p. 38). It might equally be said that the composition of Döblin's text incorporates warning signals both against the interpretation of Biberkopf's story exclusively in terms of tragedy, and also against the facile over-estimation of modern scientific perspectives (cf. Müller-Salget, 1972, p. 304; Bayerdörfer, 1983, p. 159).

The presentation of Ida's death contains important indicators of how narration in *Berlin Alexanderplatz* is generally organised. Albrecht Schöne (1963) noticed something odd about the narrating voice in this novel: it was forever quoting, and seemed to be evoking a world that consisted entirely of language. He fell back on a defence of the term 'narrator' in a minimal sense, to denote the apparent agent of narration in those portions of the text which are recognisably 'narrated'; but he also acknowledged that the 'narrator' of *Berlin Alexanderplatz* did not possess a consistent identity, any more than the characters did. We certainly feel the strong 'presence' of a narrator in the initial introduction to Biberkopf's story, but it is a narrator who mimics the role of a boxing commentator, telling us how Biberkopf 'picks himself up' after the first hard blow he receives, how he is 'almost out for the count' at one stage, and is finally 'torpedoed' with superlative brutality, so that he 'gives up the fight'. The preambles to individual Books occasionally slip into a form of rhyming doggerel: 'Das Leben findet das auf die Dauer zu *fein* und stellt ihm hinterlistig ein *Bein*' (Life finds that too cute in the long run, and cunningly trips him up: BA, p. 111), and 'Er wehrt sich tapfer und wild mit Händen und *Füßen*, aber es hilft nichts, es geht über ihn, er muß *müssen*' (He defends himself bravely and wildly with his hands and his feet, but it's no use, it's too much for him, he has to go through with it: BA, p. 177). It is a device which echoes the style of the fairground ballad, the *Moritat* of popular German tradition, in which the exploits and the ultimate demise of notorious criminals are celebrated: the moralising voice, too, is accorded its own distinctive idiom. Even the voice which conveys explicit statements of authorial intention acquires an ironic function towards the end of the novel, where it is used to interrupt the depiction of Biberkopf's agony with a showmanlike address to the reader, and with apologetic remarks about the length of the story which also draw attention to the way it has been artificially constructed (BA, pp. 486, 495, 499). Döblin remains true to the precepts of his 'Berlin Programme': the authorial interjections we encounter in *Berlin Alexanderplatz* are deployed in much the same way as all the other montage elements that constitute the text (cf. Keller, 1980, pp. 213–25; Bayerdörfer, 1983, p. 153f). His approach to narration – and this is surely the sense in which his novel does show a fundamental affinity with Joyce's Ulysses – is to use one form of diction to set off another and to show up its distinctive profile, its functionality as language.

A work which is so pointedly composed of signals and countersignals poses a special challenge, of course, to any act of interpretation. If the published commentaries on *Berlin Alexanderplatz* contradict each other in many respects, then that is because the commentators have tended to emphasise particular aspects of Döblin's work over others, according to their own predisposition. Fritz Martini (1954), Kathleen Komar (1983), and to some extent also Schöne (1963) and Kobel (1985), emphasise the spiritual dimension over the material, and see the theme of 'sacrifice' (*Opfer*) as central to the novel – but against this it should be noted that the words *Opfer* and *opfern*, as used in the text, cover the sense of simply yielding, of giving something up, as well as sacrifice for a cause. Volker Klotz (1969) emphasises the material dimension by focusing on Biberkopf's contest with society in the form of the big city, and J. H. Reid (1968) highlights the strand of political anarchism in Döblin's outlook – opposed to the centralised state, opposed to the political machinery of big parties. But here again we need to notice how contemporary issues are integrated into the overall texture of the work. When the political conflicts of Weimar Germany are evoked in the novel, they tend to present themselves in sloganised form, as elements which are again subject to the principle of mutual relativisation. When Biberkopf himself takes an interest in political agitation, through a personal contact with an anarchist group, the ultimate impression created by the encounter is once more ambivalent: on the one hand he lacks that sense of solidarity that they would seek from him, and on the other hand they do not seem to have conceptual categories that are adequate to comprehend the person he is (BA, p. 297f). Whatever might be said for each individual line of interpretation, the text does not permit any one of them finally to dominate over the others (cf. Müller-Salget, 1972, p. 296; Bayerdörfer, 1983, p. 156; Kobel, 1985, p. 282).

There are, moreover, peculiar difficulties awaiting the reader who approaches the work expecting it to be composed towards a conclusion, because the inherent tensions in the text are not resolved even at the end (cf. Durrani, 1987). When Biberkopf returns to the Alexanderplatz he is hailed as his old self as well as being presented as a new person. He is given a new name in token of his 'rebirth', but it is one that was originally given to him at baptism. He has acquired a new appreciation of human solidarity – expressed once more in terms which strongly echo biblical wisdom, namely Ecclesiastes 4:9-12 (Komar, 1983, p. 43) – but the political dimension of that solidarity still presents itself on the streets of Berlin in the form of marching batallions. The tendency towards mindless sloganising in the political sphere is answered with a rhyming counter-slogan – 'Den Menschen ist gegeben die Vernunft, die Ochsen bilden statt dessen eine Zunft' (Men are endowed with reason, it's cattle that form a club) – and yet the closing sentences of the text, which are printed in italics as if to emphasise their conclusive character, once more draw on the songs of armies marching to battle.

Döblin was challenged about the peremptory nature of this ending as early as 1931 by a Berlin student. He responded defensively, acknowledging that it must appear 'tacked on' (*scheinbar angeklebt*), that it had come about rather against his will, and that he could not resist blowing a little 'fanfare' at the end. He also joked that a proper ending could really only take place 'in Heaven', with 'another soul saved' – implying that a twentieth-century novel could not plausibly draw on expectations of redemption in the way that, for example, Goethe's *Faust* still could. And he spoke of a possible sequel which would develop aspects of the book's themes for which the figure of Biberkopf was clearly an inadequate vehicle. This proposal for a sequel – which never did materialise – is related to what he had to say about the dualism in his thinking at the time of writing *Berlin Alexanderplatz*: he was unable to resolve the dichotomy between the human mind as a passive component of the material world (*das Ich in der Natur*) and the sense of it having dominion over the material world (*das Ich über der Natur*) (*Materialien*, p. 41f). These comments point to a wider intellectual dimension to Döblin's work which has been much discussed in the secondary literature, but which it is not possible to enlarge on here. They also carry an implication for the interpretation of Döblin's novel, however, as well as echoing its principal themes. Our response as readers needs to acquire something of that dynamism which we have seen to characterise the text, neither succumbing to what Döblin calls the 'passive' and implicitly 'tragic' aspect of human affairs as depicted in the novel, nor yet seeking, in a form of hubris, to subordinate the material reality of its language to our interpretative schemes.

Döblin's text maintains its techniques of mutual relativisation and amplification, as well as the tensions between its themes, to the very end. Biberkopf emerges from his confrontation with death and with the lessons of his own past as someone who has 'learned to see' – and Döblin parodies his own theme by interpolating a fantasy advertisement for the rejuvenation of eyes (BA, p. 494). And the battle song which he chooses for his final 'fanfare' is one which rhymes *Morgenrot* with *Tod* – the intimation of renewal implied in the image of rosy-fingered dawn remains bonded to the prospect of imminent death, and vice versa. As we entertain the one thought, the text is suggesting, we should remain mindful of the other. It is by following through the implications of the montage principle to their logical conclusion that *Berlin Alexanderplatz* acquires its radical status in the history of the twentieth-century novel. There is no ultimate authority within the text to guide our perceptions of it, and any termination of the interplay of ideas will of necessity appear arbitrary, as Döblin acknowledged in his Berlin speech of 1928 (AzL, p. 124). Just as the montage technique opens up the confines of the narrative to the living world of the reading public, so too does it keep the act of reading open to the incessant dynamism of earthly existence.

REFERENCES

Page references to the collected works of Alfred Döblin are indicated in the text in the following way: AzL = *Aufsätze zur Literatur*, ed. W. Muschg, Olten: Walter Verlag 1963; BA = *Berlin Alexanderplatz: Die Geschichte von Franz Biberkopf*, ed. W. Muschg, Olten: Walter Verlag 1961.

BAYERDÖRFER, H.-P. (1983), Alfred Döblin: *Berlin Alexanderplatz*, in P. M. Lützeler (ed.), *Deutsche Romane, des 20. Jahrhunderts: Neue Interpretationen*, Königstein im Taunus: Athenäum.

DURRANI, O. (1987), The End of *Berlin Alexanderplatz*: towards the terminus of Döblin's tramway, *German Life and Letters* 40, pp. 142–50.

DUYTSCHAEVER, J. (1975), Joyce – Dos Passos – Döblin: Einfluß oder Analogie? in M. Prangel (ed.), *Materialien zu Alfred Döblin: 'Berlin Alexanderplatz'*, Frankfurt am Main: Suhrkamp.

DUYTSCHAEVER, J. (1979), Alfred Döblins Aischylos-Rezeption, *Revue de littérature comparée* 53, pp. 27–46.

HÜLSE, E. (1965), Alfred Döblin: *Berlin Alexanderplatz*, in R. Geissler (ed.) *Möglichkeiten des modernen deutschen Romans*, Frankfurt: Diesterweg.

KELLER, O. (1980), *Döblins Montageroman als Epos der Moderne*, Munich: Fink.

KLOTZ. V. (1969), *Erzählte Stadt*, Munich: Hanser.

KOBEL, E. (1985), *Alfred Döblin: Erzählkunst im Umbruch*, Berlin: de Gruyter.

KOMAR, K. L. (1983), *Pattern and Chaos: Multilinear Novels by Dos Passos. Döblin, Faulkner and Koeppen*, Columbia, South Carolina: Camden House.

MARTINI, F. (1954), *Das Wagnis der Sprache*, Stuttgart: Ernst Klett.

Materialien zu Alfred Döblin: 'Berlin Alexanderplatz' (1975), ed. M. Prangel, Frankfurt am Main: Suhrkamp.

MITCHELL, B. (1976), *James Joyce and the German Novel 1922–1933*, Athens, Ohio: Ohio University Press.

MÜLLER-SALGET, K. (1975), Zur Entstehung von Döblins 'Berlin Alexanderplatz', in M. Prangel (ed.), *Materialien zu Alfred Döblin: 'Berlin Alexanderplatz'*, Frankfurt am Main: Suhrkamp.

MÜLLER-SALGET, K. (1972), *Alfred Döblin: Werk und Entwicklung*, Bonn: Bouvier.

REID, J. H. (1968), *Berlin Alexanderplatz* – A political novel, *German Life and Letters* 21, pp. 214–23.

SCHÖNE, A. (1963), Döblin – *Berlin Alexanderplatz*, in B. von Wiese (ed.), *Der deutsche Roman vom Barock bis zur Gegenwart*, Düsseldorf: August Bagel Verlag.

STENZEL, J. (1966), Mit Kleister und Schere, *Text und Kritik* 13/14, pp. 41–4.

ZIOLKOWSKI, T. (1969), *Dimensions of the Modern Novel*, Princeton, New Jersey: Princeton University Press.

ŽMEGAČ, V. (1968) Alfred Döblins Poetik des Romans, in Grimm R. (ed.), *Deutsche Romantheorien*, Frankfurt Athenäum.

8

Experimenting with Experience
Robert Musil, *Der Mann ohne Eigenschaften*

DUNCAN LARGE

And with this, and a profound bow to his patrons, the Manager retires and the curtain rises. (Thackeray, *Vanity Fair*)

'Why, then, are we not realists?' Ulrich wondered. (IV, p. 1239)

In a radio lecture of 1958, Theodor Adorno discusses the nature of the post-Realist novel and comments on the illusion that had been inherent in the narrative technique of the traditional novel, comparing it with the 'fourth-wall' stage of bourgeois theatre. 'The narrator,' he writes, 'raises a curtain: the reader is meant to participate in events as if he were present in person' (Adorno, 1974b, p. 45). This illusionary principle had been coupled with a taboo on reflection in the novel, which had been treated as 'the cardinal sin against factual purity'. But just as the illusionary quality of narrative represen-tation was losing its power, so too was the taboo on reflexion, and Adorno cites Robert Musil's *Der Mann ohne Eigenschaften* (The Man Without Qualities) as a prime example of a Modernist novel in which reflexion not only breaks through the Realist illusion of formal 'transparency', but also moves beyond simple moralising and becomes self-reflexiveness. He sees this as the charac-teristic innovation of the period and terms it: 'taking sides against the lie of representation, indeed against the narrator himself' (*ibid*).

Formal 'transparency' is indeed clouded in *Der Mann ohne Eigenschaften*, not only by the novel's emphasis on reflexion in general and that of its hero, Ulrich, in particular (see Heydebrand, 1966), but also by its new-style self-reflexiveness which takes it definitively 'beyond Realism'. This move is already accomplished by the end of the first chapter – if not, indeed, the first page – for what immediately becomes apparent to the reader is not only a provocatively ironic tone, but also a self-consciously 'experimental' technique. It will be the task of this essay to examine both the technical and the thematic functions of the notion of experimentation in the novel, since even after the stylistic pyrotechnics of the first chapter have largely given way to a more conventional narratorial presence – to the extent that J. P. Stern (1982, p. 83) can argue that: 'compared with a writer like Borges [Musil] was not experimental enough' – experimentalism nevertheless continues to pervade the rest of the uncompleted novel. This is seen not only in Musil's use of the key words *Versuch* ('experiment', 'trial', 'attempt', and 'essay'), *Essay* and *Experiment* itself, but also in his repeated recourse to the paradigm of scientific method, the notion of the world as laboratory and associated imagery taken from mathematics and the natural sciences.

In his three celebrated opening pages, Musil deliberately flouts the conventions of scene-setting and presents us with a dazzling, disorientating chapter: 'From Which, Remarkably, Nothing Results' (I, p. 9). Yet for all that this declaration of independence seeks to relegate the rest of the novel to the status of a *non sequitur*, the defiance of the chapter title is a mischievous bluff, since through the ironic 'smoke screen' the chapter, however begrudgingly, does introduce us to a date (August 1913), a place (Vienna), two named characters ('Arnheim and Ermelinda Tuzzi') and the beginnings of a plot (a traffic accident which they witness) in successive paragraphs. What is most clearly established in this first chapter of *Der Mann ohne Eigenschaften* is an ironic tone of narration which never leaves us be with an unproblematic presentation of 'the factual' (I, p. 9) but rather badgers us with an incessant pluralisation both of 'reality' and of 'realism'

That *Der Mann ohne Eigenschaften* should treat 'reality as an ontological problem' (Heidegger, 1957, p. 209) has already attracted no little critical attention (Kaiser, 1957; Payne, 1976; Stern, 1982; Reis, 1983). What interests us here is that Musil's 'experimental' technique relies heavily for its effect on parallelism, juxtaposition and in general the 'doubling' which Jean Molino (1978, p. 63) describes as: 'an almost logical category which governs the conceptual organisation of a novelistic universe'. This is certainly a key device in Musil's armoury: on the thematic level we are soon introduced to the 'doubly' Dual Monarchy – 'It was, for example, imperial-royal and it was imperial and royal' (I, p. 33) – the Second Part is then dominated by the satirical *Parallelaktion* (Parallel Campaign), and Book Two has the twin themes of Ulrich and his sister Agatha (the 'Siamese twins') as 'doubles' and as 'hermaphrodites'.

From the technical point of view, not only is the first chapter title turned into a form of double negative when we call its bluff, but if we look more closely at the chapter itself we can see that Musil's multiple doublings produce two quite different types of effect. For on the one hand the doubling of reality results in the emergence of another, incompatible possibility which stands in opposition and thus produces interference or, in extreme cases, mutual cancellation; on the other hand, the doubling of descriptions of reality produces alternative accounts which complement each other and remain in apposition, with an additive, if still mutually relativising effect.

To take the 'oppositional doubling' of reality first, this is particularly in evidence just as Musil is apparently introducing us to his two characters in the first chapter, for with a 'post-Modern' flourish he promptly makes them disappear again:

> Assuming they were called Arnheim and Ermelinda Tuzzi – which, however, is incorrect, since Frau Tuzzi was spending August with her husband in Bad Aussee and Dr Arnheim was still in Constantinople – then we are faced with the puzzle of who they were. (I, p. 10)

As the narrator goes on to explain, he is simulating here what is actually quite an everyday occurrence: our experience of having to abandon the attempt to put a name to a face. So there is a double irony here, for the narrator is self-consciously drawing attention to the fact that his account is more life-like than Realism itself – if nevertheless still a simulation, of course. He takes us down to street level rather than hovering loftily above his characters like the omniscient Realist narrator, who is revealed to be inherently unrealistic. Indeed, the street-level perspective persists, for the link between the first and second chapters is achieved by means of an imaginary continuation of the two characters' walk to take them past the hero's house. We thus first see them from without, then become their imaginary fellow-travellers, then lose sight of them altogether when in the second chapter we realise that we in turn are being observed as the narrative perspective shifts to Ulrich, who is looking out of his window at the activity in the street.

Such 'perspective shifts' (I, p. 21) are typical of Musil's technique throughout the novel – whether they remain wholly within the fictional world, or puncture its illusion through narratorial glosses, self-reflexive passages and 'essayistic' interludes. Most effective of all in subverting Realist expectations are such moments when 'hyper-realism' and self-reflexiveness are combined, as is the case again in Chapter 18 where the sex murderer Moosbrugger is being introduced and the reader is once more exquisitely caught out:

> When his gaze fell upon this face with the signs of a child of God, over handcuffs, Ulrich had promptly turned back, slipped a few cigarettes to one of the soldiers on guard at the nearby district court, and asked about the convoy which could only have left the gate shortly before: thus he learned – : but that is indeed how such things must have happened in former times since we often find them reported in this way, and Ulrich almost believed it himself, but the contemporary truth was that he had merely read everything in the newspaper. (I, p. 69)

Ulrich's imaginary *Umkehrung is* here matched by the peripeteia of our double-take and realisation that we have been taken in. 'Ulrich almost [beinahe] believed it himself', we are told – *beinahe* and *fast* are the hallmarks of his ever un-totalising thinking – but his ruthless honesty with himself allows him no resource to self-romanticisation, whereas we have no choice but to take the incident as read until the carpet is pulled out from under our feet once again. Musil's use of the indicative here apparently confirms the 'real' status of the incident, and yet we realise that we have after all been presented with a mere chimera, one of the many unrealised narrative possibilities which Musil as all-powerful author could so easily have bestowed on us, and which he usually gives the subjunctive mood the task of conveying, as Albrecht Schöne (1966) has so convincingly shown.

In this passage Musil is applying the key concept of *Möglichkeitssinn* (sense of possibilities: I, p. 16) a cast of mind which is shared by the narrator, Ulrich and even his neo-Leibnizian God (I, p. 19), and which involves preferring 'everything which equally well could be' (I, p. 16) to what is actually the case. The narrator turns out to have been pandering to our 'unrealistic' expectations after all, then – ones which, in another ironic twist, presumably result from our reading of too many (Realist) novels. Here he calls his own bluff, though, and 'reality' (or at least its more acceptable counterfeit) manages to reassert itself over its shadowy double, which this time is what is cancelled out and dematerialises before our eyes. As Stern (1982, p. 79) argues: 'All the realistic and naturalist elements in Musil's work are subordinated to the demonstration of a reduplicated mode of the possible', and the point Musil is making with these manoeuvres is simply that 'reality' is intrinsically less interesting than all its possible alternatives. This becomes clear when the narrator continues:

> The possibility of learning something unusual from the newspaper is far greater than that of experiencing it; in other words, it is in the abstract that the more important things happen nowadays, and what happens in reality is more trivial. (I, p. 69)

This object-lesson devaluation of 'fictional truth' demonstrates the extent to which we are at the mercy of the narrator and have no way of checking the information he is giving us, just as in the example from the first chapter we have no way of knowing who the people 'actually' are. When reading *Der Mann ohne Eigenschaften* we must recognise that we have no opportunity to perform our own 'objective' control experiments in such cases of doubt.

'The narrator gave, and the narrator hath taken away' is the 'moral' of such episodes, a principle of tantalisation which Musil, in one of his unpublished drafts, sees in operation on the level of European culture as a whole. Having detailed the titles which the hero and his father share between them, Musil writes: 'These titles [*Prädikate*], which are none, are part of the giving with the one hand and taking with the other which is characteristic of the development of Europe. *Cancelled world*' (I, p. 1965). Their titles are no different from the first chapter title, and with the notion of a 'multiply cancelled world' (I, p. 1966), Musil goes a long way towards preempting in a literary context the philosophical point which Heidegger (1967, p. 30) and Derrida (1967, pp. 31, 65; 1972, p. 6) make with their practice of 'placing under erasure'. Not only does he effectively do this to the reality which he abortively sketches out in the passages which we have examined, but on a more general level he also consistently places under erasure Ulrich's *Prädikate* in the sense of predicated qualities, another implication of the ambiguous term.

We see Musil applying the notion of erasure or cancellation again in a projected preface to the novel, where he asks himself: 'Why Vienna instead of a fabricated city' (I, p. 1820) and explains: 'Because fabricating such a city would have been more trouble than a "cancelled" Vienna' (*ibid.*), That the name of the city should remain still 'legible' is crucial to Musil's satirical intent, and therefore although our adherence to it is scorned on the first page of the novel, it is nevertheless allowed to stand.

Whereas 'Vienna' is to a calculated extent 'put in brackets' on its initial presentation, on the other hand – and to come back to the opening paragraph of the novel, – what we have in this case are two different and in their own ways equally valid representations of the prevailing conditions, when Musil self-consciously reduces his cosmo-meteorological report stuffed with pseudo-technical jargon to the formulaic: 'In other words, which denote the facts perfectly well even if they sound a little old-fashioned: it was a fine August day in 1913' (I, p. 9). We are not led to believe that these descriptions necessarily cancel each other out, but rather they stand in apposition to one another and indicate that there can be multiple parallel cases of 'the right word'. The strategy is repeated later on in the year, when this time a list of historical events is reduced to: 'In a word, a lot was happening, it was an eventful time, the period around the end of 1913 and the beginning of 1914' (I, p. 359). The phrases: 'mit einem Wort' (in a word) and 'mit anderen Worten' (in other words) are such stylistic constants of Musil's narrator that the reader is always left with the lingering suspicion that 'the truth' needs ever more 'other words' to express it, and a ghostly alternative comes to hover over every statement, even if it is only suggested in the subjunctive mood: 'He could equally well have said the opposite' (I, p. 367); 'one might equally well have thought' (I, p. 918) or 'but she could equally well also have said' (I, p. 1094).

These variant descriptions levelled alongside one another in the narrative subject each other to a process of mutual accommodation which resembles nothing so much as Ulrich's accommodation itself, 'House and Dwelling of the man Without Qualities' (I, p. 11). Not only does this house already incorporate three centuries of different architectural styles (I, p. 12), but Ulrich goes on to abdicate responsibility for its overdetermined décor, paralysed as he is, like Buridan's ass (II, p. 1030), by the attractions of the *ebensogut* ('equally good' or 'equally well'):

> From stylistically correct reconstruction to complete heedlessness, all principles were available to him for it, and similarly [*ebenso*] all styles suggested themselves, from the Assyrians to Cubism. What should he choose? [...] just as he had thought up some massive and imposing design, it occurred to him that one might equally well replace it with something technically economical and utilitarian. (I, p. 19f)

This whole comic episode reads nowadays like a parody on the eclecticism of incipiently 'postmodern' architecture, but in the novel the stylistic confusion is merely a facet of the turn-of-the century 'jumble of beliefs' (I, p. 56). In the face of so many competing claims on legitimacy, it is not surprising that a bewildered Ulrich opts for an attitude of indifference – *Gleichgültigkeit* – and thereby acknowledges their 'equal validity'.

Not only does the first chapter of *Der Mann ohne Eigenschaften* give us experimental doubling with an interplay between juxtaposed linguistic paradigms which map the same reality in radically differing, as yet mutually indifferent ways, but the two 'languages' or 'discourses' (Moser, 1980) are invariably those of everyday language and the 'meta-narrative' (Lyotard, 1979, p. 31) of science. The discrepancy between the two is expressed in the 'satellite picture' of the first paragraph as well as in the humorous passage from the second paragraph, where we are told it would be important to know why in this day and age we still content ourselves with the 'inexact' commonsensical description of a nose as simply red, when we could actually measure its redness much more precisely, to within a 'micromillimetre' of its wavelength.

What is in question in both these instances is the relative imprecision on such matters which suffices in everyday life, and the competing scientific paradigm of more precise description is doubly represented by measurements of both telescopic and microscopic exactitude. On the very first page of the novel, Musil not only succeeds in marking out these two extremes within which we generally operate in the non-scientific 'middle distance' of ordinary language, but he also makes it clear that our choice to do so has a fundamental arbitrariness about it. By establishing the contingency of language in this way from the outset, Musil gives a perfect example of the effect which Richard Rorty derives from Wittgenstein's analysis of 'language-games': 'When we consider examples of alternative language games [...] it is difficult to think of the world as making one of these better than another, of the world as deciding between them' (Rorty, 1989, p. 5f).

By his dramatically effective juxtaposition of paradigms, Musil presents us with a world in the throes of a 'vocabulary-shift' of the type described by Rorty, with the scientific in the ascendant. In fact the picture Musil paints in *Der Mann ohne Eigenschaften* is one in which science has encroached on every aspect of modern life, and as Ulrich tells Clarisse: 'Scientific man is nowadays a quite unavoidable phenomenon; one can't not want to know!' (I, p. 214). This is not necessarily a happy state of affairs, though, for the scientific mode of expression has penetrated our innermost thought patterns (I, p. 1249), and the narrator hints at its threatening nature when he tells us that 'not even a dunce is safe from it' (I, p. 301).

Science is itself on trial throughout the novel, but the direction in which things are moving is evident from the futuristic nightmare which begins Chapter 8, and where 'Stress and relaxation, activity and love are accurately divided in time and weighed up after painstaking laboratory experience' (I, p. 31). Musil's strategy is to deal his hero the cards with which to play the scientists at their own game: we have seen how the narrator shows his hand of narrative experimentation in the opening chapter of the novel, but from his introduction in Chapter 2 it is Ulrich who dictates the play, and it is to him that we must now turn. Let it be noted, though, that Musil himself was particularly well qualified to play the role of dealer, which involved integrating the vocabulary of contemporary science into the novel, for his familiarity with the sciences and technology was first-hand and extensive.

In a 1926 interview on the novel-in-progress, Musil explains how the social structure of his novel are set in motion:

> when I introduce a young man who is schooled in the most advanced knowledge of his time, in mathematics, physics and technology. [...] So he sees, to his astonishment, that reality is at least 100 years behind what is being thought. From this phase difference emerges one of the major themes: *how is an intellectual person meant to relate to reality?* (I, p. 940)

Intellect (*Geist*) and science (*Wissenschaft*) are linked here as they will be throughout *Der Mann ohne Eigenschaften,* and the ethical time-lag or 'Stufenunterschied' (I, p. 274) which is to be Ulrich's main concern is also thematised repeatedly in the novel itself, starting with the discrepancy on the first page between 1913 and an apparently naïve question about the name of the city, which a disdainful narrator dismisses as hailing from the 'horde age' (I, p. 9). In this same interview, Musil typically sums up his novelistic practice as a *Versuch*: 'My novel aims to provide material for such a new morality. It is an attempt [*Versuch*] at a solution and an intimation of a synthesis' (I, p. 942).

Ulrich has the best possible scientific training, then, and Musil makes of him 'something like a prince and lord of the mind' (I, p. 152) by giving him his own background with more experience besides. On leaving school, Ulrich embarks on 'three attempts [*Versuche*] at becoming an important man' (I, p. 35), and the first two of these careers correspond to Musil's own, in the army and as an engineer. In his portrayal of the latter's mentality Musil again gives us a critique of the unscientific views of society in terms of the 'phase difference' between man's machines and his 'old fashioned' behaviour: 'a difference in development which is almost as great as that between the appendix and the cerebral cortex' (I, p. 37). The engineers, in love with machines and the future, consider themselves vastly superior to the common run of men thanks to their scientific explanations, and they simply cannot take the world seriously. We have the last laugh, though, when the narrator parodies their obsession with precision and shows up the ridiculousness of their fetishisation of the slide rule.

Although Ulrich is at first bowled over by his experience as an engineer, he becomes disillusioned by their dogmatism, shortsightedness and overblown sense of self-importance, so he distances himself from technology and makes a third *Versuch* which is classed as the most important, when he becomes a mathematician. The narrator points out that the mathematician is in rather bad odour in modern society, but he puts up a spirited defence, giving us an ironic perspective on the 'evil' of mathematics from the standpoint of the uninitiated and arguing that people's fear of mathematics is unjustified. After all, mathematics is the one career at which Ulrich perseveres for the longest time, in which he achieves 'no small success' (I, p. 41), and to which he periodically returns throughout the novel (I, p. 111), even in Part Three (I, p. 686f; I, p. 719f.). Ulrich's aim is to save science from cheap detraction out of ignorance and, more especially, to change people's lives by asserting the benefits of the scientific mentality. In this, the narrator's and Ulrich's aims are one:

> In science things are as powerful and carefree and magnificent as in a fairy-tale. And Ulrich felt: people simply don't know that; they have no idea of how it is already possible to think; if they could be taught to think afresh, then they would also live differently. (I, 41)

After his scientific training, then, Ulrich emerges with an opencast mind and a new technical vocabulary, an invaluable analytical and interpretative tool which he wastes no time in putting to good use during his year's 'holiday from his life' (I, p. 47). He has a new picture of the world which is singularly appropriate to describing the modern urban reality, which itself is so much a product of the scientific revolution in the first place. This new picture is summed up by his image of the world as laboratory (I, p. 152), which prompts the reflexion:

> Previously he had often imagined life as like a great testing-ground [*Versuchsstätte*] where the best ways of being human would have to be tried out, and new ones discovered, if it was to please him. If the whole laboratory worked in a somewhat unplanned manner and lacked overall leaders and theorists, that was another story. (I, p. 152)

The reason there is no plan to the whole, in Ulrich's eyes, is that God, the arch-experimenter who (all-too-tentatively) created the world and set up the laboratory in the first place, has deserted it. It is therefore incumbent on us to make the best of the equipment and raw materials He has left us in order to solve the problem of the world by our own efforts: 'we ourselves must work out the solution he sets us' (I, p. 358).

Already in early chapters we are told how the modern city breaks up into a 'skein of forces' (I, p. 13) or 'a community with forces running through it' (I, p. 31), and Ulrich later develops this into a full-blown theory of human interaction based on the notion of force fields (*Kraftfelder*) lifted straight out of the realm of physics. Two main implications of this theory are worked out – the first concerns the replacement of the concept of causation by a Machian theory of functions, which also strait-jackets the 'will' inside a scientific determinism and reduces the self to a merely notional nodal point; the second has to do with the application of statistics.

Equipped with his new tool, Ulrich finds he can provide Diotima with an easy answer for the vexed and hoary question of the freedom of the will: in the context of the 'force fields of feeling [...] which surround us' he explains attraction and repulsion between people in terms of 'a mutual, functional dependence like that between two elastic balls or two charged electric circuits'

(I, p. 473). Ulrich's functionalism has profound implications for the status of the self, when the definitive formulation of 'the laws of personality' (I, p. 474) is so near at hand. By this 'force-field' theory the self threatens to become completely depersonalised, the product of an act of interpretation from the general law to the particular case: 'an imaginary meeting place of the impersonal' (*ibid.*). This was already evident when we were told how Ulrich's early mistress, the major's wife, was reduced to the status of an 'impersonal centre of force' (I, p. 126), and an extraordinary consequence hits Ulrich when he is talking to Gerda shortly after his conversation with Diotima, for the two strike him as interchangeable – both are simply bodies (*Körper*) occupying the same force field:

> Basically it was the same conversation as the one he had had with Diotima; only the externals were different, behind which the one might have been the continuation of the other. And it was evidently a matter of such indifference [*gleichgültig*] which woman was sitting there; a body which, when introduced into an already-existing intellectual force field, set certain processes in motion! (I, p. 489)

For Ulrich, science is a vocabulary which enables him to describe human behaviour in morally neutral terms, since he argues that the context or 'force field' is paramount in determining not only the nature of the self, but also moral values as 'functional values' (I, pp. 37, 1880). He subsequently elaborates on this key notion at several stages, emphasising the freedom it grants *Geist* to create values (I, p. 153f), and, in one crucial passage, uses analogies from physics (force fields), chemistry (valency) and linguistics (the contextual decipherment of a polysemic word) to culminate in a textualisation of reality derived from the Nietzschean, perspectivistic practice of determining values by interpretation. This passage deserves to be quoted at length:

> The value of an action or a quality, even its essence and nature, appeared to him dependent on the circumstances which surrounded it, on the goals that it served, in a word, on the variable constitution of the whole to which it belonged. [...] Then all moral events occurred within a force field, bestowing meaning upon its constellation, and they contained good and evil in the same way that an atom contains possibilities of chemical bonding. They were, so to speak, what they became, and just as the single word 'hard' denotes four quite different entities, depending on whether the hardness is connected with love, brutality, enthusiasm or severity, so all moral occurrences appeared to him in their significance as the dependent function of others. (I, p. 250f)

The other aspect of Ulrich's new scientific theory, the role of statistics, follows on from the first, for of course the 'laws of personality' he mentions are statistical laws, and he reflects that not even the notion of personal destiny can remain unaffected by them: 'What we nowadays still call personal destiny is being repressed by collective and ultimately statistically ascertainable processes (I, p. 722). Statistics are abstractions, subject to 'the law of large numbers' (I, p. 488), and an analogy with the laboratory of the world is again made explicit: 'the balance, the sum of the experiments [*Versuche*] then no longer arises within the individual, who becomes intolerably one-sided, but the whole is like an experimental community' (I, p. 490). Statistics extrapolate a general social 'fact' from numerous individual cases but then assume a life of their own and in turn neutralise the individual case through the average. The most extreme example of this is when Ulrich hypothesises that moral principles can be described by analogy with the gas laws – reducing the individual, once more, to mere molecular significance:

> but the most important thing is that our personal, individual movement does not matter, our thoughts and actions can be right or left, high or low, new or old, unpredictable or considered: it is of no consequence [*gleichgültig*] for the mean value, and that is what matters to God and the world, not us! (I, p. 491)

Society is thus conceived as subject to the second law of thermodynamics, allowing Ulrich to formulate 'Cacanian' decadence in terms of increasing entropy, since 'with time every play of forces tends towards a mean value and a mean state, of balance and paralysis. Morality in the usual sense was for Ulrich nothing more than the aged state of a system of forces' (I, p. 251). Ulrich finds that even language falls victim to entropy, and the debasement of the terms *Genie* (genius) and *genial* (of genius) are one of his first preoccupations in the novel, leading him to abandon his career as a mathematician on reading of 'a racehorse of genius' (I, p. 44). *Menschliche Größe* (human greatness: I, p. 45) is replaced by the neutral *Größe* (size) of purely quantitative measurement (I, p. 12), with the result that the extraordinary case is marginalised – just as heroism is swamped by all the everyday actions of the average citizen (*ibid.*) – and the particularity of the individual *Sonderfall* (special case) becomes levelled down to *Gleichgültigkeit* with the lowest common denominator. The world of *Seinesgleichen geschieht* (The Like of it Happens: I, p. 81) is a fundamentally statistical one, and Ulrich ponders the question of why 'the special results from nothing special happening, and the highest meaning turns out to be something that can be arrived at by means of the average of the most profound meaninglessness' (I, p. 488).

Ulrich himself is determined to derive positive benefit from his new theories and to go beyond mere 'thought experiments', beyond the descriptive aspect of the new vocabulary to its prescriptive applications. For the main purpose of his experiments in the laboratory of the world has always been clear:

> if, while he was writing treatises on mathematics or mathematical logic, or while he was occupied with the natural sciences, anyone had ever asked him what goal he had in mind, he would have answered that only one question was really worth thinking about, and that was the question of the right life. (I, p. 2 55)

He describes himself at one point as being 'morally dissolved into a primal atomic condition' (I, p. 940), and his 'ionic' unattachedness gives him the maximum combinatory power, which Musil exploits by pitching him back into society against his will so that he can 'combine' with all the other characters who, apart from Agathe, are set off against him as counter-examples.

Ulrich's 'qualitilessness' aligns him with the 'Meister des innerlich schwebenden Lebens' (masters of the hovering [or chemically suspended] inner life: I, p. 253), one of whom is evidently Nietzsche (Allemann, 1969; Peters, 1978; Dresler-Brumme, 1987). Ulrich's existential blueprint, an 'experimental' life free from established values, owes a great deal to Nietzsche's creative 'Experimental-Philosophie' (Neitzsche, 1956, I, p. 834) and notion of '*auf den Versuch* hin leben' (living *by experiment*: Nietzsche, 1956, I, p. 441). Indeed, Hans Reiss (1982, p. 48) writes of 'Musil's conception of experimentation emanating from his own peculiar blend of Nietzscheanism and science'. Ulrich's is 'a life with interim principles' (I, p. 46), for its scientific paradigm makes any parameters of interpretation and evaluation provisional, and it always allows for – indeed expects – subsequent revision. His patchwork quotation from Emerson makes this clear: 'Men walk the earth as prophecies of the future, and all their deeds are experiments [*Versuche*] and tests, for every deed can be surpassed by the next!' (I, p. 38).

The notion of 'living hypothetically' (I, p. 249) has been with Ulrich since adolescence, we are told, and it issues into the key term *Essayismus*, both being explicitly linked to the image of a scientist testing out ('assaying') his theories:

> the present is nothing but a hypothesis which we have not yet gone beyond. What better thing could there be for him to do than keep his distance from the world with the good sense of a researcher distancing himself from the facts that would seduce him into believing in them prematurely! (I, p. 250)

The translation of the word essay by *Versuch* (I, p. 253) may not do full justice to the literary model which also underpins the term, but this other model is nevertheless made quite explicit in the presentation of the 'utopia of essayism':

> In rather the same way that an essay, in the sequence of its sections, views a thing from many sides without comprehending it completely [...] he believed he could view and treat the world and his own life most correctly. (I, p. 250)

The same can be said of Musil in his own approach to the potential of the essay as form, and in an essay with that title Adorno makes clear how admirably it suits Musil's purpose when he described how 'under the gaze of the essay every intellectual creation must transform itself into a force field' (Adorno, 1974a, p. 22).

'Even the Earth, but Ulrich in Particular, Pays Homage to the Utopia of Essayism' (I, p. 247), we are told, and Ulrich takes the injunction to 'keep his distance from the world' to an extreme of anti-realism (in the philosophical sense), arguing that 'reality has no sense any more' (I, p. 575), and that since reality is not what it used to be it ought to be abolished (I, p. 289). 'Abolishing reality' is in theory to restore to the world all the potential which it had before even God apparently sold it short in his act of creation, and the experimental-scientific mentality thus issues into what is fundamentally an aesthetic attitude.

However, any interpretative system within which moral values are merely 'functional values', and which adopts an attitude of such indifference towards reality that it can happily entertain the notion of 'abolishing' it altogether, can clearly make only the most tenuous claims to being a morality at all. As Philip Payne (1988, p. 161) argues: 'morality is incompatible with detachment – it cannot be merely an extension of the scientists' attitude of scrupulous impartiality. Morality involves commitment.' In fact, as we have seen, Ulrich's 'utopia ' – 'beyond good and evil' – has more in common with Nietzschean post-morality, for the essentially future-perfect 'morality of the next step' (I, p. 733) provides no workable moral principles that can be acted on in the present. In an essay of 1918, Musil writes of the latitude which has crept into our interpretation of 'Thou shalt not kill' (II, p. 1028; cf. I, p. 254), and throughout *Der Mann ohne Eigenschaften* he deliberately uses crime, especially murder, as a provocative motif to pursue this theme ruthlessly. For although certain redesignations and rehabilitations might seem permissible – even recommendable – there is inevitably something repellent about the notion that the gravity of the sort of crime committed by the psychopath Moosbrugger can also be reinterpreted away after the event.

It is around Moosbrugger that the crime motif crystallises, for he exerts a fascination on Ulrich, who senses a deep affinity with him and espouses him as his alter ego. In fact Ulrich goes so far as to make the claim that: 'if humanity as a whole could have a dream, then Moosbrugger would necessarily result' (I, p. 76), which proves to be not altogether unjustifiable, given the way interest in Moosbrugger ripples out from Ulrich to affect not only Clarisse, but subsequently the whole *Parallelaktion*. Ulrich uses crimes as key examples to illustrate the moral ambivalence of the 'force field' theory in both of the set-piece discussions he has on it with Diotima (I, pp. 250, 474), so much so that she asks: 'Why do you so often speak of criminals? You have a special liking for crime. That must mean something?' (I, p. 474).

The meaning is conveyed on the level of imagery by the wielding of *Messer* ('knives' and 'meters'), which forges a link between Moosbrugger's rapacious-ness and Ulrich's experimental mentality. For Moosbrugger commits his murder with a knife, and Ulrich's origins as a character lie in a figure from Musil's first diary entries, 'monsieur le vivisecteur' (Musil, 1976. pp. 1–8), who is again of Nietzschean derivation (Albertsen, 1970). It is clear that Ulrich's mentality retains vestiges of vivisectionism when we find him musing:

> If we dissect the essence of a thousand people, then we arrive at a couple of dozen qualities, sensations, processes, structures and so forth, of which they are all composed. And if we dissect our bodies, then we find just water with a few dozen substances swimming around on it. (I, p. 66)

Moreover, these speculations, reported by Clarisse to Walter, are immediately followed by the introduction of Moosbruggger in the next chapter. The implications of *Messer* are wider still, for just as Hermann Broch described Musil as 'an immensely complex mind, razor-sharp [*messerscharf*] and clear' (Broch, 1981, p. 286), so against 'the hazy type of man who dominates the present' (I, p. 249), Ulrich sets 'today's research': 'a religion whose dogmatics is imbued with and carried along by the hard, courageous, mobile, razor-cool and razor-sharp [*messerkühlen und -scharfen*] mathematical school of thought' (I, p. 39). Ulrich has the scientist's fascination with *Messer* of all kinds, though: we encountered the theme of *measurement* already on the first page, with the question of measuring the redness of a nose, and when we first met Ulrich, in the second chapter, he is measuring the traffic, watch in hand.

The indifference to reality inherent in *Möglichkeitssinn* (living hypo-thetically) and the theory of functions also has ambiguous, not to say sinister overtones for their practitioner:

> he is capable of killing without being certain that he has to [...]. He tries to understand himself differently, with an inclination towards anything which enhances him internally, even if it is morally or intellectually prohibited [...]. That is incidentally just the simple description of the fact that a murder can appear to us as a crime or as a heroic deed [...]. After this reflection Ulrich felt himself basically capable of any virtues and any wickedness. (I, p. 250f)

The ironic perspective on the 'evil' of science during Ulrich's third *Versuch*, which we alluded to above – with its 'monstrous mixture of sharpness in the particular and indifference to the whole' (I, p. 40) – turns out to have been not so wide of the mark after all. Indeed, the innate belligerence of the scientific mentality is spelled out early on, when Ulrich is still seduced by his career as a mathematician:

> His mind was to prove itself sharp and strong, and had performed the work of the strong. This pleasure in the power of the mind was an expectation, a warlike game, a kind of undefined lordly claim on the future. It appeared to him uncertain what he would accomplish with this power: it offered the potential to do anything or nothing, to become a saviour of the world or a criminal. (I, 45)

However, it is in Chapter 72 of the First Book, 'Science Smiling into its Beard or First Extensive Encounter with Evil', that the darker side of science in general is most fully revealed and Ulrich's own position becomes distinctly problematic (see Bouveresse, 1978). In this devastating chapter Musil attacks the insidious 'professional ideology' of the scientists who claim to be disinter-ested servants of the truth, and he rounds on their 'utopia of the exact life' (I, p. 304), which may well be 'a mentality of experiment and retraction,' but is 'subject to the iron martial law of intellectual conquest'. The other side of the coin from an obsession with science is not only the ease with which it can be hijacked for warlike purposes, but the essentially warlike and invasive cast of mind which it fosters: 'the mind [*Geist*]' is 'a very manly saint with incidental vices of a warlike and hunterly kind' (I, p. 305).

There is a fundamental ambivalence at the heart of the imagery Musil associates with the scientific mentality, which is on the one hand exhilarating but on the other deeply suspicious and destructive, indeed Medusan: '*Science with the evil eye*' (I, p. 1979). 'Ulrich had considered science a preparation, a toughening up and a kind of exercise' (I, p. 46), we are told, but science's ideal of impassibility and toughness easily turns into something more predatory, as in its hope 'that a far-off day will come when a race of intellectual conquerors will descend into the valleys of spiritual fertility' (*ibid.*). The Nietzschean overtones of this appeal to the 'blond beasts' (Nietzsche, 1956, II, p. 786) of the future are strong, and in a passage from the posthumous papers Musil notes Nietzsche's influence on his formulation of this complex problem: 'Mathematical morality: the legacy of Nietzsche' (I, p. 899). The passage quoted above stresses the 'monstrousness' (*Ungeheuerlichkeit*) of the scientific mentality, and Walter repeatedly accuses Ulrich of being 'inhuman ' (I, pp. 65, 67). Ulrich's physical fitness gives him the condition of a panther (I, p. 46), but the ambivalence of his 'inhumanity' is compounded by further associations with beasts of prey, for he is by turns also a jaguar (I, p. 42) and wolf (I, p. 357) – even to Agathe he appears 'an intellectual beast of prey' (I, p. 1245).

Ulrich remarks to Diotima that our morality is 'an utterly legitimate average and collective value' (I, p. 572), but the norm is a position of safety, and he no longer sees it as worth striving for. He wants to dispense with safety nets and live dangerously (Nietzsche, 1956, II, p. 166), and the consequence is his quest for the exotic, the exception, the extreme; he is consistent in leading the experimental life to the full and he embraces its dangerous ethic of subversion. His *Möglichkeitssinn* is transgressive of the moral code, as is apparent from the first presentation of the iconoclastic 'man of possibilities' *(Möglichkeitsmensch)* in Chapter 4, for whom the creative finds its outlet in the breaking of taboos and a crime can be (relatively glibly) reduced to a 'social slip' (I, p. 17). 'Science is amoral' (I, p. 960), Ulrich confirms to Agathe, and what society terms 'immorality' has an invaluable critical role: 'it shows us that life can also be led differently' (I, p. 959). But this leads him merely to restate the *Möglichkeitsmensch* position that everyone secretly wants to commit crimes and that criminals are just the fall guys of society.

Ulrich's comment to Agathe, 'We are both moral imbeciles!' (I, p. 961) sums up best this highly dubious outlook. For irrespective of Moosbrugger's own rehabilitation, his actions can never be redressed – after all, his victim does not live to see her individual case incorporated into the annual crime figures. It is Arnheim who immediately responds to Ulrich's talk of 'a life of experiment' by putting his finger on its intrinsic danger: 'what's it like in wars and revolutions? Can the dead be woken again when the experiment has been carried out and is taken off the schedule?!' (I, p. 636). Ulrich weakly replies that probably even a *Versuch* needs always to be taken seriously, but one cannot avoid the impression that Arnheim, by being more 'realistic' in the colloquial as well as Musil's more technical sense, here provides a necessary counterweight to Ulrich's mistaken excesses.

Finally we must turn to consider more closely the third, unfinished part of the novel, subtitled 'The Criminals', in which it seems at times as though Ulrich is at last distancing himself from the experimental ideal. After his father's funeral his breakthrough with his mathematical research (I, p. 720) has an almost valedictory feel to it and is symbolic of a change of attitude, for what interests him is the irrational flash of inspiration which allows him to solve his problem, and which he likens to falling in love. In Part Three, Ulrich comes down critically on science a number of times (I, pp. 1039, 1144), and his comment on scientific method, 'everything on earth is laid waste and flattened so that it can be dominated' (I, p. 1092), is quite typical of these pronouncements. He prefers to think of his quest now as a 'search for feeling' rather than a 'life of research [...] in the light of science' (I, p. 1039), although he is well aware that Agathe's moving in with him represents merely the substitution of one form of experimental life for another: 'Ulrich realised that with this experiment [*Versuch*] the experiment [*Versuch*] of his "life on holiday" had to end' (I, p. 801). The narrator likens Ulrich and Agathe's 'journey to the edge of the possible' to the irrational 'moment' in a mathematical calculation (I, p. 761), and their search (*Suchen*) is formulated in terms of one final joint *Versuch* to find a new morality, their own utopia.

The construction of a utopia has already been likened to a scientific experiment:

> It is a similar process to a research scientist observing the change in one element of a composite phenomenon and drawing his conclusions from it; utopia means the experiment in which we observe the possible change in one element and the effects that it would generate in that composite phenomenon we call life. (I, p. 246)

But for Musil's narrator a utopia is also an inherently transgressive act of the imagination, an 'immoral experiment [*Versuch*]' (I, p. 247), and this is borne out by the nature of Ulrich and Agathe's common search. Their utopia would seem to be relatively innocuous – a flirtatiously incestuous relationship as 'Siamese twins'; an erotic and ecstatic self-indulgence. As they turn away from the public to the private they restrict their 'crimes' to acts of petty lawlessness and the private transgression of taboos: Agathe toys with the idea of killing her husband Hagauer and forges their father's will (I, p. 799); Ulrich theorises about reasons for stealing a cigarette case (I, pp. 796, 956). But their *Versuch* is the culmination of the experimental-scientific mentality in the novel and, as such, it is also the high-point in the association of science, crime and war, which have been linked throughout.

In his 1926 interview, Musil is quite clear that his 'twins' are doomed to fail in their project: 'this attempt [*Versuch*] to preserve the experience, to fix it, fails. Absoluteness cannot be retained (I, p. 940). He also underlines the fact that this failure is symbolic of the spiritual bankruptcy and more cataclysmic failure of society as a whole, as it teeters over the brink into the Great War:

> The mobilisation, which tore apart the world and our thinking to such an extent that it has not been possible to patch them up to this day, also brings the novel to a close. [...] The fact that war came, that it had to come, is the sum of *all* the conflicting currents and influences and movements that I show. (I, pp. 939, 941 – my emphasis)

This indictment is still in evidence in Musil's posthumous notes, where 'All the lines lead to war' becomes a kind of refrain (I, pp. 1851, 1902).

Writing of another Modernist master, Richard Ellmann (1986, p. 76) argues that James Joyce 'did not regard himself as an experimenter', and that the ways in which he radicalised literature were instead 'solutions to the literary and intellectual problems he set himself.' In the sense that Musil, too, knew at least the direction in which his plot was to head, his was also a search for the solution to a problem – but his approach to deriving it was fundamentally experimental (Allemann, 1969, p. 183). As Schöne (1966, p. 296) remarks, 'the very creative process presents itself as an experiment: as an extended sketching-out, trying-out [*Versuchen*], rejecting, shelving and testing of possibilities. Musil writes *and thinks at the same time that it could equally well be different.*'

What is more, this process is not completed by the time we begin reading, and the narrator taunts us to join in and treat the fictional world as provisional, watch the fictional reality being doubled, cancelled and otherwise relativised by all the unrealised possibilities which occasionally make their unscheduled appearances. Of course the process is not completed by the time we finish reading, either, for the novel disintegrates into fragments which mark the open-endedness of a 'partial solution', and Musil's approach to the end-position he had set himself remains asymptotic.

As far as Ulrich is concerned, science, and especially physics, may give him a new vocabulary for interpreting the modern world as laboratory, and his periods of training may equip him for an exhilarating existential experiment, but by remaining consistent within the terms of the experimental mentality and taking it to its amoral conclusion with Agathe, Ulrich in his own way sets up a scientific nightmare. It is less concrete than the futuristic dystopia of Chapter 8, but he becomes nonetheless an apologist for violent crime – even after his own mugging in Chapter 7, which one might have expected to make him less tolerant. Ulrich makes the mistake of applying the moral detachedness of the experimental-scientific mentality too far outside the confines of its fairy-tale world (I, p. 41), and its *Gleichgültigkeit* leads him in reality up the same blind alley as the *Parallelaktion*, which is ultimately hijacked by the vested interests of the military-industrial complex. In failing to complete the novel Musil showed himself to be unable to bridge the gap between 'ironist' theory (Rorty, 1989, p. 73) and ethical practice, although as he himself argues in an unpublished note, perhaps the task is itself an impossible one: 'The

explanation of what is meant by the word experiment [*Versuch*] or indeed essay
will be found in the book itself; it is essentially something unrealisable' (I, p.
1352).

REFERENCES

References to Robert Musil, *Gesammelte Werke* (2 vols), edited by A. Frisé,
Reinbek bei Hamburg: Rowohlt 1978, are given by volume and page number
only in the text. (The paperback edition in nine volumes has identical
pagination, with vols 1–5 corresponding to *GW* I, and volumes 6–9 corresponding to *GW* II.)

ADORNO, T. W. (1974a), Der Essay als Form, in *Noten zur Literatur
    (Gesammelte Schriften, Band II)*, Frankfurt: Suhrkamp.
———— (1974b), Standort des Erzählers im zeitgenössischen Roman, in *Noten
    zur Literatur*.
ALBERTSEN, E. (1970), Jugendsünden? Die literarischen Anfänge Musils (mit
    unbekannten Texten), in Dinklage, Karl, Albertsen, Elisabeth and Corino,
    Karl (eds) *Robert Musil: Studien zu seinem Werk*, Reinbek: Rowohlt.
ALLEMANN, B. (1969), *Ironie und Dichtung*, 2nd ed., Pfullingen: Neske.
BOUVERESSE, J. (1978), La science sourit dans sa barbe … , *L'Arc* 74 (*Robert
    Musil*), pp. 8–31.
BROCH, H. (1981), *Hermann Broch: Briefe 3 (1945–51)*, ed. Lützeler, P. M.
    Frankfurt: Suhrkamp.
DERRIDA, J. (1967), *De la grammatologie*, Paris: Minuit.
———— (1972), *Marges de la philosophie*, Paris: Minuit.
DRESLER-BRUMME, C. (1987), *Nietzsches Philosophie in Musils Roman 'Der Mann
    ohne Eigenschaften' : Eine vergleichende Betrachtung als Beitrag zum
    Verständnis*, Frankfurt: Athenäum.
ELLMANN, R. (1988), James Joyce in and out of art, in *Four Dubliners*, London:
    Cardinal.
HEIDEGGER M. (1957), *Sein und Zeit*, 8th ed., Tübingen: Max Niemeyer.
———— (1967), *Zur Seinsfrage*, 3rd ed., Frankfurt: Vittorio Klostermann.
HEYDEBRAND, R. VON (1966), *Die Reflexionen Ulrichs in Robert Musils Roman
    'Der Mann ohne Eigenschaften'*, Münster: Aschendorff.
KAISER, E. (1957), Der Mann ohne Eigenschaften: Ein Problem der Wirklichkeit,
    Merkur 11, pp. 669–87.
LYOTARD, J-F. (1979), *La condition postmoderne: Rapport sur le savoir*, Paris:
    Minuit.
MOLINO, J. (1978), Doubles: Sur la logique de Musil, *L'Arc* 74 (*Robert Musil*),
    pp. 63–74.
MOSER, W. (1980), Diskursexperimente in Romantext: Zu Musils *Der Mann
    ohne Eigenschaften*, in Baur, U. and Castex, E. (eds), *Robert Musil:
    Untersuchungen*, Königstein: Athenäum.
MUSIL, R. (1976), *Robert Musil: Tagebücher*, ed. Frisé, A. Reinbek: Rowohlt.
NIETZSCHE, F. W. (1956), *Friedrich Nietzsche: Werke in drei Bänden*, ed.
    Schlechta, K., Munich: Hanser.
PAYNE, P. (1976), Robert Musil's reality: a study of some aspects of
    'Wirklichkeit', *Der Mann ohne Eigenschaften*, *Forum for Modern Language
    Studies* 12/4, pp. 314–28.
———— (1988), *Robert Musil's 'The Man without Qualities' : A Critical Study*,
    Cambridge: Cambridge University Press.

PETERS, F. G. (1978), *Robert Musil: Master of the Hovering Life. A Study of the Major Fiction*, New York: Columbia University Press.

REIS, G. (1983), *Musils Frage nach der Wirklichkeit*, Königstein: Hain.

REISS, H. (1982), Musil and the writer's task in the age of science and technology', in Huber, Lothar and White, John J. (eds), *Musil in Focus: Papers from a Centenary Symposium*, London: Publications of the Institute of Germanic Studies.

RORTY, R. (1989), *Contingency, Irony, and Solidarity*, Cambridge: Cambridge University Press.

SCHÖNE, A. (1966), Zum Gebrauch des Konjunktivs bei Robert Musil, in Schillemeit, J. (ed.), *Interpretationen 3: Deutsche Romane von Grimmelshausen bis Musil*, Frankfurt/Hamburg: Fischer.

STERN, J. P. (1982), 'Reality' in *Der Mann ohne Eigenschaften*, in Huber, L. and White, J. J. (eds), *Musil in Focus: Papers from a Centenary Symposium*, London: Publications of the Institute of Germanic Studies.

9

Accounting for History
Thomas Mann, *Doktor Faustus*

RITCHIE ROBERTSON

Modernism is an art of fragmentation. But what does the artist do when faced with real, physical fragmentation? In the period from 1943 to 1945, when Mann was writing his novel, he was aware of fragmentation in space: the destruction of German cities, the division of its territory among four invading armies. And he was also aware of fragmentation in time, since recent German history seemed to consist of alarming discontinuities: defeat in 1918, the establishment of a fragile democracy, and its transformation into a Fascist state resting on mass support and committed to brutal internal repression and external aggression. Modernism by itself could neither register nor explain the enormity of these events. If he was going to explore the origins of the German catastrophe in its cutural and intellectual history, Mann needed an art of continuity. However, he could not simply return to the Realism that had served him in *Buddenbrooks*. With its stress on the continuity of generations, and its coolly ironic perspective, such Realism was too leisurely, too secure, to cope with a drastically altered reality. For a novelist like Mann, Germany's history could only be grasped by a device foreign to both Realism and Modernism, namely myth. And so Mann had recourse to the quint-essentially German myth of Faust, who sells his soul to the Devil in return for twenty-four years of power and pleasure, and then is carried off to hell; and he related the Faust myth to German history by means of a highly elaborate allegory.

In *Doktor Faustus* all three modes of representation – Modernism, Realism, and myth – are allowed to interact. Myth alone would have brought Mann dangerously close to the Nazis' irrationalist revival of Germanic mythology; it had to be controlled by the intellectualism of Modernism. But Mann also suggests deep doubts about the value of Modernism, wondering how far it is complicit with the new world of inhuman totalitarianism. Hence the Modernism of *Doktor Faustus* is englobed within a Realist narrative. The Faustian composer Adrian Leverkühn does not tell his own story, except in a few letters, in his written record of his dialogue with the Devil, and in his final speech before his collapse. It is told for him by Serenus Zeitblom, a Realist figure reminiscent of the narrators in nineteenth-century fiction by Storm or Raabe.

These diverse materials required intellectual control. But ever since *Tonio Kröger*, where the writer is estranged from ordinary people by his frosty detachment from their emotions, Mann had found the intellectualism of modern, and especially Modernist, art both unavoidable and intensely problematic; and he articulates this problem in *Doktor Faustus* by making his central figure a Modernist artist. Mann's conception of the crisis of modern art is modelled on the scheme put forward by Schiller in *Über naïve und sentimentalische Dichtung* (On Naïve and Reflective Poetry), a treatise on aesthetics, that Mann valued highly (Reed, 1974, p. 139). Schiller contrasts the 'naïve' artist, who is in a direct relationship to nature and depicts reality freshly and without obtruding his own personality, and the 'reflective' artist who is estranged from nature, depicts reality as falling short of an ideal standard, and obtrudes his own personality and reflections into his work. In adopting this scheme, Mann assumes that the 'naïve' artist composes freshly and spontaneously, while his reflective counterpart risks being hampered by intellectualism – itself a long-standing theme in German aesthetic discussion (Reed, 1969). An associated text, which, unlike Schiller's, is mentioned in the novel, is Kleist's essay *Über das Marionettentheater* (On the Puppet Theatre), which laments that human beings are hampered by consciousness from regaining the instinctive sureness of puppets or animals. Kleist's speaker concludes that having been expelled from the Eden of unreflective spontaneity, man must go all the way round the globe and re-enter Eden from the other side, thus passing through experience in order to regain innocence on a higher level. Leverkühn reads this (VI, p. 410) for his *Gesta Romanorum*, which is to be performed by puppets, and which is supposed to be Leverkühn's breakthrough from coldness to feeling in art (VI, p. 429).

The legend of Faust had long appealed to Mann as a means of expressing the privileged and dangerous position of the artist. After finishing the *Joseph* tetralogy he looked through old notes and considered returning to the problematic of the artist, treated so thoroughly in *Der Tod in Venedig* (Death in Venice). His plan of describing a Faustian artist went back even further – to 1901. He copied out a note which read as follows:

> *Alte Notiz*: Figur des syphilitischen Künstlers: als *Doktor Faust* und dem Teufel Verschriebener. Das Gift wirkt als Rausch, Stimulans, Inspiration; er darf in entzückter Begeisterung geniale, wunderbare Werke schaffen, der Teufel führt ihm die Hand. Schließlich aber *holt* ihn der Teufel: die Paralyse. (Quoted in Voss, 1975, p. 15).

> (*Old note*: figure of the syphilitic artist: as Doctor Faust who has sold his soul to the Devil. The poison has the effect of an intoxicant, stimulant, inspiration; transported by ecstasy, he can compose wonderful works of

genius, with the Devil guiding his hand. In the end, however, he is *carried off* by the Devil: paralysis.)

Moreover, the Faust legend seemed quintessentially German. Several great German writers – not only Goethe, but also Lessing and Heine – had tried their hand at it. The figure of Faust had been used to justify German imperialism and aggression (Schwerte, 1962). Now, with the collapse of Germany, it seemed an appropriate vehicle for reflections on the deep ambivalence of German history. For Mann, moreover, rewriting a pre-existing narrative was a way of disciplining himself. In his previous major works, *Der Zauberberg* (The Magic Mountain) and the *Joseph* tetralogy, the narrative drive that had carried *Buddenbrooks* along had become submerged in the narrator's playful elaborations. The Faust legend, however, has an irremovable narrative drive. From Faust's pact with the Devil, the story heads relentlessly towards his damnation.

Mann uses the figure of Faust initially to dramatise the problems of the modern artist. An essential feature of the Faust legend is Faust's desire for forbidden knowledge. The legend is characteristic of the Reformation and the Renaissance, when theological certainties were being questioned and curiosity about the empirical world was defying the Church's injunction *noli altum sapere*, 'do not seek to know what is above you' (Ginzburg, 1990). And Mann appropriately goes back to the original version of the legend, the 1597 *Volksbuch* (chap book) about Faust, which he read in a modern edition with a useful introduction (Voss, 1975, p. 24). His Faust is closely associated with the Reformation. Before turning to music, Leverkühn studies theology at Halle, with which, as Mann reminds us, the old university of Wittenberg, associated with Luther, had been amalgamated in 1815 (VI, p. 117). Mann makes virtually no use of Goethe's *Faust*: the only parallel is that Leverkühn's father, like the medical father of Goethe's hero, is interested in the secrets of the natural world. Goethe's Enlightenment Faust could be of no use to Mann. After all, in *Faust Part One* Goethe's hero loses interest in hidden knowledge and relies on the Devil's help to re-enter ordinary life; and throughout the adventures of *Part Two* we know, if we remember the 'Prologue in Heaven', that he is not going to be damned. More serviceable was Heine's *Der Doktor Faust: Ein Tanzpoem* (Doctor Faust: a Dance Poem), which Mann read while working on his novel (XI, p. 218), for the knowledge sought by Heine's Faust is above all erotic, and he is tempted by a female Devil called Mephistophela, who bears some resemblance to Leverkühn's Esmeralda.

In Mann's view, art was closely linked with forbidden realms of experience, particularly with erotic experience. He thought it the artist's duty to explore morally dubious terrain and question the complacent certainties of the bourgeois public. He knew, too, that the origins of artistic inspiration may be sensual and shameful. In *Der Tod in Venedig* the high-minded Aschenbach, after a long period of artistic sterility, writes some of his best pages while ogling Tadzio, who is romping on the beach. In *Doktor Faustus*, creative sterility is no longer the psychological problem of an individual; according to Leverkühn, it constitutes the crisis of modern art.

The erotic aspect of music is deeply problematic for Leverkühn. His first experience of music has an erotic tinge: he, his brother, and young Zeitblom are taught to sing canons by the stable-maid Hanne, whose flapping breasts (*Waberbusen*: VI, p. 41) introduce a note of coarse eroticism (Fetzer, 1990, p. 26); this is recalled later when Leverkühn complains about the inherent 'Stallwärme, Kuhwärme' (stable warmth, bovine warmth) of music and speaks of the need to cool it down (VI, p. 94). This dislike of emotional warmth appears also in his aversion to music which presents itself as the spontaneous outpouring of feeling. He even hates the word 'inspiration' (VI, p. 38). Conscious of the manipulation involved in composition, he disbelieves in the conception of 'das Werk als solches, das selbstgenügsam und harmonisch in sich geschlossene Gebilde' (the work as such, the construction, self-sufficing, harmonically complete in itself: VI, p. 241). As he makes clear in a letter to his teacher Kretzschmar, he cannot take seriously the current ideals of beauty, harmony, melody, in music; his awareness of the technical devices involved prevents him from enjoying music straightforwardly and puts him at an ironic distance from it. 'Warum muß es mir vorkommen,' he asks, 'als ob fast alle, nein, alle Mittel und Konvenienzen der Kunst *heute nur noch zur Parodie taugten*?' (Why must I think that almost all, no, all the methods of *art are today only fit for parody*? – VI, p. 180)

This view of modern art as in danger of being defeated by its own intellectualism had long been central to Mann's understanding of his own work. He was helped to apply it to music by another California exile, Theodor Wiesengrund-Adorno. In the typescript of Adorno's *Philosophie der neuen Musik* (Philosophy of Modern Music) Mann found an account of the situation of modern art which seemed remarkably close to his own view (XI, p. 172). In a passage that Mann was to quote in the dialogue between Leverkühn and the Devil, Adorno maintains that nowadays tonality, the medium of all traditional music, now strikes even a relatively insensitive ear as false and clichéd (Adorno, 1949, pp. 40–1; cf. VI, p. 319; Bergsten, 1974, p. 100). The only way forward, he argues, is to abandon the Romantic notion that the artist's subjectivity can organise itself freely, and to subject musical material to thoroughgoing rational organisation (Adorno, 1949, p. 56).

Leverkühn regards naive art – direct, spontaneous, warm – as no longer attainable. He echoes Schiller in admitting that he lacks the *robuste Naivität* necessary for an artist (VI, p. 178): instead he has a restless intellect that soon gets bored. He can move forward by intellectualising his compositions, and he does this in a variety of ways: one is to promote the relationship between music and words, as he does in his songs and operas (VI, p. 218); another is to insist on the importance of order in music, whence his affection for the eccentric German-American composer Beissel who drew up strict hierarchies of notes. He also makes great use of parody: in his opera *Love's Labours Lost*, in his puppet–opera *Gesta Romanorum* (a parody of Wagnerian music-drama: Stein, 1950, p. 270), and also in his private letters and conversation. His great musical breakthrough, the *strenger Satz* or strict style (of which more later), is just such a rational organisation of musical substance as Adorno advocated. By themselves, however, these devices would merely confirm Leverkühn's artistic sterility. Before he can resolve the crisis of modern art by his masterpieces, Leverkühn must receive an infusion – something corresponding to the 'inspiration' he despises – from a mysterious, deadly source. And this brings us back to Leverkühn's role as Faust and to the erotic basis of art.

Leverkühn's equivalent of the Faustian pact with the Devil is his liaison with the prostitute 'Esmeralda'. Having met her in a Leipzig brothel where he was led by a devilish-looking guide, he then seeks her out in Hungary and disregards her warning that she is infected with syphilis. Zeitblom thinks that he was driven by a 'Verlangen nach dämonischer Empfängnis, nach einer tödlich entfesselnden chymischen Veränderung seiner Natur' (a longing for demonic conception, for a chemical change in his nature which should be liberating and deadly: VI, p. 206), that is, not only by erotic attraction, but by a (semi-conscious) feeling that contact with her would infuse him with creative power. This should not sound absurd. There were good reasons for connecting Nietzsche's syphilitic infection with the bursts of creative euphoria he experienced in later life, and other examples of syphilitic geniuses were either known (Hugo Wolf) or conjectured (Beethoven) (Bergsten, 1974, pp. 83–5). Besides, the connection with genius and illness was a favourite theme of Mann's: the musically gifted Hanno Buddenbrook dies of typhus; residence at Davos brings out both tuberculosis and genius in Hans Castorp (Weigand, 1933). In Leverkühn's case the stakes are much higher. A believing Christian, he takes the view (more reminiscent of Augustine than Luther) that sex is intrinsically evil and marriage a means of domesticating it (VI, p. 249). The close association of music and the erotic therefore makes it a devilish art. So it is appropriate that the Devil – whom we can take as a projection of Leverkühn's unconscious, since everything he says can either be traced to Leverkühn's memories or develops ideas already expressed – should explicitly promise the restoration of naive creativity through syphilis (VI, pp. 315–16). The price is the eventual collapse into general paralysis of the insane which overtakes Leverkühn after twenty-four years, the period in which the traditional Faust was allowed to enjoy power and pleasure with the Devil's help.

There is another price, however, which the Devil expressly demands: Leverkühn is forbidden to love anyone. In the *Volksbuch* the Devil supplies Faust with *succubae* (spirits in female shape), of whom Helen of Troy is one; this explains the mysterious reference to Hyphialta in Leverkühn's final speech (VI, p. 663). Leverkühn has a homosexual relationship (there is no telling how close) with the violinist Rudi Schwerdtfeger, who acts as go-between when he unrealistically proposes marriage to Marie Godeau. It seems, however, that Leverkühn is actually manipulating Rudi into a situation where the violinist will be shot by his jealous ex-lover Ines Institoris, and that he is doing so because, having disobeyed the Devil by loving someone, he is obliged to kill the person he loves (cf. XI, p. 167). His love for his little nephew Nepomuk is also punished, and, cruelly, the punishment is inflicted on the child, who dies of meningitis; the agony the child suffers is like an intensification of Leverkühn's syphilitic migraines. By comparison with this devious yet inexorable tragedy, Goethe's *Faust*, in which the hero always gets another chance, seems almost trivial. The climax of Leverkühn's tragedy is his artistic triumph, the seventy-five-minute oratorio *Dr Fausti Weheklag* (Dr Faust's Lament), in which the rigorous organisation of every note releases the utmost expressive power. And what it expresses is the composer's conviction of being damned for writing it. It was wholly appropriate that earlier, in evoking Leverkühn's *Apocalipsis cum figuris*, Mann should recall the figure of the Despairing Man in Michelangelo's *Last Judgement* (VI, p. 476); and it was appropriate for Adorno to insist that in evoking the *Weheklag*, Mann should reduce its suggestion of hope to the faintest possible intimation (XI, p. 294).

What is the musical breakthrough that Esmeralda and the Devil enable Leverkühn to accomplish? Mann's own appreciation of twentieth-century music was very limited (Carnegy, 1973, pp. 11–12), but Adorno explained to him Schönberg's technique of twelve-tone composition, which is substantially the technique that Leverkühn expounds to Zeitblom on the day of his sister's wedding (VI, pp. 255–8). Schönberg proceeded as follows (as a musical layman, I quote the summary by Stein, 1950, pp. 257–8):

> According to [Schönberg's theory], each musical work is based on a characteristic succession of all twelve tones in the tempered scale, independent of any 'key', and related only to one another in the particular juxtaposition chosen anew for each composition. Announced at the opening, this series of twelve tones becomes the sole frame of reference for the entire work, all themes and voices being derived from it.
>
> The unique feature of the twelve-tone system is formal economy, since not a single note, nor any succession of notes can occur in the composition which does not directly stem from that particular series of twelve tones which the composer has chosen as the structural core of his work. This represents a kind of uncompromising unity which is not present in any other type of music. Within this strictly unified formal pattern, however, the possibilities for variety are endless.

This is broadly the technique Leverkühn expounds. Although there are also considerable differences between Leverkühn's *strenger Satz* and Schönberg's methods (Carnegy, 1973, pp. 46–54), the similarity is sufficient to let Leverkühn 'be' Schönberg as well as Faust. For this reason, Schönberg is one of the few composers never mentioned in the text.

Leverkühn's method rests on strict organisation. Instead of relying on Romantic inspiration, the composer must impose extremely strict rules on his work and allow variation only within narrow limits. Romantic subjectivity is replaced by rational, even mathematical objectivity. But since, as Leverkühn insists, objectivity and subjectivity are dialectically related, this technique makes it possible to attain a new freshness and directness of subjective expression. And this, we learn much later, is triumphantly achieved in *Dr Fausti Weheklag*, in which, according to Zeitblom, 'der Umschlag von strengster Gebundenheit zur freien Sprache des Affekts, die Geburt der Freiheit aus der Gebundenheit, sich vollzieht' (the change from the strictest constraint to the free language of feeling, the birth of freedom from bondage, is accomplished: VI, p. 644).

Is *Doktor Faustus* itself a verbal analogue to Leverkühn's compositions? Commentators have been eager to argue that the novel is structured according to a kind of *strenger Satz*. But their arguments seem to rest on dubious analogies between musical and literary composition. For example, Gunilla Bergsten points out that if you count Chapter 34, which is divided into three parts, as three chapters, then the novel contains forty-nine chapters, and Chapter 25, the dialogue between Leverkühn and the Devil, therefore comes right in the middle of the book (Bergsten, 1974, pp. 226–7). This is true enough, but on the other hand such numerical symmetry is extremely crude and simple, and hardly deserves comparison with the intricate arithmetical relationships possible in music (see Butler, 1970, pp. 168–9). Subsequent investigators claim to have found much more elaborate numerical symmetries in *Doktor Faustus* (Puschmann, 1983). The agnostic reply is, first, that such arguments need to be supported by external evidence, interpreted by adequate philological standards, since the dedicated numerologist can always find the desired patterns in the text; second, that even if Mann did play the numbers game, that is a trivial aspect of his work and only remotely related to the specifically literary mode of communication through narrative structure and verbal nuance.

A more serious analogy between *Doktor Faustus* and Leverkühn's works also stems from Gunilla Bergsten. She argues that Mann's technique of assembling leitmotivs corresponds to Leverkühn's deliberate planning of his works, and that the leitmotivs themselves correspond to the twelve tones which are allowed to return in variations (Bergsten, 1974, p. 229). Wolf-Dietrich Förster has argued this case less tentatively. He claims that just as Schönberg derives all the themes and voices in a composition from his original twelve tones, leaving not a single 'free' note, so *Doktor Faustus* is based on a complex of themes and motives to which everything in the novel can be reduced (Förster, 1975, pp. 698–9). In its thematic unity, Förster concludes, *Doktor Faustus* is a perfect model of *Dr Fausti Weheklag*; like Leverkühn's oratorio, the novel is 'eigentlich undynamisch, entwicklungslos' (actually undynamic and devoid of development: *ibid.*, p. 700, quoting VI, p. 645); and its principal theme is that of 'identity'.

Much in this argument is dubious, not least the assumption that a theme in music is the same thing as a theme in literary criticism. A musical theme is sensuously present to the ear, whereas a theme like 'identity' is a high-level critical abstraction. And a musical theme is highly individual, whereas a literary-critical theme is highly general: if one tells somebody who has not yet read *Doktor Faustus* that it is a book about identity, one has given a completely uninformative description. Besides, one could as easily argue that *Doktor Faustus* is about difference, or a hundred other abstractions; and one could easily find a hundred other novels that could as plausibly have 'identity' as their theme.Indeed, the word 'theme' in literary criticism has become almost vacuous (Levin, 1979). Moreover, if *Doktor Faustus* really could be reduced to a tight complex of themes and motifs, as Förster maintains, it would be extremely boring. Part of its success, as I shall argue later, is due to the presence of unmotivated features that create the illusion of reality. And finally, few books could be less 'devoid of development' than *Doktor Faustus*. It is a dynamic narrative which becomes richer in unexpected developments as it approaches its grisly climax.

I have spent some time disputing with Bergsten and Förster because Bergsten's book (for the most part, a very valuable one) has exercised prolonged influence on criticism of *Doktor Faustus*, and because Förster's assumptions are so widely shared. It must be admitted that the subordination of narrative to theme is widespread in twentieth-century literary criticism, and for the good reason that this is so common a feature of Modernist texts. But to what extent is *Doktor Faustus* a Modernist text? Mann undoubtedly wanted it to bear comparison with ambitious Modernist works. His diaries show that he was always glancing over his shoulder at the work of Joyce in particular (Mann, 1982, p. 627; XI, p. 205; Vaget, 1989). In 1944, reading a study of *Finnegans Wake*, he expressed the fear that his work might be mere traditionalism by comparison (Mann, 1986, p. 85).

The most important claim that *Doktor Faustus* can make to full-blown Modernism is its use of montage. Mann uses the word in his diaries (Mann 1986, p. 16) and describes more fully in *Die Entstehung des 'Doktor Faustus'* (The Genesis of 'Doctor Faustus') how he employed this technique to incorporate all manner of data from real life into the book, in order both to suggest authenticity and to open up new perspectives. He speaks of his *Montage-Technik* and *Montageprinzip* (XI, p. 165). Montage is the technique of assembling a whole from prefabricated parts (Klotz, 1976). Modernists who use the term to describe artistic creation are replacing the nineteenth-century metaphor of organic growth with an aggressively twentieth-century metaphor of mechanical production. Admittedly, Realist writers who venture beyond their own experience always have to collect and insert second-hand information: Flaubert relied on archaeological studies to reconstruct ancient Carthage in *Salammbô*, Zola inserted second-hand information about mining equipment and agricultural economics into *Germinal* and *La Terre*. Similarly, Mann turned to encyclopaedias for help in constructing a composite Central German town (Voss, 1975, pp. 47–52) and consulted Paul Tillich about the study of theology in Halle at the beginning of the century (Bergsten, 1974, pp. 42–51). The unusual element in Mann's procedure is that he incorporated his sources largely verbatim in the text, as can be seen from the parallel passages quoted by Bergsten. The word 'montage' might suggest that the text draws attention to its own heterogeneity, as Döblin's *Berlin Alexanderplatz* does by juxtaposing such diverse discourses as those of advertising and the Bible, or as Broch's *Huguenau* does by interweaving unconnected narratives with a treatise on the disintegration of values in modern civilisation. In so far as Mann's borrowings are meant to be recognised and thus destroy the illusion of an intregral work of art, then we have montage. In so far as they are meant to be absorbed into the novel's fabric and sustain the Realist illusion, then we have a method thoroughly familiar to the nineteenth century. We have, in other words, the technique of the leitmotiv, the recurrent phrase used to identify a character or signalise a theme, which Mann claimed to derive from Wagner, but which is in fact a long-established literary devise (Vaget, 1989; Reed, 1974, p. 74). Bergsten argues the former case – that the borrowings are meant to be recognised – for the novel as a whole. However, Mann has incorporated this material into his text with more skill than Bergsten perceives (cf. Voss, 1975), and often, as with the examples given above, the reader need not and perhaps should not notice its heterogeneous origins.

It is a different matter, however, with the many cultural allusions that Mann has worked into the text. These are clearly meant to be noticed and understood. For example, Leverkühn's choice of songs to set to music alludes in various ways to his own situation. The most obvious example is Brentano's 'O lieb Mädel, wie schlecht bist du' (Sweet maid, how wicked you are), but his other Brentano compositions are also relevant to the story (Fetzer, 1980). Blake's 'The Sick Rose' clearly alludes to Leverkühn's own illness, and Keats's 'Ode on Melancholy' reinforces a theme already introduced by Dürer's *Melencolia*. Such allusions are at the opposite end of a spectrum from such borrowings as those from Tillich. In between, there are a number of doubtful cases. Is the reader supposed to notice that the Devil quotes verbatim from Adorno's *Philosophie der neuen Musik* (which was not published until two years after *Doktor Faustus*)? Is anything to be gained by following up the references to medieval apocalyptic literature that Leverkühn uses for the *Apocalipsis* (VI, p. 474), especially since Mann simply took these references from a newspaper article (Bergsten, 1974, pp. 119–20)? Or was Mann counting on the fact that even his most artfully hidden borrowings would eventually be unearthed by scholarship, the findings of which would then be integrated into the aesthetic understanding of the novel?

One set of references that the reader certainly needs to understand is the correspondence between Leverkühn's life and that of Nietzsche. Among the novel's allusion-complexes, this is second in importance only to the Faust references. Like Leverkühn, Nietzsche was lured into a brothel, where he may well have contracted syphilis; after a prolonged alternation of prostrating illness and feverish creativity, he suddenly collapsed into hopeless insanity and spent the last eleven years of his life, unable to recognise anyone, in the care of his sister, as Leverkühn is tended by his mother. Mann mentions further borrowings (XI, pp. 165–6). Leverkühn's dialogue with the Devil contains quotations from Nietzsche's *Ecce Homo* (VI, p. 316; Bergsten, 1974, p. 76). The triangular relationship among Leverkühn, Marie Godeau, and Rudolf Schwerdtfeger, who reports Leverkühn's marriage proposal to Marie and then gets engaged to her himself, is modelled on the relationship of Nietzsche, Lou Andreas-Salomé, and Paul Rée (XI, p. 166). Zeitblom's visit to the insane Leverkühn is modelled on Paul Deussen's account of his last visit to Nietzsche (VI, p. 674; Bergsten, 1974, p. 74). Even Leverkühn's diet is based on Nietzsche's. The more one recognises these quotations, the more one realises that *Doktor Faustus* not only takes the Faust legend as the representative German myth, but uses Nietzsche as a representative German figure; and since Leverkühn's life recapitulates Nietzsche's, it is important that Nietzsche, like Schönberg, is never mentioned in the text. Even here, however, Mann does not simply lard the text with lumps of untransmuted source-material. Another of Nietzsche's visitors, Erwin Rohde, described the invalid's appearance as 'den halbblödsinnigen Ecce homo fast ganz' (almost entirely the semi-cretinous Ecce homo: Bergsten, 1974, p. 74); Mann accordingly gives Leverkühn 'ein Ecce homo-Antlitz', thus associating Leverkühn both with Christ and with the author of *Ecce Homo* (VI, p. 674; Reed, 1974, p. 360).

Another reason for doubting whether Mann adopted Modernist techniques wholesale is that his mentor Adorno provided him not only with a description of atonal music, but also with a critique of it. Adorno judges Schönberg dialectically. On the one hand, the sheer difficulty of twelve-tone music liberates it from the trivialising power of the culture industry. On the other hand, the rational organisation of sensuous musical material forms a disturbing parallel to the destructive control of nature by technical rationality which Adorno and his collaborator Horkheimer were soon afterwards to denounce in *Dialectic of Enlightenment* (Adorno, 1949, pp. 36, 65). Mann invites us to take a similarly ambivalent attitude to Leverkühn's innovations. We are left in no doubt that they are masterpieces; but, although their author is entirely remote from politics, his work seems alarmingly complicit with the anti-humanism that is gaining ground in contemporary Germany.

Not only does Leverkühn reject nineteenth-century music as banal; he hints elliptically at a Nietzschean critique of ninteenth-century civilisation. He rejects Zeitblom's antithesis between culture and barbarism; he points out that sometimes in history barbarism has been compatible with very high culture; and just as he himself wants to regain naïve spontaneity in composing, so he wishes that civilisation as a whole could return to *Naivität* (VI, p. 83). His teacher Kretzschmar gives a lecture celebrating the primitive elements in music, and Leverkühn proves that he has absorbed Kretzschmar's teaching by

reintroducing medieval and even older forms of expression into his compositions. In addition, Leverkühn rejects the individualism which he thinks
reached its extreme point in Beethoven, and wishes art to be placed in the
service of an overarching organisation, a modern counterpart to the medieval
Church.

Leverkühn's life is remote from politics, but if his ideas were realised
politically, they would take the form of an authoritarian, perhaps totalitarian
state in which notions of humanity, compassion, and self-control counted for
little. This would be the kind of society Nietzsche envisaged as superior to the
comfortable mediocrity of nineteenth-century Europe. And such a society is
enthusiastically imagined, and welcomed as inevitable, by the group of right-
wing intellectuals, the Kridwiss circle, whose meetings Zeitblom attends in
Munich in the early 1920s. Mann has made the parallels between Leverkühn's
music and their ideas very clear by describing the *Apocalipsis cum figuris* in two
sections, between which he inserts an account of the Kridwiss doctrines. He
tells us in *Die Entstehung des Doktor Faustus* 'daß ich die Analyse des
schlimmen Endwerkes mit der Darstellung unheimlich verwandter
Zeiterlebnisse des guten Serenus (den erzfaschistischen Unterhaltungen bei
Kridwiß) verschränken wollte' (that I wanted to juxtapose my analyses of this
grim final work with an account of the uncannily connected contemporary
experiences undergone by the good Serenus (the ultra-Fascist colloquies in
Kridwiss's home): XI, p. 243).

The intellectuals who meet in Sixtus Kridwiss's flat rejoice in the end of
bourgeois humanism, of 'Bildung, Aufklärung, Humanität' (education, enlightenment, humanity: VI, p. 485). These highly cultured men are in love
with violence. They deride the notions of impartial justice, objective truth and
scientific inquiry, and want a new version of medieval theocracy. One of their
number is Dr Chaim Breisacher, who had earlier sung the praises of
everything primitive. But the Kridwiss circle are not reactionaries: the
dictatorship to which they look forward has the gloss of novelty, and it is truth
and justice that seem drearily old-fashioned. Leverkühn's *Apocalipsis* similarly
innovates by restoring the primitive. Rejecting nineteenth-century musical
traditions, it returns to medieval polyphony. Its strict organisation, like that of
the totalitarian society envisaged by the Kridwiss group, permits the expression of primeval, even animal emotions. It combines the primitive with the
ultra-sophisticated: 'Wie oft ist dieses bedrohliche Werk in seinem Drange,
das Verborgenste musikalisch zu enthüllen, das Tier im Menschen wie seine
sublimsten Regungen, vom Vorwurf des blutigen Barbarismus sowohl wie der
blutlosen Intellektualität getroffen worden!' says Zeitblom (How often has this
intimidating work, in its urge to reveal in the language of music the most
hidden things, the beast in man as well as his sublimest stirrings, incurred the
reproach both of blood-bolstered barbarism and of bloodless intellectuality! –
VI, p. 496).

Mann makes completely explicit the analogy between the *Apocalipsis* and the Kridwiss group's apocalyptic fantasies. This is an extreme and disturbingly specific instance of the moral dubiety that Mann attributed to all art, and which he illustrated in *Der Zauberberg* by meditating on the morbid depths concealed in Schubert's seemingly innocuous 'Lindenbaum' (Linden Tree). More specifically, it illustrates the anti-humanist character which is generally acknowledged in many masterpieces of Modernism. Just as Modernist tower-blocks, sited amid the wreckage of traditional neighbourhoods demolished by developers, dwarf and alienate their human users, so the great works of Modernism austerely prohibit the pleasures of following a narrative and sympathising with fictional characters. And Mann's analogy also reminds us that many Modernists have been anti-humanist also in their political choices. In Germany we need only think of the 'reactionary Modernism' (Herf, 1984) represented by Gottfried Benn and Ernst Jünger, and of the abject acceptance of totalitarianism displayed on a high aesthetic level by Brecht's *Die Maßnahme* (The Measures Taken). It is, unfortunately, an evasion of Mann's insight to assert that, as a work of genius, 'such music can never be anything other than an illumination and a delight' (Stern, 1975, p. 13). Leverkühn's *Apocalipsis* cannot be heard with disinterested aesthetic pleasure: in appreciating it, one is also to some degree affirming its anti-humanist values.

A retreat to humanism, however, means (in the terms offered by the novel) reaffirming the values of Zeitblom, the proclaimed humanist. Much of the time Zeitblom is a caricature figure. His classical values often take the form of pedantry: he chose his wife partly because her name was Helene, and he has an affair with a shop-girl in order to practise classical ideals of sexual freedom. When he uses his classical learning to interpret the message on the ring that Frau von Tolna gives Adrian, he actually misses its point (Oswald, 1948). Moreover, his humanism seems desperately impoverished. It is remarkable how seldom he mentions the classics. Introducing himself to the reader, he associates himself with the Reformation humanists Reuchlin, Crotus von Dornheim, Mutianus and Eoban Hesse (VI, p. 10). Apart from Reuchlin, who was a famous Hebrew scholar, Mann probably knew nothing about these people beyond their names, which he found in David Strauss's life of Ulrich von Hutten (Voss, 1975, p. 132); so the reader can hardly be expected to consider it a distinguished pedigree. Mann may have considered modelling Zeitblom on the humanist Erasmus (Lehnert, 1984), but this has not been carried out. Although Zeitblom is nominally a Catholic, he does not seem at all religious, and appreciates Dante much less than Leverkühn does. Nor does he care for natural science, complaining that non-human nature is illiterate (VI, p. 28), and that the horrors of the physical world are remote from human values (VI, p. 363), whereas Leverkühn (albeit ironically) celebrates the vastness of the universe in his setting of Klopstock's 'Frühlingsfeier' (Celebration of Spring). Zeitblom seems to inhabit a cramped little world, and Leverkühn has some reason for rebuking the pettiness of his *Homo Dei* conception (VI, p. 364).

Another surprising omission from Zeitblom's humanism is any connection with the Weimar classicism of Goethe, Herder and Schiller (Koopmann, 1988, pp. 109–24). Mann knew from the *Volksbuch* that Faust was born near Weimar, but did not use this reference (Voss, 1975, p. 43). Weimar is mentioned only once, but very significantly. Writing on 25 April 1945, Zeitblom reports that an American general has forced the population of Weimar to file past the nearby concentration camp, Buchenwald, and accused them of passive complicity in its horrors (VI, p. 637). This is surely a broad hint that Weimar classicism, with its belief in the perfectibility of man, ignored the power of evil and cannot offer guidance in the present (cf. Ball, 1986).

By implication, then, Zeitblom represents an aspect of Germany which was too weak to oppose the demonic forces that issued in Nazism. Leverkühn, on the other hand, represents those forces, though on a much higher moral, intellectual and aesthetic level. Zeitblom represents humanism by functioning as a social type (a humanist schoolteacher), as is usual with characters in Realist fiction; whereas Leverkühn represents the demonic forces allegorically. Thus Thomas Mann is taking a step beyond Realism; but, like the composer Leverkühn, he is also taking a step back and reviving a pre-Realist mode of representation. And so, throughout the novel, a Realist portrayal of German history, focused by Zeitblom, runs alongside an allegorical portrayal of German history in the person of Leverkühn.

Why did Mann make his Faust a musician? Music was the art in which Germans had excelled, from Bach, via Beethoven and Wagner, down to Brahms and Wolf, Mahler and Schönberg. Hence it focuses Leverkühn's deeply German character. Mann remarks in the lecture 'Deutschland und die Deutschen' (Germany and the Germans, 1945) that the Faust legend is flawed by not connecting its hero with music. Quoting Kierkegaard's *Either-Or* (the book Leverkühn is reading when the Devil pays him a visit), Mann asserts that music is 'dämonisches Gebiet' (demonic territory: XI, p. 1131; Kierkegaard, 1959, I, p. 63). Adorno, whose study of Kierkegaard Mann read in 1944, gave him additional help by interpreting the twelve-tone technique in particular as a superstitious belief in fate, comparable to astrology and gambling; this passage, marked by Mann in his typescript, does not appear in the published version (Wisskirchen, 1986, p. 177).

Leverkühn is identified as quintessentially German by his association with the Reformation period. The description of his home town Kaisersaschern emphasises its late-medieval atmosphere (VI, p. 51). He is repeatedly associated with Dürer: the descriptions of his parents are based on Dürer portraits; at Halle he has in his room the 'magic square' shown on Dürer's *Melencolia* (VI, p. 125); the 'Abbot's Room' at Pfeiffering is modelled on Dürer's room at Nuremberg; and his *Apocalipsis* is based on Dürer's series of woodcuts. (Elema, 1965). As the Devil reminds him, it was in the Reformation period that syphilis appeared in Europe (VI, p. 309). When he goes to Halle,

Leverkühn immerses himself in a similar atmosphere by studying theology. Zeitblom assures us that it belongs to the medieval world, and cannot compromise with the demands of science and reason (VI, p. 121). There seems no reason to reject this view as an example of Zeitblom's limitations. After all, Mann would have found a similar view in Heine's *Zur Geschichte der Religion und Philosophie in Deutschland* (A History of Religion and Philosophy in Germany), which he read while working on the novel: 'Von dem Augenblick an, wo eine Religion bei der Philosophie Hülfe begehrt, ist ihr Untergang unvermeidlich' (As soon as religion seeks help from philosophy, its doom is inevitable. – Heine, 1968–76, III, p. 578). And the Halle theologians we meet are archaic figures. The Devil-like Schleppfuss, recalling Naphta from *Der Zauberberg*, combines modern psychology with medieval Catholic theology (which Mann smuggles into the novel by making Schleppfuss, a Protestant, lecture on the psychology of religion). Ehrenfried Kumpf embodies the more brutal aspects of Martin Luther, whom Mann, relying largely on Heine's characterisation of him, considered an incarnation of the German character (XI, p. 1132; Hansen, 1975, p. 270). Though superficially very different from Luther, the refined Leverkühn resembles him in being fascinated by the ambivalences of theology. At Halle he learns that the study of God requires an acquaintance with evil, and that freedom can only be manifested through sin. His theology becomes increasingly paradoxical until his last work is based on the hope that the deepest despair, the conviction that one has forfeited God's grace, may in fact entitle one to grace. For this negative theology, however, Mann was indebted not to Luther but to Kierkegaard, as interpreted by Adorno (Wisskirchen, 1986, p. 193). Although Kierkegaard was an isolated figure, his religious thought develops from Protestant theology and has had considerable influence on mainstream theology in the twentieth century. Nietzsche, another isolated thinker, was the son of a Protestant clergyman, and was understood by Mann as continuing some of the ethical concerns of Protestantism after the death of God. Thus Leverkühn is to be seen as representative of the Protestant tradition in German religion and philosophy.

Leverkühn's deeply German character, however, is presented as a kind of failure. As Hans Rudolf Vaget has shown in a crucial study (Vaget, 1977), Leverkühn is initially endowed with European sympathies, and he has an important prototype in the Emperor Otto III, whose grave Mann transfers for fictional purposes from Aachen to Kaisersaschern. Mann had read about Otto III in a study of the German character by Erich von Kahler, *Der deutsche Charakter in der Geschichte Europas* (The German Character in the History of Europe, 1937), a book whose importance for *Doktor Faustus* has still to be fully explored (Travers, 1991, p. 155). He takes care to give us via Zeitblom the essential information about this Emperor:

> Als er im Jahre 1002 nach seiner Vertreibung aus dem geliebten Rom in Kummer gestorben war, wurden seine Reste nach Deutschland gebracht und im Dom von Kaisersaschern beigesetzt – sehr gegen seinen

Geschmack, denn er war das Musterbeispiel deutscher Selbst-
Antipathie und hatte sein Leben lang unter seinem Deutschtum
gelitten.

(He was driven out of his beloved Rome and died in misery in the year
1002; his remains were brought to Germany and buried in the cathedral
in Kaisersaschern – not at all what he would have relished himself, for
he was a prize specimen of German self-contempt and had been
tormented all his life by being German. – VI, p. 51)

The young Leverkühn too is a self-hating German. This conception of
him is plain from a diary entry of 30 May 1944: 'Adrians Neigung zum
musikalisch Internationalen, bei persönlicher Scheu davor. Antipathie gegen
das Deutschtum. (Otto III)' (Adrian is inclined towards musical
internationalism yet personally shy of it. Antipathy towards the German
character. (Otto III). – Mann, 1986, p. 61). Leverkühn argues logically
against the irrationalist Francophobia of the students in the Winfried-Bund.
He complains that the Germans are a confused nation who always want to
reconcile irreconcilable opposites (VI, p. 115); yet his own theology of
paradox later conforms to this pattern. His first compositions are settings of
non-German poets, including Blake, Keats and Verlaine. His *Meerleuchten* is
first performed outside Germany, in Geneva. One of his greatest friends is
the Anglophile Rüdiger Schildknapp, who, however, later slips into the
background. After his infection Leverkühn loses interest in the world
outside Germany. He rejects the blandishments of the impresario Saul
Fitelberg who wants to lure him to Paris. Many (though not all) of his
compositions are based on German models: his settings of Brentano and
Klopstock, his *Apocalipsis* based on Dürer, and above all *Dr Fausti Weheklag*.
In this he is like Nietzsche, who wanted to be a 'good European' but became
(in Mann's opinion) a quintessential German. And in this light we can see
that Kaisersaschern's various associations give it a twofold symbolism.
Through Otto III and the Holy Roman Empire it symbolises German
universalism, openness to the rest of the world; through its late-medieval
atmosphere it symbolises the narrow, petty, provincial spirit that Mann
thought one of Germany's worst features. He thought that this spirit was
embodied in Luther's anti-roman, anti-European animus (XI, p. 1133), and
also, in a degraded form, in Hitler. It had managed to abuse for its own ends
the Germans' valuable qualities. Thus Zeitblom reflects, on learning that
German technicians have invented a new torpedo, that German ingenuity is
now in the service of a regime which 'den Intellektuellentraum von einem
europäischen Deutschland durch die allerdings etwas beängstigende, etwas
brüchige und, wie es scheint, der Welt unerträgliche Wirklichkeit eines
deutschen Europa ersetzt hat' (replaced the intellectual's dream of a
European Germany with the upsetting, rather brittle reality, intolerable, so it
seems, to the rest of the world, of a German Europe: VI, p. 229).

In addition to this general correspondence between Leverkühn and Germany,

Mann seems to have built into the novel a number of analogies between Leverkühn's life and contemporary events in German history (Brode, 1973). Some are explicit. The German attempt in 1914 at a 'Durchbruch zur Weltmacht' (breakthrough to world power: VI, p. 408) is clearly related to Leverkühn's attempt at an artistic *Durchbruch* (VI, p. 428). Zeitblom discerns a symbolic parallel between the decline of Leverkühn's health and the decline of Germany's fortunes in 1918 (VI, p. 454). In spring 1919 Leverkühn's illness leaves him, and his spirit, like a reborn phoenix, attains freedom (VI, p. 468); it was in February 1919 that the Weimar Parliament assembled, and in August 1919, when Leverkühn completes the *Apocalipsis cum figuris*, the Parliament approved the constitution of the Weimar Republic. Leverkühn's new burst of creativity thus corresponds to the birth of true democracy in Germany. Most of the analogies between Leverkühn's life and Germany's history, however, are indicated only by puzzlingly specific dates. For example, his visit to Italy at the end of June 1911 coincides with the Agadir crisis; his plans to marry Marie Godeau, a French-speaking Swiss, coincide with the Locarno Conference of 1925, which aroused hopes of closer ties between Germany and France; Schwerdtfeger's sudden death in February 1925 coincides with that of President Ebert; Leverkühn collapses in 1930, when the Nazis were becoming a major force in politics, and his eleven years of insanity overlap with Nazi rule. These analogies, however, should not be overestimated; they serve to supplement the overall correspondence, but in themselves they are external and uninformative.

Mann's use of allegory has provoked a number of criticisms which cannot be discussed here: I shall refer the reader instead to critical surveys which supply convincing answers (Vaget, 1977; Travers, 1991). The most important criticism, however, is that since Mann finds ambivalence everywhere, and since Leverkühn's fine though inhuman music corresponds allegorically to the advent of Nazism, Mann is implying that Nazism has some good to it (Voss, 1975, p. 20). Now, Mann's ambivalence often means that evil is not the other face of good, but a perversion, a degradation of good; and this can apply to the 'German' character of Nazism. And although Mann's detractors might wish him to have inserted clear instructions about how to interpret his novel, Mann differs from Leverkühn in not subjecting his materials to rigorous control: there is some freedom to generate unexpected meanings, and as readers we are allotted an active part in the construction of meaning, even at the risk of sometimes misconstruing it.

Two other considerations in defence of the allegory are these. Leverkühn's history does not always march in step with German history, but sometimes anticipates it – for example, Leverkühn's artistic breakthrough is much more successful than Germany's military breakthrough; hence Leverkühn's expression of contrition in the *Weheklag* indicates what Germany ought to do after the annihilation of Nazism. Moreover, the allegory does not apply solely to Germany: early in the novel Zeitblom is at pains to emphasise that all human beings are capable of regression to the primitive – 'die altertümlich-volkstümliche Schicht gibt es in uns allen' (this ancient layer of folk consciousness exists in all of us: VI, p. 54).

Alongside the historical allegory, spanning almost a thousand years of German history (from Otto III to the Third Reich), we have Zeitblom's Realist account of the segment of history he lived through. A classically educated schoolteacher, he represents the German *Bildungsbürgertum* at a late stage, when it has become narrow and conservative in its outlook (cf. Ringer, 1969). Nevertheless, he is not on the whole an unreliable narrator; if he were, the novel would be unintelligible. Although his humanism invites irony, his comments on history are those of a decent though unheroic intellectual who has learnt through experience. He took early retirement in 1934 because of his lack of sympathy with the Nazi regime. Twenty years earlier, he shared the general enthusiasm for war, and in retrospect he depicts his excitement with some detachment (VI, pp. 405–9). He describes the naïvety of pro-revolutionary intellectuals in 1918 (VI, p. 453) and later, as we have seen, the enthusiastic acceptance of barbarism by the academics of the Kridwiss circle. His narrative is interspersed with reports on the progress of the Second World War. Early on, he remarks that although the Allied bombing of Germany is terrible, the Germans are receiving the treatment they gave others (VI, p. 50). It is not clear how to distinguish irony from patriotism in his later remarks about 'dem glückhaften Wiederaufleben unseres Unterseeboot-Krieges' (the fortunate revival of our submarine warfare: VI, p. 229) in which two foreign passenger ships full of civilians have been sunk; but he may be quoting the word *glückhaft* ironically from the newspaper in which he finds this information. After all, he goes on to describe the intensified destruction of German cities as a Last Judgement (VI, p. 231). Near the end of the novel he roundly curses the Nazis who have corrupted Germany, but adds that their regime was not wholly alien to the German character (VI, pp. 638–9). This confession of shared guilt precedes Leverkühn's two confessions, one expressed musically in *Dr Fausti Weheklag*, and the other made to his assembled acquaintances in a parody of Faust's last speech to his disciples. Here again, Realism complements allegory. Leverkühn's double confession raises the story to the plane of tragedy and myth; but in case the use of literary forms should seem like the evasion of real historical responsibility, Zeitblom acknowledges that responsibility in plain, sober language.

In other ways, Realism was an essential component of Mann's undertaking. While planning and writing the novel, Mann read, not the great works of Modernism but classic Realist fiction: from the German tradition, Gotthelf, Stifter, Keller, Fontane, and from the wider European tradition, Balzac, Conrad and Dostoyevsky. He explains: 'Mit großer Epik Fühlung zu halten, gleichsam die Kräfte in ihr zu baden, ist geboten, wenn man selbst erzählerisch Ernstes erstrebt' (To keep in touch with great narrative fiction, to bathe one's energies in it, as it were, is imperative when one is engaged on a serious story-telling project. – XI, p. 186). And in describing the genesis of *Doktor Faustus*, he talks about 'das eigentümlich *Wirkliche*, das ihm anhaftet' (the strange sense of the *real* that attaches to it: XI, p. 165). Commentators have acknowledged his success in creating 'a highly structured fiction, enriched by wit and anecdote and anchored in a variety of individual lives full of bizarre Dickensian idiosyncrasies and contradictions' (Stern, 1975, p. 10). This effect of reality is indispensable to a novel that aims to account for an all-too-real historical catastrophe.

Among Mann's diverse means of achieving Realism, one is the standard nineteenth-century devise of the social type. Thus Zeitblom, as we have already seen, typifies the *Bildungsbürgertum*, while the Kridwiss circle typify the reactionary mode of the 1920s. Similarly, Baron von Riedesel typifies a conservative attitude to culture, which is trumped in a superb comic scene by the primitivism of Dr Chaim Breisacher; while Helmut Institoris, the sickly art-historian who enthuses about Renaissance supermen, represents the cult of the strong man which eventually helped to legitimise Hitler. Many of these people have real-life originals: all the members of the Kridwiss circle, for example, have been identified (Bergsten, 1974, p. 40–1); but that does not diminish their typicality. A few real people are mentioned by name: when they belong to the musical world, like Bruno Walter, their names serve to authenticate Leverkühn's career; when they are not well known, the references to them may be taken as private compliments, as with the reference to Mann's Zürich friend Frau Reiff (VI, p. 554; Bergsten, 1974, p. 30), or private jokes, as with the story about Herr von Gleichen-Russwurm and the mouse (VI, pp. 561–2); this last is founded on a real incident which was even more extraordinary than Mann realised (Weigand, 1984). The inclusion of real people in a novel is a technique which must be practised sparingly. If it is overdone, then, by a curious aesthetic paradox, credibility vanishes and we are left with the characteristic post-modern phenomenon of pastiche (Jameson, 1991, p. 17). Mann, however, stops well short of post-modernism.

The novel's Realism is most firmly guaranteed by the presence of Zeitblom as narrative voice. He holds together materials so heterogeneous that without him they would constitute a barely coherent collage – Leverkühn's compositions, his letters, his dialgoue with the Devil, and the social gatherings in Munich and elsewhere, and reflections on German history. Thus he serves to integrate the novel. He also humanises it by serving as an intermediary between the reader and a world which seems strange and alien, yet also oppressively real. And he assists Mann in another means of creating the reality-effect, which is to leave the composition of a novel rather rough at the edges. A smooth and polished text too clearly testifies to its author's manipulation of the material. Zeitblom certainly cannot be called an over-expert narrator. He frequently apologises for his clumsiness (e.g. VI, p. 32). On the pretext that he is not writing a novel (VI, p. 393) he reports conversations in indirect speech where dialogue would have been more interesting; the novel's dialogue scenes are among its best, and it is a great pity that the discussions among the Kridwiss circle are not given in dialogue form: Mann's narrative integration of theoretical materials is here less than fully successful (*pace* Voss, 1975, p. 158). On the other hand, an inexpert story-teller can draw the reader's attention to important aspects of the novel with a degree of explicitness that would be intolerable in an impersonal narrator but is forgiveable in an amateur story-teller like Zeitblom: to the three time-levels, for example (VI, pp. 334–5), or to the close relation between the *Apocalipsis* and the speculations of the Kridwiss circle. In any case, some clumsiness is acceptable, even desirable, in a Realist novel. It needs particles of reality which escape being sucked into the machine of thematic integration. The anecdote about the children's doctor, a digression for which Zeitblom apologises (VI, p. 40), is such a particle. On a larger scale, the same can be said of Rüdiger Schildknapp, who is described at great length and plays no significant part in the action. A novelist more conscientious about formal unity might have removed him, or amalgamated him with Rudi Schwerdtfeger; but in the novel as we have it we can accept Schildknapp, along with Bullinger, Zink, Spengler, and many other minor characters, as being there because they are there – part of the dense population of the novel.

If we hold together the Modernist and Realist aspects of *Doktor Faustus*, we can see it as a pivotal work in literary history. It makes great use of techniques of intellectual construction associated with Modernism, but also reanimates myth. Its intellectual self-awareness keeps the myth remote from the irrationalism with which the Nazis mobilised national mythology. It expresses deep doubts about the inhuman element in Modernism, and complements its Modernism with the densely Realist portrayal of varied characters against a background of recent history. And by using Zeitblom as a narrator it englobes its Modernism within a Realist narrative. *Doktor Faustus* affirms the positive advances made by Modernism and also, perhaps more strongly, the lasting value of Realism.

REFERENCES

Quotations by volume and page number are from Thomas Mann, *Gesammelte Werke*, 12 vols, Frankfurt: Fischer, 1960. Translations from *Doktor Faustus* are based on *Doctor Faustus: The Life of the German Composer Adrian Leverkühn*, translated by H. T. Lowe-Porter, London: Secker & Warburg, 1949, modified occasionally; translations from other texts are my own.

    The genesis of *Doktor Faustus* can be followed through the relevant volumes of Mann's diaries, and is described by Mann himself in *Die Entstehung des 'Doktor Faustus'* (in vol. XI of his works); though the subtitle of this account, *Roman eines Romans*, warns us that it is itself a calculated piece of self-presentation. An up-to-date survey of studies of *Doktor Faustus* will be found in Volkmar Hansen, *Thomas Mann*, Sammlung Metzler 211, Stuttgart: Metzler, 1984.

ADORNO, T. W. (1975), *Philosophie der neuen Musik* [1949], in *Gesammelte Schriften*, vol. 12, ed. Rolf Tiedemann, Frankfurt: Suhrkamp.

BALL, D. J. T. (1986), *Thomas Mann's Recantation of 'Faust': 'Doktor Faustus' in the Context of Mann's Relationship to Goethe*, Stuttgart: Heinz.

BERGSTEN, G. (1974) *Thomas Manns 'Doktor Faustus': Untersuchungen zu den Quellen und zur Struktur des Romans*, 2nd edn. Tübingen: Niemeyer.

BRODE, H. (1973), Musik und Zeitgeschichte im Roman. Thomas Manns *Doktor Faustus*, *Jahrbuch der Deutschen Schiller-Gesellschaft* 17, pp. 455–72.

BUTLER, C. (1970), *Number Symbolism*, London: Routledge & Kegan Paul.

CARNEGY, P. (1973), *Faust as Musician: A Study of Thomas Mann's Novel 'Doktor Faustus'*, London: Chatto & Windus.

ELEMA, J. (1965), Thomas Mann, Dürer und Doktor Faustus, *Euphorion* 59, pp. 97–117.

FETZER, J. F. (1980), Nachklänge Brentanoscher Musik in Thomas Manns *Doktor Faustus*, in D. Lüders (ed.), *Clemens Brentano: Beiträge des Kolloquiums im Freien Deutschen Hochstift 1978*, Tübingen: Niemeyer.

FETZER, J. E. (1990), *Music, Love, Death and Mann's 'Doktor Faustus'*, Columbia, SC: Camden House.

FÖRSTER, W.-D. (1975), Leverkühn, Schönberg und Thomas Mann: Musikalische Strukturen und Kunstreflexion in *Doktor Faustus*, *Deutsche Vierteljahrsschrift für Litertur– und Geistesgeschichte* 49, pp. 694–720.

GINZBURG, C. (1990), The high and the low: the theme of forbidden knowledge in the sixteenth and seventeenth centuries, in his *Myths, Emblems, Clues*, tr. J. and A. Tedeschi, London: Hutchinson.

HANSEN, V. (1975), *Thomas Manns Heine-Rezeption*, Hamburg: Hoffmann und Campe.

HEINE, H. (1968–76), *Sämtliche Schriften*, ed. Klaus Briegleb, 6 vols, Munich: Hanser.

HERF, J. (1984), *Reactionary Modernism: Technology, Culture, and Politics in Weimar and the Third Reich*, Cambridge: Cambridge University Press.

JAMESON, F. (1991), *Postmodernism, or, the Cultural Logic of Late Capitalism*, London: Verso.

KIERKEGAARD, S. (1959), *Either/Or*, tr. David F. Swenson and Lillian Marvin. Swenson, 2 vols, Princeton: Princeton University Press.

KLOTZ, V. (1976), Zitat und Montage in neuerer Literatur und Kunst, *Sprache im technischen Zeitalter* 60, pp. 259–77.

KOOPMANN, H. (1988), *Der schwierige Deutsche: Studien zum Werk Thomas Manns*, Tübingen: Niemeyer.

LEHNERT, H. (1984), The Luther-Erasmus Constellation in Thomas Mann's *Doktor Faustus*, *Michigan Germanic Studies* 10, pp. 142–58.

LEVIN, R. (1979), *New Readings vs Old Plays*, Chicago: University of Chicago Press.

MANN, T. (1982), *Tagebücher 1940–43*, ed. P. de Mendelssohn, Frankfurt: Fischer.

MANN, T. (1986), *Tagebücher 1944–46*, ed. I. Jens, Frankfurt: Fischer.

OSWALD, V. A., Jr. (1948), Thomas Mann's *Doktor Faustus*: the enigma of Frau von Tolna, *Germanic Review* 23, pp. 249–53.

PUSCHMANN, R. (1983) , *Magisches Quadrat und Melancholie in Thomas Manns 'Doctor Faustus': Von der musikalischen Struktur zum semantischen Beziehungsnetz*, Bielefeld: AMPAL Verlag.

REED, T. J. (1968), Critical consciousness and creation: the concept *Kritik* from Lessing to Hegel, *Oxford German Studies* 3, pp. 87–113.

REED, T. J. (1974), *Thomas Mann: The Uses of Tradition*, Oxford: Clarendon Press.

RINGER, F. K. (1969), *The Decline of the German Mandarins*, Cambridge, Mass.: Harvard University Press.

SCHWERTE, H. (1962), *Faust und das Faustische: Ein Kapitel deutscher Ideologie*, Stuttgart: Klett.

STEIN, J. M. (1950), Adrian Leverkühn as a composer, *Germanic Review* 25, pp. 257–74.

STERN, J. P. (1975), *History and Allegory in Thomas Mann's 'Doktor Faustus'*, inaugural lecture, London: H. K. Lewis.

TRAVERS, M. (1991), Thomas Mann, *Doktor Faustus* and the historians: the function of 'Anachronistic Symbolism', in D. Roberts and P. Thomson (eds), *The Modern German Historical Novel*, New York and Oxford: Berg.

VAGET, H. R. (1977), Kaisersaschern als geistige Lebensform, in W. Paulsen (ed.), *Der deutsche Roman und seine historischen und politischen Bedingungen*, Berne and Munich: Francke.

VAGET, H. R. (1989), Thomas Mann und James Joyce. Zur Frage des Modernismus in *Doktor Faustus*, *Thomas Mann Jahrbuch* 2, pp. 121–50.

VOSS, L. (1975), *Die Entstehung von Thomas Manns Roman 'Doktor Faustus'*, Tübingen: Niemeyer.

WEIGAND, H. J. (1933), *Thomas Mann's Novel 'Der Zauberberg'*, New York: Appleton-Century.

WEIGAND, H. J. (1984), Die tote Maus oder Nachtrag zur 'moralischen Verwirrung der Zeit': Schillers Urenkel in Thomas Mann's *Doktor Faustus*, *Deutsche Vierteljahrsschrift für Literatur- und Geistesgeschichte* 58, pp. 470–4.

WISSKIRCHEN, H. (1986), *Zeitgeschichte im Roman: Zu Thomas Manns 'Zauberberg' und 'Doktor Faustus'*, Thomas-Mann-Studien 6, Berne: Francke.

A Post-Realist Aesthetic
Günter Grass, *Die Blechtrommel*

MICHAEL MINDEN

The *Tin Drum* appeared in 1959 and caused a sensation in literary circles, because it seemed blasphemous and obscene or even pornographic to some, but also because it offered what might well have appeared impossible in the preceding decade, a literary representation of ordinary German involvement with the crimes of the Nazis. It was unashamedly a work of literature and did not moralise in any obvious way, yet it confronted the recent German past, and, perhaps even more disturbingly to its first generation of readers, recognised that this confrontation had extremely pressing implications for the post-war West Germany of the economic miracle.

The great stylistic achievement of the novel is to have found means of representing recent German history without either trivialising it or demonising it. It contrives to show that 'monstrosities are human' without allowing the insight to be diminished by 'the lethargy that comes from repetition and familiarity' or itself diminishing 'the feeling of outrage' or our 'capacity for interpretation' (Stern, 1987).

At the same time it is an extremely personal work, since it evokes the lost world of Grass's youth, pre-war Danzig, a predominantly German free city which had ceased to exist in the form in which Grass had spent his childhood years there, becoming in 1945 the Polish city of Gdansk. Indeed, this circumstance helps to focus upon the particular blend of fantasy and realism which characterises the novel: the historical fate of Danzig has meant that objective irretrievable pastness – Danzig as it was just isn't there any more – and subjective irretrievable pastness – the memories of childhood – are superimposed upon each other. The effect of this is to mix together the mythological quality which early childhood takes on in the memory with objective representation of history: two kinds of pastness produce an ambiguous and poetically richly productive play.

The novel is remarkable for its visual quality. Grass elaborates his complex ramified narrative by means of a succession of images, which impose a certain coherence upon the enormous variety of material dealt with, and which also repeatedly arrest and enthral the reader. Many of the chapter titles refer to individual motifs around which the narrative is worked ('Moth and Light Bulb', 'Herbert Truczinski's Back', 'House of Cards'). One of the thematic turning points of the whole work is the description of a horse's head dragged from the bay, full of eels which are feeding on it, and which are in turn dragged forth from their carrion to be taken home, cooked and eaten themselves (Reddick, 1975, pp. 25–9). Heads and tails recur throughout the novel, setting up complex and differentiated thematic contexts (Thomas, 1985). Colours, cupboards, nurses' uniforms, etc. generate the narrative rather than adorn it. It is not surprising that the film version of the novel, made in 1979 by Volker Schlöndorff, with advice from Grass, is perhaps uniquely successful among film versions of literary works. It simply takes up and realises the tendency towards vivid visualisation through which the novel works anyway.

Yet there is one aspect of the novel which the film could not retain, and that is its narrative perspective, although, perversely, one has to say that the narrator is himself more a visual image than a realistic character. The representation of German history is entrusted by Grass to Oskar Matzerath, who decides at the age of 3 to stop growing, observes the world with an adult's mind within a child's body, interprets it with a grown man's sophistication but an infant's amoralism, and relates to it via his tin drum on which he drums up ... the *images* of his autobiography. What the film could not turn into visual terms was Oskar's point of view, from which the world he presents is refracted in his own untrustworthiness as a person (how can you trust someone who tells you he decided to stop growing at the age of 3?). The objective world of Danzig, Düsseldorf and the historical period is visible to us only through the tissue of self-defensive and self-deluding lies offered us by Oskar, narrating (drumming) his own story from within the temporary and unfortunately ever more precarious haven of a hospital bed in an insane asylum. It is accessible to us only via Oskar's remarkable linguistic performance.

But there are also limits to Oskar's language. The novel is divided into three parts, at the end of each one Oskar falls silent. The end of the first registers with incomparable literary power the inability of narrative, of 'es war einmal' (once upon a time), to stand up to the real brutality of history, which silences all the tin drums in the world. In the other two books the ease with which dominant ideologies can appropriate any voice, even one as individual as Oskar's, is conveyed: as a means to his own survival, Oskar works both for the Nazi propaganda machine, and for the market economy. At the end of the second book Oskar has reached the point in his story at which his final flight from Danzig must be recounted. This is the moment he chooses to hand over the narrative to his nurse Bruno. At the end of the novel itself Oskar, once more in flight, hands over a substantial portion of the narrative to another voice, while the closing sequence is an anticipation of his own silence after the end of the novel, when, we are persuaded to imagine, he will be at the mercy of the black cook, a witch of German children's folklore who awaits him when the words finally run out.

The first two books of *Die Blechtrommel* offer a relatively homogeneous historical/fantastic evocation of Danzig. The third book moves to Düsseldorf, and addresses the post-war situation. It is thus distinct from the first two books (the film ended, with a certain stylistic inevitability, with Oskar's departure from Danzig). The final book is often regarded as inferior to the first two, but in fact it is just different. Perhaps the most sensitive remark concerning the heterogeneity comes from Ralph Manheim in an unpublished manuscript which he kindly allowed me to see: 'It has been felt that, as an emanation of Danzig, Oskar is out of place anywhere else. But precisely therein lie the pathos and interest of Book III.' He may be at home there, but he may not stay there. Book III is Oskar's attempt to grow up, which fails pathetically, and becomes instead a formulation in a major key of the theme of existential and historical homelessness which has been present in a minor key throughout the novel. If the final book is less poetically assured than the first two, it is more effectively satirical, and besides, its uncertainty is meaningful: while firmly rejecting any attempt on the part of either Oskar or post-war German society, to take refuge from responsibility in any form of regression, it nevertheless refuses to prejudge or foreclose the only really important question: how can and must the past relate to the present in preparation for the future?

It is comparatively easy to describe Die Blechtrommel, but it is not easy to analyse it. The difficulty can be concentrated into one, crucial, question: how are we to understand the relation between the author of the work, Grass, and the author in it, Oskar? The latter is obviously an artificial construct. You cannot read the book without seeing that he is not a realistic character in the traditional sense. He is 'a persona not a personality' (Thomas, 1985, p. 19). His function is to supply the aesthetic focus for the representation of the epoch, and the key characteristic of this function is Oskar's seemingly amoral stance. We naturally then ask, what did Grass intend by this device? Does Grass narrate from a position of moral stability which eludes Oskar? If so, he must inhabit another world from that perceived through the medium of Oskar, in which one is denied such stability, and to concede this would be to undermine the authority of the text. Grass is not Oskar, certainly, but how are we to understand Grass's function in constructing Oskar as a function for certain aesthetic aims, which the novel triumphantly fulfils? The core question can be put in abstract terms: how does the moral relate to the aesthetic in Die Blechtrommel?

To this the natural answer would be to refer to the idea of the Artist. Grass is an artist who has created Oskar and through him the world. If the authority of Oskar's irony is undermined by his apparent deceit and self-deception,

Grass's irony is not. He is the 'supreme godlike ironist' (Thomas, 1985, p. 25) who stands above his creation, controlling it. Indeed, it is this very control which is his legitimation as an Artist, and which answers our moral question posed above, by ruling it out of court. The aesthetic sphere entailed in this construction of the Artist is defined by a special relation to morality. In the eighteenth century Schiller argued that morality, though not transcended by the aesthetic, is suspended for the time and space of the effective appearance of the aesthetic in the form of the aesthetic production. Something of this view survives even today. For the German Romantics a little later, and ever since, irony was part of the equipment of the Artist: irony means being elsewhere, and by being 'supremely' ironic you are always elsewhere and thus morally never answerable. On the other hand, aesthetically, the credit for the creation of an artistic artifact rests entirely with you, and this in turn increases the sense that a special aura surrounds the activity of the Artist.

It may well be that with one part of his mind Grass would himself endorse this view. He has, after all, always been rather proud of his schizophrenic tendencies: 'Voraussetzung für künstlerisches Tun – mehrmals gespalten zu sein' (Requirement for all artistic activity – to be split into several different selves), said Grass in a televised debate in 1977. But I don't think we as readers and would-be interpreters may legitimately acquiesce in it. We cannot, I suggest, take this construction of the Artist as read, and proceed from that perhaps unavowed supposition to pass off *description* of Grass's startling literary achievement as *analysis* of what it means in aesthetic or moral terms. To see the artist as creator and controller is part of an ideological configuration, an *episteme*, in Foucault's term, which Grass's text refuses and contests on each page. To construct the artist in this way is, in short, to subscribe to the Enlightenment notion of human autonomy and moral freedom from which, historically, it evolved. It is to make the unproblematic assumption that the author 'owns' his meaning with – precisely – godlike authority. But the novel shows us human beings subject to the twin tyrannies of sex and history from the round of chase and persecution of the originary scene in the Cassubian potato fields to the threat of the *schwarze Köchin* at the end. Although Grass may well subscribe to some humanist values, if we are to judge by the fractured moral world the *Tin Drum* shows us, he is very far from embracing them all as a unified model of Man's place in the world.

As a contemporary reviewer noted at the time with outrage 'nowhere do we find a father figure' (Müller-Eckhard, 1959). Indeterminate paternity is indeed one of the most insistent motifs of the novel. Oskar does not know who his father is, Oskar does not know if he is a father himself. No more fundamental indication of the breakdown of familiar order could be imagined, and the implication must surely be – as the contemporary critical outrage indirectly testifies – that the order here scattered is that moral and aesthetic authority which once made it possible for the artist to be constructed as autonomous and as owning the language he used, and made it possible for him to pass his meaning undiminished along the paternal line of succession, as it were, to his heirs/readers.

Although Grass certainly does, in a sense, believe in the artist controlling and being answerable for his work, this is to be understood in the context of an aesthetic of craftsmanship rather than against the background of the excesses to which the idea of the artist has been subject since the effloresence of Individualism at the end of the eighteenth century. In a significant essay on his own aesthetic, written in 1956, during the composition of *Die Blechtrommel*, he rejects 'the immoderation of the would-be genius' (*genialische Maßlosigkeit*: Grass, 1963, p. 9) and praises instead the performance of the – significantly female – ballerina who effaces her subjectivity, exercising and disciplining her body until it becomes a medium of expression and representation surpassing the most auratic efforts of the Artist: 'Einsam zeichnet sie ihre Figuren und erreicht zwischen der dritten und vierten Pirouette jenen Grad der Verlassenheit, den selbst das deutscheste Dichtertum nicht erreicht' (In her solitude she traces her figures and reaches, between the third and fourth pirouette, that stage of abandonment that not even the most German of poets ever reach. – Grass, 1963, p. 6).

If Grass, then, both explicitly, and implicitly in his fiction, distinguishes himself from the kind of artist we are used to in the nineteenth century, can we perhaps understand his relation to his creation Oskar by looking at an older model of authorship, predating the modern epoch in which the Artist came about? In fact, there is much to be said for this view. In so far as the *Tin Drum* can be understood in relation to the history of the *Bildungsroman*, the novel of formation or development – a history which is in some respects a history of those 'most German of poets' – it appears to mark a return to the form of picaresque novel which the *Bildungsroman* superseded with its view of organic individual development. Grass acknowledges his allegiance to Grimmelshausen, the author of the great German picaresque novel, *Der Abenteuerliche Simplicissimus Teutsch*. The picaresque novel lived with the subject's partialness, showing an individual not accommodated and led into growth and development by the world, but buffeted and hurt by it, and hurting and striking back where possible. Here too a kind of amoralism reigns. For the writers of the baroque as well as for Grass the world does not display an ultimate consonance with the regularities of human development: rather, it is a vale of tears.

Oskar would then be an image through which Grass conveys the objective moral agony – the vanity – of the world to which he, Grass, is also subject. In this model of authorship images do not well up from within the interior of the Artist's subjectivity to become manifest as art in and for the objective world. They are shared concretisations of a common perception of partialness and fragmentation. Grass's images would then have something of the quality of baroque emblems, images originating not from the will and act of the creative individual, but from a common stock. Indeed in some cases, such as the motif of the moth drumming on the light bulb at Oskar's birth, or the cupid and the hour-glass, Grass is actually adapting conventional baroque vanity emblems (Weber, 1991, pp. 1–6). Authorial skill resides not in the creation of but in the elaboration of these images. Concrete figures (such as the horse's head violated by eels or the impalement of Truzcinski) embodying the vanity of the world are the objective starting-point for narrative, rather than its adornment or elucidation. They have priority over narrative. Structurally, they offer the potential for development as allegory in the baroque manner (Weber, 1991). It is the drum, not the drummer, from which the ramified narrative springs. This model is, in this sense, objective by contrast to the institutionalised subjectivity of the Artist. Grass's novel does seem to have more in common with *Simplicissimus* than with *Wilhelm Meisters Lehrjahre* (Wilhelm Meister's Apprenticeship).

Yet the Grass of *Die Blechtrommel* is a writer of the Second World War, not of the Thirty Years War. Although there are certainly affinities between those times, as between the practice of Grass and that of Grimmelshausen, it obviously will not do simplistically to equate two distinct epochs of history. The crucial difference in our context is that whereas then the particular relationship between the moral and the aesthetic with which we are concerned was not opaque, owing to the overarching religious context in which both categories received their status and meaning, in Grass this is not the case, since, in the twentieth century, the religious context is only vestigially present.

The third option to which we turn is therefore, historically speaking, the most logical. Between Oskar and Grass, between the moral and the aesthetic, we seem to discern, if nothing else, a dissociation. Can we perhaps align Grass with that form of Modernism which affirms the plurality of language, its detachment from the intentions and person of the author, and which becomes instead the enactment of the materiality of language itself, a circulation of pure difference? If we cannot reconcile the Grass we read with the humanistic individualist notion that 'I own meaning', can we perhaps see him in terms of the Modernistic assertion that 'no one owns meaning'?

In this model the presence of Oskar in the text would correspond to nothing more individually or humanly significant than the linguistic necessity of pronouns. Language bears the traces of the individual human subjects who speak it, and the fact of Oskar is a registration of that linguistic circumstance, and does not otherwise impede or contain the autonomous movement of language itself. Language carries within it the identification codes of individual speakers, but does not originate in or with them. Indeed, speakers only exist, so this view would have it, as effects of language. Oskar's dispersal in language is, of course, evident on every page of the novel in the circumstance which no reader can overlook, that he is sometimes encoded in the first person *Ich* but just as often in the third person *Er*, or in his proper name: 'Oskar'.

This grammatical scattering reduces, quite possibly to zero, the effectiveness of Oskar to manipulate and control language. For all his *claims* to be in charge of his life, he is manipulated and controlled not only by the circumstances of his biography, but by language itself. Morality now subsists only as the traces, in language, of diverse moralities. It is no surprise that the accusation of immorality greeted the novel's spectacular first publication.

There is something to be said for this view. Grass's use of language incontrovertibly distances him from conventional narrative realism. Language for him is not – as it is for, say Fontane – transparent upon a shared reality, but often opaque, tending toward the self-referential, a play of the signifier. Just as, in privileging images above narrative, he proceeds metaphorically in the conventionally metonymic space of the novel, he also proceeds paradigmatically in the syntagmatic space – the 'and then ... and then' – of narrative realism. That is to say that words are included which the ordinary activity of narrative would consist in eliminating. To take – quite literally – an example at random, in this case from the famous account of the assault on the Polish Post Office: 'Zweiunddreißig Karten wurden gemischt, abgehoben, verteilt, ausgespielt' (thirty-two cards were shuffled, cut, dealt and played) – p. 279/232. To be sure, there is a trace of narrative here, namely the stages of a game of cards. But stylistically the other function prevails. These four verbs make up a semantic field, a paradigm store of 'things you can do with cards'. any one verb would have served the purpose of the narrative, 'sie spielten Skat' would have done fine. But here the obvious verb is postponed until the end, and even then it functions plurally, punningly, since 'ausgespielt' allows a variety of connotations from 'all played out' to 'played off against each other'. Examples of non-referential, or only marginally referential use of language could be multiplied.

Yet here again we cannot believe that we have arrived at a satisfactory formulation of our problem. *Die Blechtrommel* is not quite *Finnegans Wake.* That Grass's own views on the role of the artist, such as those expounded in the essay on the ballerina, preclude the description of his mode of discourse as non-referential cannot be taken as decisive given the nature of the debate (in fact, in some senses his views are not so far from those of Joyce). Nor does the fact on its own that there is a powerful narrative dynamic in Grass's novel automatically exclude him from the school of such Modernism, since it is almost as hard to imagine language without narrative as it is to imagine it without pronouns. But there are nevertheless two factors which, when taken in combination, speak unanswerably against the identification of Grass's writing with extreme deconstructive Modernism. First, the overpowering presence of an historical and geographical referent, Danzig and then Düsseldorf, before during and after the Second World War, and secondly, the unmistakable moral commitment which speaks through the aesthetic configuration in a way we are here seeking to understand. The range of effects created by Oskar's detachment from what he sees (or, if one wishes, from what is seen through him) goes from irony to the grotesque, but undeniably it passes through satire on the way (Thomas, 1985), and it is hard to imagine genuine satire without moral involvement on the part of the satirist. These two factors are intimately linked, since it is the nature of what happened in those places at those times which generate – indeed, demand – the moral involvement manifest in and through the aesthetic reality, the undeniable literary fact, of the novel.

Let us therefore try to formulate a type of relation between the aesthetic and the moral, between Grass and Oskar which is not open to the objections we have outlined, and which meets the perceived fact and experience of his writing. Perhaps the most effective way of doing this is to relinquish the strict dissociation between them, with which we have been working hitherto. When you think about it, Grass and Oskar do have much in common, and I don't mean by this merely the shared autobiographical background. What they have in common is a fact we have recognised from the start, namely that they are both authors. But more than this, they are a peculiar sort of author, combining some of the qualities of the post- and pre-Enlightenment models of authorship which we have briefly rehearsed. On the one hand, in the manner of the Artist, they tell their own stories, but on the other, their work is a performance, a rhythm of repetition and variation. Oskar both tells his own story discursively and 'drums' it, Grass tells Oskar's story, and through it that of an historical period, and 'performs' it by means of the linguistic and thematic devices we have been talking about, in the litany of recapitulations which animates his style.

But, the reader will object, Oskar is a liar and self-deceiver, how can he be in any sense at all cognate with the empirical Grass? The answer may be that Oskar's dissembling, his chief characteristic, is not to be taken as a swerving away from the truth, but as a particular instance of properties which condition all utterances, regardless of the truthful intention or otherwise of the speaker. His irony must be seen as 'a paradigm for all utterance: I can appropriate meaning to my own purposes only by ventriloquizing' (Clark and Holquist, 1984, p. 15). This view of the nature of language would provide a theoretical context for the reader's immediate sense that, although the novel is all about lies, language is nevertheless being made to work: that is to say is *not* evading moral responsibility. Language and literature are always performance, taking place in the real world in a specific context, implicating not only what is being spoken about, but, at every turn, also the person who is speaking. Our linguistic activity, our appropriation or ventriloquising of meaning, is the means by which we answer for 'our own particularity in the face of everything else' (Clark and Holquist, 1984, p. 64). Language and literature are parallel and intrinsically moral activities, since both are a matter of authorship, of the self and of the text, and this authorship – here we are close to Sartrean Existentialism – produces my ethical identity: 'ethics is not abstract principles but the pattern of actual deeds [including linguistic ones] I perform in the event that is my life' (Clark and Holquist, 1984, p. 64).

Thus, the comment with which we started out that Oskar is obviously an artificial construct and not a character in the traditional Realist sense, loses its force as an argument against associating Grass with his creation. Nobody is a character in the traditional Realist sense, if that is taken to imply an unchanging, irreducible essence of personality, the humanist, secular version of a soul. The self is not a substance or essence, but exists 'only in a tensile relationship with all that is other and, most important, with other selves' (Clark and Holquist, 1984, p. 65). Near the end of the *Tin Drum* Oskar tries to console himself in the face of existential terror with thoughts of 'alle die da meine fragwürdige Existenz einrahmten, die da an meiner Existenz scheiter- ten' (all those who had framed my questionable existence, those who had come to grief on the shoal of my existence: p. 709/578). Selves condition, realise, curtail each other, they are in process together, 'never convergent but always reciprocal' (Clark and Holquist, 1984, p. 64). Ethical activity is the fashioning of a coherent performance of the relation between self and other, in other words: authorship.

These reflections are drawn not only from French Existentialism, to which Grass was undoubtedly exposed, writing in the Paris of the fifties, but from a cognate body of thought with which Grass was probably not familiar, but which in a number of ways is closer to his own view than Existentialism, namely that of M. M. Bakhtin (1895–1975). Although Bakhtin wrote in some obscurity in Stalin's Soviet Union and has only subsequently acquired a reputation among western theorists, his work is relevant to that of Grass because it addresses in theoretical terms the – historical – issues Grass confronts in literary practice. Bakhtin wrestled throughout his life with ways of reconciling precisely the three models of authorship with which we have been briefly concerned here. He combines an unquestioned commitment to the aesthetic and spiritual qualities of language, and thus to the question of literature as art, with the attempt to come to terms with post-Saussurean linguistics, that is to say language as a system of arbitrary differences, as well as with the investigation of pre-bourgeois humanist models of authorship – Menippean satire, Rabelais – with an eye to their relevance for literature in a post-bourgeois context (i.e. the Marxist Soviet Union), without sacrificing all the values of bourgeois literature or the value of its greatest productions.

Bakhtin is best known for certain central ideas which have become major contributions to the language of literary criticism and theory. Most prominent amongst them is the notion of the carnivalesque, elaborated in a book on Rabelais, published in 1965 and going back to a dissertation of 1940. The carnivalesque offers the most obvious link between Grass and Bakhtin. In carnival Bakhtin identifies a social institution which offers an alternative time and place to the official institutions of dominant ideology. In the Middle Ages the great periods of carnival were spaces in which the serious feudal and ecclesiastical culture were contradicted. Carnival, in short, is a word for forms of non-official expression of uncentralised communal experience. In this sense

Oskar's famous drumming feat beneath the rostrum at the Nazi rally is an archetypally carnivalesque performance, in that it converts an official congregation, shaped and informed by an ideology on the way to very comprehensive dominance, into a shared experience of music with no significance beyond the pleasure of the moment and the physical delight of the dance. 'Gesetz ging flöten und Ordnungssinn' (Gone were law and order. – p. 139/117). The relevance of Bakhtin at this point is underscored when one remembers that he formulated his notion of carnival in tacit opposition to another form of mid-twentieth-century totalitarianism – Stalinism.

It is very important that Oskar's subversive act is not itself ideological. This is one of the many morally difficult or recalcitrant passages in the novel. One wishes to impose a sense upon the episode that Oskar is mounting opposition specifically to Nazism, but the text refuses this: 'Nein, nein, Oskar war kein Prophet, Hunger verspürte er!' (But Oskar was no prophet, he was beginning to feel hungry! – p. 140/118). What is being opposed to Nazism is simply Oskar's irreducible physical being: his pleasure, his drumming, his melody. Physicality is a dimension of the Bakhtinian carnivalesque. In carnival the body is liberated from the ideological constraints which normally define and regulate it, restored to its immediacy, but deprived of its high cultural dignity. Emphasis falls upon its orifices and apertures. The literature of carnival is a literature of physicality, eating, drinking, defecation and sex, of grotesque realism. Here too, of course, we recognise a specific characteristic of Grass's work. The body is present not in its classical integrity, but as a site of events and changes, signalling its openness to the flux of the material world. Herbert Truzcinski's back is an anthology of the knife wounds it has sustained; Korneff's boils ripen and burst prodigiously with Oskar's help; Oskar's growth is first arrested then distorted in the form of a hump; Oskar forms an idolatrous attachment to a severed finger. Eating is perhaps the most significant of the motifs focusing the interchange between body and world: Matzerath is an obsessive and perfectionist cook; Oskar is forced to eat some revolting soup; his mother stuffs herself to death on fish, as a response to the eating of a horse's head by eels and the cycle of rapacious sexual appetite which it recapitulates: 'Und aus lauter Liebe nannten sie einander Radieschen, liebten Radieschen, bissen sich, ein Radieschen biß dem anderen das Radieschen aus Liebe ab' (And from sheer love they called each other radishes, they loved radishes, they bit into each other, out of sheer love one radish bit off another's radish. – p. 237/198). Yet food for Grass (famously a passionate cook) is not merely a vanity motif: it is also a sign of the accommodation of man to the physical world, its preparation, a model for art itself:

> Es ist uns zur Selbstverständlichkeit geworden, ein Stück Hammel nicht
> in rohem, noch blutigem Zustand barbarisch zu verschlingen. Nein, wir
> braten, kochen and dünsten es, tun immer noch ein Gewürz in den
> Topf, nennen es am Ende gar und schmackhaft ... so sollte nun endlich

den anderen Künsten dieselbe Ehre wie der Kochkunst zuteil werden. (We would never think of barbarously devouring a piece of mutton in its raw and still bloody state. Certainly not, we roast, boil and steam it, we add another spice to the pot, and pronounce the dish finally cooked and tasty ... Should we not now accord the other arts the honour we accord the art of cooking? – Grass, 1963, pp. 13–14).

These points of convergence between Grass's practice and Bakhtin's theory are made in support of the general case that the latter can be held to be relevant to the former. They do not yet in themselves help us with our specific question about the relation of morality to aesthetics in *Die Blechtrommel*. But we have already addressed it in the Bakhtinian concept of self-authorship, which now needs to be taken in the context of two further basic aspects of Bakhtin's thought, in which his more celebrated treatments of Rabelais and Dostoevsky are grounded. This will, I think, establish a strong enough parallel with Grass to serve our purpose here. First, the fact that both authors have a positive view of a world without absolutes. The specific mix of (approval of) enormous narrative vitality and the absence of metaphysical consolation links them: food is the triumph of life over death, however temporary it may be. In this Grass can be seen to be closer to Bakhtin than to Sartre, since the former affirms as alterity what for the latter, as for Marx is alienation (Clark and Holquist, 1984). The second is precisely this idea of the positive value of alterity, namely the concept of *dialogue*, of the mutuality of all utterance, the idea not that 'I own meaning' or that 'no-one owns meaning' but that 'we own meaning' (Clark and Holquist, 1984, pp. 11–12). The inevitably performative aspect of utterance, its specific, concrete location in the material world, a given time and place, might seem on a certain view to make truth unattainable and communication impossible. This would approximate to the sort of reading of Grass which sees in him a nihilist or cynic. But Bakhtin stresses instead the implication that every linguistic act will always be (at least) two-sided, 'a territory *shared* by both addresser and addressee' (Clark and Holquist, 1984, p. 15). The absence of absolutes is compensated for by the dialogue of co-existing differences, a field of unfinalisable heterogeneity which offers a necessary, powerful and intensely productive alternative to the finalised and centralised discourses of official ideology. It is in these 'pre-located' discourses that one would normally look for the systematic ethics we find missing in the author-persona Grass–Oskar. In the absence of the certainty of fathers there is no option but to author oneself, and to author oneself is always inevitably to be in relation to others. Bakhtin supplies the theoretical vocabulary with which to talk positively about a discourse other than the finalised discourse of the fathers, without thereby foregoing moral coherence.

The first page of *Die Blechtrommel*, as is always noted, undermines the truth value of everything Oskar is going to say by locating him in an insane asylum, and having him identify himself as an inveterate liar. It is less often noted that it also situates Oskar's performance throughout the 700 pages to follow as a dialogue in the Bakhtinian sense. Oskar has a nurse, Bruno, to whom he tells his autobiography: 'Der Gute scheint meine Erzählungen zu schätzen, denn sobald ich ihm etwas vorgelogen habe, zeigt er mir, um sich erkenntlich zu geben, sein neuestes Knotengebilde' (He seems to treasure my stories, because every time I tell him some fairy tale, he shows his gratitude by bringing out his latest knot construction. – p. 9/11). Bruno makes figures out of pipe-cleaners, in terms of which he *answers* the performance of his charge. Performance answers performance, neither with a claim to truth, but both in relation to one another, a mutual validation which is independent of the truth content or otherwise of the representations involved. This relationship is at once curious, anomalous, gratuitously eccentric and – one intuitively feels – representative of the way the text constructs itself and its relation to others. It only becomes fully meaningful in the Bakhtinian context. That there is no categorical difference between ordinary human subjects and Artists, authors both, is satirically conveyed in the words which directly follow those just quoted: 'Ob er ein Künstler ist, bleibe dahingestellt' (I wouldn't swear that he is an artist). Similarly, one of the most powerful and moving scenes in the often criticised later part of the book concerns the dialogue in performance which happens between Oskar and his fellow-lodger, the magnificently squalid Klepp. Oskar is moved to take up his drum again for the first time after the post-war hiatus in his playing, which has represented his tragic and pathetic attempt to become an adult. He drums his life story for Klepp, only to register with a shock of recognition that Klepp has picked up a flute and is playing Oskar's autobiography too:

> und Oskars Herz drohte zum Stein zu werden, als ich vernahm, wie aus Klepps Flöte der Oktoberregen rieselte, wie Klepps Flöte unter Regen und vier Röcken meinen Großvater, den Brandstifter Josef Koljaiczek aufspürte und wie dieselbe Flöte die Zeugung meiner armen Mama feierte und bewies.
>
> (and Oskar's heart nearly turned to stone when I heard the October rain trickling from Klepp's flute, when, beneath the rain and the four skirts, Klepp's flute discovered Joseph Koljaiczek the firebug and celebrated, nay represented, the begetting of my poor mama. – p. 612/499)

Again, a curious and yet characteristic moment, this time one in which two distinct selves come together within a single performance. The experience is a regenerative one for both participants, and in agreeing to form a jazz band on the strength of it, the two musicians demonstrate their allegiance to an institution – jazz – which provides a theoretical structure for a coexistence of simultaneous differences, for a performance at once unifying but not homogenising, a mingling of free subjectivities. It is no surprise that this resolve is soon undermined by the centripetal tendencies of the dominant market ideology of post-war Germany …

Even so, taking the broad view, Oskar is not an example to be emulated. One factor above all others stands in the way of identifying him unproblematically with the Bakhtinian model in which irreducible particularity is affirmed as the ground of dialogue, and the world is grasped in the never-ending process of mediation between non-convergent differences. This factor is Oskar's guilt. This is all the more damaging to our argument in view of the circumstance that the guilt is associated with the very dissembling which we have tried to see in a positive light. Oskar feels guilty because, far from taking on the moral responsibility for his uniqueness in the face of everything else, he uses it to distance himself from everything else (Thomas, 1985). He remains a 3-year-old, arrested at a narcissistic stage on the very threshold of socialisation, precisely in order to avoid any such involvement. It is only the lure of the drumsticks which stops him from returning to the womb once and for all, which is what he nevertheless spends the space of 700 pages wishing he could do. He displays a veritable longing for the inwardness (witness his fascination with cupboards and other restricted interiors) denied him by the novel's commitment to surfaces and the visual. Moreover, rather than affirming the fatherlessness of his situation, he wishes fervently both to identify his father, and to identify himself as a father. In so far as he does affirm the state, in the sense of setting himself up as a double parricide (one of the rarest crimes imaginable!), it is only, again, in association with extreme feelings of guilt.

I should not have spent so much time adducing the Bakhtinian model of the relation between aesthetics and ethics, however, had I actually felt it to be so little relevant. We need to return one last time to the relation between Grass and Oskar, and reinstate a distinction between them, only this time with the benefit of the Bakhtinian model. Oskar is a Bakhtinian in reverse. He wishes not to affirm the nature of the world as Bakhtin sees it, but to deny it. He wants to opt out of answerability. However, since the world as we are persuaded to see it by the novel demands this answerability, Oskar inevitably fails. As John Reddick showed in his classic study of Grass's Danzig Trilogy, Oskar's attempt to be detached leads only to a tragic and terrifying isolation (Reddick, 1975, pp. 63–82). By his very efforts to be uninvolved, Oskar points up the dialogic nature of human existence. This, of course, makes of the performance of the Grass author-persona, the text as a whole, by inversion, a positive one, since it makes this significant failure visible, by 'performing' it. This is not to say that Grass is free of the guilt which Oskar feels, nor that Oskar is without the capacity for positive performance that Grass displays. The parallel between them for which I wish to argue, holds. It is a matter of the distribution of emphasis. As for Oskar's ability to perform actively despite his basic desire to disappear into the sub-social 'sweetness' of his hospital bed, his disruption of the Nazi rally is counter-example enough. But what of Grass's guilt? The answer is that this guilt is identifiable, in a post-Freudian world, with the mother fixation. In the case of Oskar this is satirically explicit enough (to opt out of the world – to want to return to the womb); in Grass's case we could deduce it from the general principle (in the same way that we must assume that Grass is subject to the world Oskar represents, if we wish to respect the text's authority), even if Grass had not himself talked about his mother complex in interviews. The point about the root nature of this guilt is not its reality or its unanswerable pervasiveness, it is its absolute obviousness. It is Romantic art which reveals the mother as the ultimate secret. For Grass it is inalienably a determinant both of his personality and of his great artistic, imaginative, imaginary gift (Grass, 1979). Oskar's drum, we recall, is a gift from his mother. It both separates him from, and connects him with, the world. So it is too with Grass's text. This is the paradox of this performance in writing: it is life-affirming and life-denying at the same time. In Thomas Mann this was the central theme. In Grass, it is a circumstance, a fact of life among others.

This chiastic symmetry between Oskar and Grass can be couched in terms of subjectivity and history. For Oskar, the mother fixation is positive, but the source of (almost) overwhelming anguish, whilst the events of the day are simply expressions of the eternal undifferentiated cycle of (masculine) violence, betrayal and ideologically-inspired cruelty. The subjective view predominates, the historical one shades off into myth, an imaginary appropriation of the world. For Grass the opposite is the case. For him (and he shares with Bakhtin the opinion that psychoanalysis is short of a vital social-political dimension), the mother fixation is simply a condition of subjectivity and not further remarkable, while the events of the day, and especially, of course, the inescapable moral issues they generate for him and his readers, in the acts, the performances, of reading and writing, are what matter. History predominates over subjectivity.

But history cannot do *without* subjectivity nor vice versa. Grass and Oskar complement each other in their different emphases. The simultaneous differences, which are brought into relation within the specific textual constitution of the *Tin Drum* are: subjectivity and history. Seen from the subject, history is always the same, cyclically meaningless. Seen from history, the subject is irreducibly particular. The individual on his own is a banal phenomenon, whose whole secret is the desire for the return to the womb balanced in lifelong contradiction with the terror of extinction which that would entail. But history, the single monumental historical narrative, is similarly banal in its centripetal homogenisation of the infinity of selves which constitute the actual space of reality. It is only in relation, in dialogue with each other, that either makes sense. To produce this dialogue is both the aesthetic and the moral triumph of the *Tin Drum*.

REFERENCES

Page references for quotations from Grass's novel are identified in the text by two page numbers separated by an oblique stroke. The first of these refers to the German first edition, *Die Blechtrommel*, Darmstadt and Neuwied: Luchterhand 1959, and the second to the English translation by Ralph Manheim, *The Tin Drum*, Harmondsworth: Penguin Books 1965.

CLARK, K. and HOLQUIST, M. (1984), *Mikhail Bakhtin*, Cambridge, Mass.: The Belknap Press of Harvard University Press.

GRASS, G. (1963), *Die Ballerina*, Berlin: Freidenaur Presse.

GRASS, G. (1979), Am liebsten lüge ich gedruckt, *Der Spiegel*, 2 April 1979, pp. 219–25.

MÜLLER-ECKHARD, E. (1959), *Kölnische Rundschau*, 3 December 1959.

REDDICK, J. (1975), *The 'Danzig Trilogy' of Günter Grass*, London: Secker & Warburg.

STERN, J P. (1987), Günter Grass's uniqueness, in Patrick O'Neill (ed.), *Critical Essays on Günter Grass*, Boston, Mass.: G. K. Hall.

THOMAS, N. (1985), *Grass: Die Blechtrommel*, London: Grant & Cutler.

WEBER, A. (1991), 'Günter Grass's use of baroque literature', unpublished Ph.D. dissertation, Cambridge.

A Dialogic Reality
Uwe Johnson, *Mutmaßungen über Jakob*

MARY E. STEWART

Uwe Johnson – a writer still much less well known in this country than he deserves – was born in 1934 in Cammin, Pommerania, and grew up in Mecklenburg which of course then became part of the German Democratic Republic. He studied in Rostock and Leipzig and began to write narrative prose, but to achieve publication he was forced to move to West Berlin in 1959. In that year his remarkable novel *Mutmaßungen über Jakob* (Speculations about Jakob) first appeared, dealing with some of the emotional and political pressures facing the individual in East Germany, yet seeing also the falsity of construing the East–West divide as a confrontation between evil and good. Thus Johnson began a literary career which made him for a long time *the* writer on divided Germany, and also earned his prose the reputation of being complex and difficult.

His writing was to include several further novels and short prose pieces, all of them rooted in his home country and its problematic history, past and present *Das dritte Buch über Achim* (The Third Book about Achim, 1961), for example, concerns the profound problems facing a West German journalist attempting a biographical portrait of a famous East German cyclist; *Zwei Ansichten* (Two Views, 1965) tells a wry kind of Romeo and Juliet story across the Berlin Wall. Although Johnson subsequently spent several years living in America and later England, his writing continued to focus largely on Germany. His major work, the tetralogy *Jahrestage* (Anniversaries), which was published at widely spaced intervals over the years 1970 to 1983, is an extraordinary virtuoso interweaving of multiple narrative planes. Its title points to 'anniversaries' of violence and protest, hope and struggle, linking Germany past and present and the USA in a panoramic view of culture, politics, history, time, innocence and experience, fact and fiction. The last period of Johnson's life was spent in virtual seclusion at Sheerness on the Isle of Sheppey, where he died in February 1984; its flat, watery openness perhaps reminded him of Mecklenburg, for he never lost traces of its dialect in his language, and figures from his 'homeland' people his work from beginning to end with extraordinary vitality and authenticity.

In fact one of the 'odd' things about Johnson's work is that figures from his first published novel, *Mutmaßungen über Jakob*, are taken up and followed further in something one tends to find in lower-grade 'blockbuster' writing in response to popular requests for sequels, and which is thus more characteristic of the simplest kind of Realist writing than of the serious Modernist novel. In Johnson's case, however, it is evidence of a central quality of his writing – a very profound and positive belief in humanity: not a facile optimism, but a deep respect for those who attempt to retain some kind of integrity, though of course he also thereby raises many questions about fictionality. In many ways in his writing Johnson challenges all blinkered thinking about how we construe 'identity', and not least in the way he mixes what may seem to be on the surface naïve 'belief' in his figures with a highly artificed mode of narration. Yet his loyalty to his characters certainly has none of the more cynical playfulness of a Günter Grass, whose Oskar Mazerath reappears in *Die Rättin* (The Rat) as a video-dealer. Johnson lacks Grass's humorous voice, but compensates for lacking that kind of reader-appeal with an ability to produce moments of challenging, involving, memorable plasticity within a narrative complexity which indeed frustrates naïve reading, yet rewards critical engagement with great breadth and seriousness.

There is no doubt that reading *Mutmaßungen über Jakob* for the first time is a bewildering experience. It presents a seemingly unshaped montage of various narrative forms: dialogues take place between initially unnamed and unplaced speakers, and are intermixed with monologic first-person sections, again from unnamed speakers. Interspersed amongst this diversity there are also sections of apparently traditional third-person narration, from an unlocated narrative voice. It is no surprise, perhaps, that soon after the publication of the novel a rash of 'keys' and chronologies to the work appeared, trying to disentangle who said what and when! And critics have made a bewildering range of attempts to place the novel. Some talk blandly but unhelpfully about 'existential confusion', 'the complexity of modern life', but this text does not offer us the kind of city montage – including much extraneous material – that we find in Döblin's *Berlin Alexanderplatz*, for instance: in that sense it represents far less 'confusion'. Other critics again, seeing that the novel does indeed deal with the East–West divide in Germany, insist on fixing it in the purely political plane, interpreting it as some kind of judgement on the relative merits of the two systems. Admittedly, there is some truth in both critical extremes, but both miss a lot of the novel's specificity. To point, as many critics have, to similarities between William Faulkner and Johnson, merely emphasises a general sense of 'sound and fury'. Equally, if one's prime concern is – like Popp's (1967) – to disentangle all the textual layers or techniques, to recover the 'story' in every detail, one is implicitly suggesting that Johnson has somehow unnecessarily jumbled up what might have been more simply told. The aim of this chapter is to show the complex modes of narration as an essential and positive aspect of the text, generating rather than obscuring possibilities of meaning – which include both the specific/political and the 'existential' – and working creatively, rather than obstructively on the reader.

For readers unfamiliar with this complex work it is nevertheless perhaps helpful as a starting-point to have a brief outline of the events over which it plays. It focuses on the life and death of Jakob Abs, a dispatcher for the East German Railway: that is, someone who oversees part of the network and ensures trains slot in as they should. A Stasi (State Security) official – Rohlfs – puts pressure on Jakob to enlist the services of Gesine Cresspahl, a childhood friend from Jerichow in Mecklenburg. It was with her and her carpenter father that Jakob and his mother lived as wartime refugees from further East, though in the meantime Gesine has left for the West and is working for NATO in West Berlin. With Rohlfs' intervention a phase of disruption begins to affect many lives; Jakob's mother is frightened at being asked about Gesine and flees West – a refugee once again. Jakob, already serving the state with his quiet, efficient work ethic, resists Rohlfs' approaches. But Gesine suddenly turns up in the East to see Jakob, upset and confused by news of the 1956 Hungarian uprising, and together they go under cover of night to their shared childhood home, Gesine's father's house in Jerichow – all the while, of course, under observation by Rohlfs. In Jerichow matters are complicated by the fortuitous presence of Jonas, an East German academic attracted to Gesine. Jakob argues his position with Rohlfs and manages to extract a free passage for Gesine back to the West. Later he visits her there, and is in his turn 'confused' by the West's attack on Suez. On his return to work he is killed crossing a railway line, and the speculations of the title begin. Those most closely associated with Jakob reflect on him, events and themselves, trying to elucidate what has happened, since it is hard to accept that a man with Jakob's experience and practical acumen has 'simply' met with an accident. This is, it must be emphasised, only the very barest outline of what the Russian formalists called the *fabula*, the raw material, which any attentive reader can glean. What matters is just *how* these events are mediated to us – the significance of the various narrative modes in themselves and of the way in which they are interwoven.

How then are we to make sense of its structure? At first reading the novel certainly does have a kind of superficial 'whodunnit' appeal. At one level it is the basic hermeneutic code which holds the whole together, that familiar logic of question and answer, enigma and solution which is part of everyone's reading experience; in Johnson's text the various and rapid changes of perspective create expectations of clarification to come, tempt one to try to piece a 'story' together. The repeated interruption of one narrative thread by another voice provokes the question, 'Just what did happen?' by continually depriving us of unbroken narration and seeming to defer the 'truth', as popular detective fiction does by omitting or masking essential facts. Yet no answer is provided at this level, no final 'truth' is offered beyond what one can guess from the very first page, the fact of Jakob's death; moreover, if one insists on playing the role of the naïve reader, the consumer of nicely-resolved traditional plots, then what one can recuperate from this text in terms of 'story' – as in my summary above – seems perilously close to banality. One is left with at best a run-of-the-mill pseudo-political thriller, at worst a weak variant of Socialist Realism's concern with the dignity of the working man. Either conclusion mocks the reader's self-congratulatory cleverness at 'piecing things together'.

What other interpretative approach might one then apply? Do we perhaps, after all, have yet another instance of textual complexity derived from and in a general way reflecting that of modern life itself? Might we take Johnson's text as a variation on the now common device of the unreliable narrator? If we try to apply this kind of model as a meta-language to explain the novel's specific form, then again there are surprises or disappointments in store, because on careful reading its 'confusion' is emphatically not that of texts which seek to reflect a world grown totally unreadable. Johnson's text is far from resistant to organisation in that sense; it eventually resolves itself into a structure of separate and identifiable narrators and speakers. Nor, moreover, does it contain only highly subjective accounts, mimetically reproducing purely individual comment. As well as dialogues and monologues there are, as already indicated, also occasional passages of third-person narrative which are not easy to ascribe to any of the identifiable narrators. They seem, rather, to be produced by a quite traditional 'observational' – if not more broadly authoritative – narrator, and thus to pull in quite another direction from the other 'voices', towards a simpler, consensus view of reality. To cite just one example from many, Jakob is here described at work, as Jonas enters and finds him busily in communication with the other dispatchers:

> Jakob hob die rechte Hand über die Schulter, ohne sich umzuwenden; diese Bewegung hatte etwas sehr Gefälliges und Höfliches in sich und Jonas sah daß es hier nicht auf den Händedruck ankam. [...] Jakob saß ergeben gegen die biegsame Lehne seines Drehstuhls gestützt mit den Händen im Schoß und führte seine Gespräche als sei er auf der Treppe eines Mietshauses angehalten worden und lasse sich die Neuigkeiten eines fremden Tages erzählen ohne Interesse ohne Ungeduld, hier saß er nun einmal.

> (Jakob raised his right hand over his shoulder without turning round; this gesture had something very obliging and polite about it and Jonas saw that actually shaking hands was unimportant here. [...] Jakob was leaning – quietly concentrated – against the flexible back of his chair with his hands in his lap and was carrying on his conversations as though he had been stopped on the staircase of a tenement, and was

letting someone tell him all about their day, without interest or
impatience, he was simply sitting there. – p. 234)

There is not a trace of undermining irony or self-consciousness in any of
these passages; they seem indeed to be careful but also very straightforward –
that is, not somehow ideologically angled – descriptive narrations, and if this
one might just conceivably be construed as reality viewed essentially from
Jonas's perspective, then others cannot be so assigned. Perhaps their function
might be seen as to provide some kind of basic authorial guidance and linkage,
but such a view is hard to maintain in the end. This unidentified narrative
voice clearly lacks – or refuses to assume – the traditional narrator's ability to
co-ordinate material, in this case to assign all the monologues and dialogues to
specific speakers. As Riordan (1989) has shown, there are problems over
defining just how far the narrator's insight reaches and some arguments for
talking of his potential omniscience. However, that debate is more important
in relation to Johnson's subsequent development as a writer; what matters for
the reader here is the effect of being made to experience a sense of confusion
and disorientation. Even these straightforward scenic sections are very limited.

In fact when one looks more closely, these apparently simple passages have
a very fine balance. The descriptions of Jakob are never expanded in detail and
mass to the point where their vividness or weight, their 'presence', becomes so
striking as to indicate a particular, definable view of reality such as one finds
in a Balzac or a Sartre, for instance, with their programmatic foregrounding of
amassed detail. Nor do these brief sections of narrative really advance the
'plot' in any obvious way: they are more like silent moments of camera stillness
in film, giving momentary respite between more active scenes so as not to
over-tax our concentration. In that sense they also perhaps help to establish a
narrative contract between text and reader; that is, they help to engage us, to
persuade us to take the novel's world seriously. Yet that cannot be their prime
function, because it is more fully and sustainedly achieved by the use of
subjective voices that are ultimately identifiable: they are the reader's strongest
guarantee of some kind of *vraisemblance*. So these sections, in their immediacy
and plasticity, seem to be no more and no less than the simplest kind of 'sign'
of the existence of a tangible world and Jakob's one-time presence in it.

The text does not, then, allow us simply to class it as 'existential confusion',
as reflecting a totally fragmented world, for it contains at least some diegetic
passages which cannot easily be assigned to individual speakers. Yet we
cannot, on the other hand, use these as some kind of firm grounding for
interpretation, as the reliable guide to some kind of 'meaning' that they might
seem to offer in a traditional Realist text; they are too limited for that. In a
sense what they do most obviously is draw our attention to the internal
'movement' of the text, to the difference of its other parts. The fascinating
thing is that Jakob who is almost always the focus of these passages – is also
seen in a very different way by the end of the novel, or rather during the
process of one's reading, since the 'story' is not revealed strictly chronologi-

cally. We know as simple fact that Jakob has died, but we do not know how he came to die, let alone know how to begin evaluating his death; in other words, a simple realism seems ultimately quite inadequate to encompass him. Or, to put it slightly differently, at one level the novel seems to inhabit a world where there is no strain between signifier and signified, between act and meaning, and this is reflected in the apparent artlessness of such passages as that quoted above, as in the ability of other narrators, notably Jonas, to talk of Jakob in terms of simile: 'wie eine Katze, so unbedenklich' (like a cat, so unself-conscious: p. 75). Yet by the end of the novel this unity of signifier and signified seems to have been lost. Jakob's life, pre-eminently one in which he seems to 'fill' his context, to be at ease, to have a strong presence for others, is terminated in a way which is utterly pointless and wasteful. He does not even die trying to do anything specific, other than go from A to B. What is more, his end comes in the context that he apparently knew best – another kind of divorce between act and meaning, and evident directly perhaps in the mist that enveloped that 'known', rendered it literally alien. And that mist exists for us as readers too; for us, as for Jakob, recognisable 'signs' are obliterated, we do not know what to make of the death. So where one could speak earlier of Jakob's accessibility to simple realism and simile, now – at the end of our reading – he has become in a sense 'metaphorical'. We cannot say 'Jakob's death means …' or 'Jakob's death is like …'; we can only conjure up, as it were, free-floating speculations, play with ideas associatively, or else echo what are significantly the very first and almost the last words of the novel – a kind of helpless, circular repetition, 'aber Jakob ist immer quer über die Gleise gegangen …' (but Jakob always went diagonally across the lines: pp. 7 and 304).

This movement within the novel from simile to metaphor, from a sense of physically grounded reality mediated through diegesis to subjectively focalised speculation, raises many and varied problems; issues of politics, identity and cognition are all implicated in it and constantly intertwined. If we take the political level first, we might say that it clearly represents the ultimate impossibility of maintaining a 'realist' position – 'this is the way things are' – and thus of choosing in any clear-cut, simple way between East and West. Jakob is not allowed to preserve his political 'innocence', his preference for being and doing over thinking; the mist in which he dies is also a metaphorical political mist in which he and we already flounder. Significantly, perhaps, we have no way of knowing whether the train that hits him comes from East or West, and this symbolic indication of the confused East–West divide is also referentially underpinned by the knowledge we glean in passing of broken families. For those travelling in both directions the trains could be said to bring together and to divide.

There are, however, perhaps more profound issues raised by the movement from simile to metaphor, questions of how reality is experienced in a broader sense, though politics are never lost sight of, as we shall see. Jakob is clearly experienceable: Gesine, Jonas and Rohlfs all react strongly to him, as does the reader, responding to the continuing appeal of well-handled description. Yet Jakob is finally also beyond all interpretation. Each speaker has a different way of grasping him, but by that very token no-one has a full understanding. Jakob exists very palpably, 'realistically', in the sections of diegesis, beyond and in a different way from all that can be said about him in mediated, personalised discourse, and even in a sense beyond diegetic narration, for we are given only glimpses and not from an omniscient narrator – this is clearly a very partial image of him. Yet if all that these various, individually inadequate cross-bearings on Jakob finally add up to is a general statement on the unfathomable nature of human individuality, then it has all been said before and more inventively by earlier authors, such as Joyce. Certainly Johnson does indeed show that individual life is a complex combination of realities and perspectives. However, the 'speculations' about Jakob which form so much of the text are *not* concerned with such existential issues, with trying to fathom what might be the totality or scope of Jakob's inner self, his identity in that sense. The focus seems rather to be on his (literal and figurative) *Beweggründe*, what moves him to public action and motivates him, the relationship between self and world as he lived it.

Jakob embodies initially a relatively direct and straightforward relationship between self and context. Aware, of course, of the problems of everyday life in the communist system, he copes by preserving a conscientious, practical personal efficiency. The loss of this directness has more than just factual political significance, though it does offer historically accurate detail of how the Stasi invaded private lives. Jakob is made by Rohlfs' pressure to think more about his relationship to the state, about freedom, duty and choice. His previous cat-like self-possession is made 'knowing' from the minute he signs the first document, pledging to reveal nothing of his contact and conversations with Rohlfs. Having grown up under the Nazis, Jakob's stance hitherto has been not to try to 'read' the world; he tries to maintain this during the Hungarian uprising when he refuses – unlike some colleagues to hold up troop movements and make 'symbolic' gestures. His way is to act 'literally', hence his accessibility to traditional diegesis. But Jakob is forced by Rohlfs' ideological demands into a more complex and problematic relationship with his world, and one that becomes more confusing and disorienting still when he visits Gesine in the West. Two events are important: the Suez invasion takes place, and he also hears old Nazi songs being sung in a bar. While he might perhaps have expected to meet Capitalism as the alternative political ideology, its similarity at that moment to Communism in terms of external aggression renders any notion of 'alternative' patently absurd. Furthermore, what he finds in the bar suggests not a different and competing world view, but an apparent insensitivity to implied values and meanings – not artlessness, but carelessness. Whether his death is then accidental or intentional, its striking enactment of 'disorientation' serves as a metaphor for loss of personal direction, of any possibility of achieving a secure sense of identity from the integration of self and social context. In fact, precisely this problem of self-understanding and self-definition is reflected in all the other main characters too, as much in the manner of their presentation as in what they say.

All of them are in some sense isolated, cut off from any sense of secure context. Their differing reactions to Jakob draw attention to their essential separateness as beings, but such 'existential' isolation is not really foregrounded, so much as the disharmonious relationship with their specific individual backgrounds, which seems to condition the nature of their experience. To take Gesine, for example: her monologues are characterised by frequent imaginative returns to childhood, and her view of Jakob is coloured by her own problems in relating. She seems to have no real roots in East or West – reflected in her americanised German – and is in some senses the archetypal exile. Her own unfulfilled need to belong somewhere perhaps underlies her stress on intense, enveloping experience: 'ich liebe dich wie den Regen' (I love you like the rain: p. 220) is one expression of her love for Jakob, as of the longing for a sense of immediacy which Jonas cannot provide. Such intensity accords value to personal emotion, and it is noticeable that it is often Gesine's voice which will intervene in another passage of narration with some telling, personal detail which brings a figure alive. Yet this reliance on feeling is also wilful and blind, can paralyse and isolate. Reality for Gesine seems to be what engages her fully and spontaneously, but her sense of self is thus at best mood-dependent, at worst dangerously naïve. She seems, for instance, unaware of the extent to which she has already absorbed Western values, uncritically. She is 'free' politically, but not truly autonomous, always affected by wider historical forces which she resents, but which pervade her life nevertheless, their effects the more insidious for being denied or displaced into emotional volatility.

In Jonas's case the monologues are conspicuous by their frequency, as though he finds musing easier than communication. Indeed, our first glimpse of him is as a train passenger, aimlessly occupied by thoughts and observations. His near-lethargy reflects a rather more cynical view of context than Gesine's emotional attitude; through him we are given a dissection of academic purposiveness as no more than arbitrary attribution of significance to activity. Several times in the novel we glimpse him writing, which is symptomatic of his distance from active, involved existence: even the Cresspahl cat has the power to dominate him! Jonas is a man who has lost all faith in Communism, that is, in ideology as a single source of meaning, but he is both too cerebral and too cynical to try Gesine's attempted path of personal intensity. Not surprisingly it is he who muses specifically on the emptiness of terms such as 'freedom': 'You can't resign from physics', he says (p. 135). In other words, neither the meta-language of politics nor a self-centred world view has any validity for him, leaving him in a limbo of pointlessness and indecision.

For Rohlfs, on the other hand, experience *is* ideology, anchored in a structure that gives it determinate meaning. He recognises other codes, can quote from Mörike and understand the yearning for emotional intensity, but he puts the wider context above the personal, derives the value of the latter only from the former. He has a vision of history as a great movement forwards, and self as a necessary function within it. Despite Jakob's assertion that he cannot *experience* that movement but only individual moments, Rohlfs view at least seems to relate man to his context, to offer him a defining role. Yet hints of a Nazi past make the reader wonder whether his belief in 'historical inevitability' is really an answer to the problems of relating. Has he bridged the problematic gap between self and world, or is his ideological security really an escape from personal responsibility and guilt, an evasion of context? His monologues, by their very presence, show him as more reflective than one might expect of an ideologue, and their detail reveals a sensitive and intelligent man. He experiences others as individuals, even while he has to treat them as units. He is a man who thus at the very least pays a constant price for commitment to a cause, in the painful gap between empathy and the need to manipulate, between presently-felt immediacy and submission to the dictates of past and future.

All these figures thus foreground problems of isolation, rootlessness or loss in three ways: in what they have to say about themselves and others, in the use of monologues to say it, and in the way their interventions structure the text, whether Gesine's voice repeatedly 'interrupting' the text to add a brief personal touch to an event or figure, or Jonas's frequently lengthy, meandering thoughts. All this indicates that Johnson is not so much just a narrowly political writer, as a politicised one, in the sense of being very concerned with the individual's interaction with his or her world. His characters do very much belong to the 'two Germanies', but their varied problems also touch on issues which have more general bearing too. The complex modern world of warring values, painful generation gaps, physical and emotional dislocation: all this imposes a kind of distorted 'contextuality' upon us; we are neither at one with our world, nor free within ourselves. This is strikingly emphasised by filmic devices in the text; Jakob's being held under observation from a window without knowing it (p. 25f) is redolent of far more than Stasi exploitation. The overt political pressure put on him and exemplified in this act of 'framing' is a parallel to the mental and emotional pressures experienced by many in the modern world who struggle to escape or feel excluded from or cannot find their proper context, their 'frame'. Self-interpretation is fraught with problems, both for the figures in the text and for the reader in the literary 'environment' of his/her reading of the novel. It seems able only to move to and fro around its central factual content – Jakob's death – with a constantly shifting focus, where nothing is stable, neither narrative voice nor time-scale. This abdication of any kind of directive omniscience of course suggests a concern for fullness and balance, a deep respect for the individual view as for the complexity of reality, but it also evokes a kind of extreme *Ratlosigkeit*, of perplexity. The use of dialogue – assertion and contradiction – to open the novel draws our attention very directly to the idea of 'telling stories' and helps to mark out how far the text actually deviates from any simple 'telling'. As Riordan has emphasised, the whole novel is indeed *about* the uneasy process of interpretation, about trying to place things, lives in context, and not only on an individual scale. Societies cannot escape the search for orientation either, and the novel includes one very striking instance of broader political re-interpretation: in the now-famous Twentieth Party Congress in Moscow, which effectively rewrote the history of Stalinism. David Lodge (1990), writing about quite another text, describes very succinctly how such 'difficult' novels as Johnson's engage the reader in the same process of rethinking:

> the meaning inheres in the hermeneutic process itself: the reader's activity in interpreting and making sense of the story, responding to the clues and cues provided by the text, constantly readjusting a provisional interpretation in the light of new knowledge, re-enacts the efforts of the characters to make sense of their own lives. (Lodge, 1990, p. 162)

The recognition that there can be no such thing as simple, unreflective or context-free 'being' relates in Johnson's novel not only to the messy complexities of the socio-political world, but to the relationship of language itself and reality. In the traditional realist novel language seems to envelop and embody the world unproblematically. Here our attention is drawn constantly to the theme of ongoing communication as opposed to resolved 'truth'; the central image of the railway system hints at it, the plot dramatises it in the many conversations past and present, and the whole structure of the novel makes it an unavoidable issue. The shifting narrative voice stops any one voice from dominating and thus suggesting that there is ultimately a finite, 'right' view. Equally, the constant interruption of one discourse by another stops us as readers from adopting a superior, unifying position of insight; we cannot produce a coherent source of meaning either by exercising our own differentiating judgement or by our smooth assimilation of the text – as we can with Hesse's novel *Der Steppenwolf*. This focuses our thinking firmly on the *act* of communication itself as well as on the complexion of the individual self-interpretations involved. The initial anonymity of the speakers helps to sharpen this focus. Brought up as we are on traditional notions of character typology, we naturally struggle to work out who they might be, but they do not allow us to enter the text, as a Realist novel does; we react to them as to another filmic device, the voice-over, which we often cannot initially locate or evaluate and must simply listen to. In other words, Johnson foregrounds again and again the now well-established Modernist view that language does not simply copy or reflect life, does not somehow transcribe its meaning directly and offer us 'transparent windows on reality' (Lodge, 1990, p. 51); meaning is problematic and exists only within discourse itself. As Catherine Belsey (1980, p. 61) puts it, 'The world is intelligible only through discourse: there is no unmediated experience'. Meaning in the very broadest sense – not just the 'meaning' of one's own life – is thus something that we and the novel's characters alike have to wrestle with, through the meeting of discourses: it is not a pre-existing 'given' which we disclose by means of language. Indeed, one might say that to live is to be engaged in an endless act of adjustment and re-interpretation within language.

Seeing such broad issues exemplified in the novel is not, however, to argue that its setting in divided Germany is somehow quite incidental; on the contrary, it is peculiarly appropriate. The way each 'side' of the political divide reacts to the other is a prime example of how language itself works, as a 'system of differences with no positive terms' (Belsey, 1980, p. 38). Each side has a different set of cultural/political symbols for the same physically existing world, and they derive what is perceived as their meaning not from some quintessential 'rightness', but from their contrastive interplay with those of the other side. Capitalism has meaning only because other ideologies, in this case Communism, exist, and vice versa. Each lays claim to 'truth', but Johnson's focus precisely on where and how they meet, in the senseless human miseries of a divided Germany, reveals their mutually dependent relativism – and the relativism inherent in all languages and interpretative systems. This is immensely important, for only when we recognise it are we able to see that 'no linguistic forms are ideologically innocent or neutral' (Belsey, 1980, p. 6). This is what Johnson explores very directly in his next novel, *Das dritte Buch über Achim* and its debate on biography, but it is not just a German issue or one that is ceasing to be relevant with the end of the Cold War and its competing political ideologies. Nor is it ultimately a negative stance, even though there is no possibility of escape out of language into some other cognitive system. To render us aware of ideology in all discourse is certainly to detach us from any complacent assumption that we can afford to leave any statement, however common-sensical, unquestioned. However, it is also to liberate us into full awareness of difference, of the possibility of exploring a plurality of attitudes and ideas, the richness of the multitude of human voices and their potentially creative interaction.

This realisation enables us to explore another and more positive – though not 'better' – reading of Johnson's novel. We have seen so far how its structure may be said to reflect the modern experience of deracination and consequent isolation, a loss of innocence in social, political and linguistic terms. Yet the experience of reading the text does not in the end leave one with an impression of Kafkaesque helplessness before the opaqueness of things. Though the reader may at first be thoroughly disoriented, deprived of virtually all security, Johnson never goes as far as Kafka, as we can see at quite a simple level of the text. One feature common to both authors' work is a strong sense of the physical presence of the external world. In Kafka's work this seems to impinge painfully and puzzlingly on the individual – subjectively experienced but certainly 'there' in the powerful sense of otherness that most of the protago-nists share. In *Mutmaßungen über Jakob*, however, we seem to have a more 'normal' but equally powerful presence – that of everyday objects and places, trains, stairs, rooms, chairs, cars, and above all the physical presence of Jakob himself, described via something akin to traditional diegesis.

The rest of the text tells us we must be wary of taking any discourse as simply 'given' and these sections are certainly value-laden within the overall discourse of the novel. As we have already seen, they allow us – indeed encourage us to operate momentarily on the level of conventional intelligibility, to have a sense of undeniable and uncomplicated space and time. Earlier we saw how this is then undermined by the change from simile to metaphor and the constant intervention of highly subjective discourses: reality is pluralised. Encouraged by our sense of the multiplicity of Johnson's text, however, we can reverse our view and see the function of these 'simpler' sections not merely as a measure of this change, but as important in themselves. One might say that these diegetic sections act as a positive counterweight to the indeterminacy of the rest of the text. When examined closely, they certainly bear traces of traditional narrative insight, but there is no attempt to emulate classic Realism's claim to an all-seeing authenticity, to what Holquist (1990, p. 18) calls 'ontological privilege'. These sections are framed in a variety of discourses and thus revealed as discourse themselves. Yet they do stand out in the otherwise mimetic manner of the novel, as though challenging us to consider their validity – perhaps even necessity – as an additional form of discourse. They are perhaps the most obvious sign that Johnson will not give up the search for sense and value while not retreating into realism in the fullest sense of the word, he seems to be asking whether Realist discourse does not have something to say about the sheer 'presentness' of day-to-day trivial experience, about the 'worthwhile-ness' of the ordinary, the weight and importance of human existence beyond all the anguish and pain.

This quality – what one might call the essential humanity of Johnson's writing – is very evident in its central figure, Jakob. While the novel undoubtedly engages us in a variety of complex discourses, perhaps our first and strongest reaction on putting it down – if we are really honest – is a quite straightforward sense of loss, almost of personal deprivation. Jakob has 'lived' for us as much as for the personalised narrators; moreover, his death is given a peculiar poignancy by the first-person memories of him, for they emphasise the 'pastness' of the past. We are used to narrative in the past tense, to the usual story-telling convention of the 'epic preterite' which is used to bring any tale alive, so that we do not really experience conventionally-narrated events as past. When the past tense is used by an individual speaker, however, it regains its specific reference to past time. Jakob's life is given extra and perhaps exemplary weight by this emphasis on its passing, and we are made very aware of the act of recollection as a primary human need.

We seem, then, to have two poles of reading: one emphasising reality seen as physical displacement in space and time, the other as endless discourse, the former in the end perhaps not so much undermined by as justifying the latter.

Human life is worth the effort of living it, its very resistance to our understanding the measure of its 'weightiness': this is a view particularly evident in Johnson's later work *Jahrestage*, where he is not ashamed to present history both as vivid experience and interpretation. But we can look at this balance in a more interesting way. If we consider the title *Mutmaßungen über Jakob* for a moment, we can see that in a sense it has three aspects: there is Jakob, the object of speculation, there are the unnamed enactors of speculation about him, and the speculations themselves. The title thus enshrines a view of cognition as an ongoing process of interaction between subject and object; in other words, we have here something very like Bakhtin's view of consciousness as 'dialogue'.

As Holquist puts it, for Bakhtin 'existence [...] is a shared event' (p. 28); 'in dialogism, the very capacity to have consciousness is based on *otherness* [...] it is the differential relation between a center and all that is not that center' (p. 18). The self is an unfinished process of addressivity, 'the event of constantly responding to utterances from the different worlds I pass through' (p. 48). While we each experience life from a unique position in space, are our own 'centre', we are not alone and thus not complete in ourselves, for whatever we observe is shaped by the place from which we see it. We need the perspective of the 'other' if we are to escape solipsism, and Holquist quotes Bakhtin's nice example of an observer looking at another observer. You can see things behind my back that I cannot see, and I can see things behind your back that are denied to your vision' (p. 21). 'I am able to "conceive" or construct a whole out of the different situations we are in together' (p. 36f). The 'self', then, is not a circumscribed entity, but an activity: not self *plus* other only, but also the ceaselessly adjusted *relation* between self and other. 'The world addresses us and we are alive and human to the degree that we are answerable, i.e. to the degree that we can respond to addressivity' (p. 30). Each of us, of course, is addressed uniquely, but by engaging in dialogue with the world we become part of a larger whole.

In the light of this we can see *Mutmaßungen über Jakob* as an essentially 'dialogic' text. The novel actually opens with dialogue in the usual sense of the word, and that sort of 'present' conversational exchange is taken up many more times, as a kind of icon of the deeper dialogue with which the text is concerned: the unceasing process of responding, of allowing oneself to be 'addressed' by the world. This is in fact what each of the main 'living' figures – Jonas, Gesine, Rohlfs – is engaged in, despite the fact that we have looked at their utterances so far as 'monologue'. Each is wrestling, not just with unclear facts about Jakob's death, but with self-understanding made possible only through the experience of the 'other' – in Jakob, in their social contexts. It is interesting in this context to observe how Johnson handles their monologues, for while their separate voices suggest isolation and loneliness, that is not emphasised as much as it could be. We are *not* really dealing here with stream of consciousness, a mode which is perhaps best suited to underline isolation.

Instead, the monologues seem rather to *be* monologues in the proper sense: speeches addressed to someone, too well-formed and articulate to be unshaped thoughts, and also marked by hints of self-justification or self-defence, that is, by a sense of someone else's presence as potential critic or judge. It is not clear to whom they are addressed – whether to the reader or to some kind of internal interlocutor, an imagined speech-partner: perhaps to both. In either case the effect is interesting. If we posit the reader as partner, then he/she is being challenged directly to participate in a dialogue with the characters, to be addressed by them as the 'other' rather than just watch *their* processes of engagement. If we imagine internal collocutors, whether conscience or some imagined absent friend, then it emphasises Johnson's rather Bakhtinian view of what we have in common, the life force as a drive to be engaged in addressivity, in interchange, as the only way of knowing ourselves.

In fact 'dialogism' seems to pervade every aspect of the text. Jakob's death and the stress on his 'pastness' emphasise the uniqueness of each individual's place in time and space, which ends when life ends; but that uniqueness also forms the 'other' to which all his acquaintances respond – life as dialogue goes on. Moreover it goes on beyond the scope of the text. The 'story' is not finished with the last page because nothing is resolved – not for the figures and certainly not for the reader! The circularity that we noticed earlier and considered as a sign of perplexity is also an invitation to repeat our own dialogic engagement with the text again and again. Even in terms of simple plot there is no end, and new dialogues have begun, for Gesine – whom Jakob wished to protect from Rohlfs – has met him, thus opening up particularly interesting possibilities of challenge and self-development for both. In the 'monologues', too, there is even more sense of dialogue than we have noted already; not just the intimated presence of an interlocutor in their linguistic formulations, but also an element of tension, inner dialogue. Gesine's sections, we might say, contain a dialogue between her two selves as adult and child; Rohlfs' sections reveal the tension between a past self he would like to deny and a present/future self; Jonas wrestles with the age-old problem of aligning action and insight – and all of them with the personal versus the political. This constant foregrounding of 'dialogue' cannot be overlooked, and it is surely one of the most positive and humane aspects of the text. It seems to address precisely the issue symbolised by the confrontation of two ideologies in divided Germany, and by the pressure put on Jakob which is the very impetus of the plot: the dangers of one-voicedness, of ideology. Ideology is dangerous, not just because it can cause people overtly to demand specific and perhaps harmful acts from others, as Rohlfs does from Jakob. It is dangerous because it seeks to impose a unique interpretation on the world, to suppress the individuality that most of us feel is the very condition of life, and to freeze humans in a static form of imposed 'meaning' that serves only the self-regard of those in power. Johnson's writing is quintessentially directed against ideology: not in the superficial, limited sense that he produces explicit theoretical arguments against Communism or Capitalism, but in what we might call the 'polyphony' of his work and its dialogism. To believe that 'meaning' is an ongoing and interactive process is to be, as Holquist rather neatly puts it (p. 35), 'intransigently pluralist', to celebrate the richness and variety of human life.

In some ways, then, this seems a paradoxical novel. It tends constantly towards a view of the painful and unresolved entangledness of human life in the modern world, towards scepticism about the power of language to capture that world and make sense of it. Yet what remains with the reader is a strong sense of presence: the individuality of the figures engaged in the search to understand, even if they are far from being 'fully rounded characters' in the traditional Realist sense. In the very diversity of their individual problems, and in the echoes of simpler referentiality offered by the images of Jakob, there is an extraordinary vitality which proclaims a belief in human value. This is not in the end an unhopeful book; simple realism, ideological fixation, emotional or intellectual internalisation are all in a sense rejected as inadequate ways of grasping reality – but reality has weight nevertheless, it is worth the process of enquiry. What may seem meaningless or impenetrable in the individual moment, a subject of speculation rather than certainty, acquires added value and new meaning by its continued existence in memory, its participation in other dialogues. It is in this process that meaning lies, not in the 'closed' text of a conventional biography: it is quite right that Jakob's life-story remains in purely factual terms unfinished. For Johnson, as for Bakhtin, nothing is ever utterly lost or without significance.

NOTE

This chapter is based in part on work which appeared in *London German Studies III* (1986), ed. J. P. Stern. I am grateful to the Institute of Germanic Studies for allowing me to draw on it.

REFERENCES

References given by page number only relate to the first edition of *Mutmaßungen über Jakob*, Frankfurt: Suhrkamp 1959.

BELSEY, C. (1980), *Critical Practice*, London & New York: Routledge (New Accents Series).

BOND, D.G. (1989), The dialogic form of Uwe Johnson's 'Mutmaßungen über Jakob', *MLR* 84, pp. 874–84.

HOLQUIST, M. (1990), *Dialogism: Bakhtin and his World*, London & New York: Routledge (New Accents Series).

LODGE, D. (1990), *After Bakhtin: Essays on Fiction and Criticism*, London & New York, Routledge.

POPP, H. (1967) *Einführung in Uwe Johnsons Roman 'Mutmaßungen über Jakob'*, Stuttgart: Klett.

RIORDAN, C. (1989), *The Ethics of Narration: Uwe Johnson's novels from 'Ingrid Babendererde' to 'Jahrestage'*, London: MHRA & Institute of Germanic Studies (MHRA Text & Dissertations, Vol. 28/ Bithell Series of Dissertations, Vol. 14).

The Reconstructed Subject
Christa Wolf, *Kassandra*

JOHN GUTHRIE

'The writer, the unique point of reversal from object to subject and back to object.' (Anna Seghers)

Although the novels discussed in this volume are all distinct in many ways from each other, Christa Wolf's *Kassandra* seems different from all of them again. Not only because of its length, for it is by far the shortest of them and shorter indeed than the average German novel, but also by virtue of the fact that it is a novel written by a woman about a woman. If we take the work in its entirety, it is at the opposite end of the spectrum, then, to a novel like *Effi Briest* where the (male) narrator seems so much a part of the society he is depicting. Christa Wolf's novel is distinguished by the consistency of its first-person narrative, its pronounced foregrounding of the subject and its unique relation to a series of lectures on poetics by the author, the *Voraussetzungen einer Erzählung: Kassandra* (Conditions of a Narrative: Cassandra), which form the theoretical basis and a kind of preamble to Kassandra's story itself. We shall return to that part of the work in the course of our discussion. On the other hand, certain similarities with other novels treated here cannot be overlooked. As with Musil and Thomas Mann, there is the notable tendency towards essayism (evident in the *Voraussetzungen*), and as with Mann, or Grass, a concern with mythology and the fate of Germany (and Europe) in what is a *Zeitroman*. Like Musil's *Törleß*, the novel deals with a state of heightened awareness (to begin with, that of childhood), and like Kafka's novels the text does not always yield literal meanings, showing that reality is structured by language. Like many other novels in the German tradition, Christa Wolf's *Kassandra* is concerned with an outsider figure who has many signs of the artist's temperament. Finally, like Rilke's *Malte*, it is a novel in which the senses play a vital role, and in which the main character is confronted by death.

We may discern three important aspects of *Kassandra*. Firstly, there is Kassandra's struggle, which may be viewed as an exemplary struggle for autonomy, a theme quite independent of the ancient myth. Secondly, we may see this struggle as the progress from the object to the subject of history, with a concomitant stress on subjectivity coinciding with the author's own aesthetic views. And thirdly, developing from here, we may look at the whys and wherefores of the recreation of this subject, the reconstruction of the myth, structural as well as linguistic.

But first, some account of the plot is necessary. The story begins at its end. After a brief introduction by the narrator we find Kassandra (Cassandra), daughter of Priamos (Priam) and Hekabe (Hecuba), before the gates of Mycenae, about to be killed by Agamemnon's wife Klytaimnestra (Clytemnestra). Agamemnon, now slaughtered by Klytaimnestra, had taken Kassandra captive after the fall of Troy and brought her to Greece. By means of a series of extended flashbacks, Kassandra gives an account of her childhood and youth in Troy, her first love, her desire to become priestess. We learn about the beginnings of the ten-year war between Greece and Troy and its progress. Three expeditions (or 'ships' as they are called) stick out in Kassandra's mind, representing the build-up to the war, with the third supposedly bringing Helen from Greece to Troy, but in fact not doing so at all. The deception of the people then propagated deepens the rift between Kassandra and the court around her father, dominated as it is by aggressive warmongers. As the war progresses, its *raison d'être* (ostensibly the retrieval of Helen by the Greeks, but in reality the control of the Dardanelles) is forgotten, and Greeks and Trojans become more alike. Kassandra witnesses many of the atrocities of war at first hand, goes against the grain of Trojan policy, prophesies defeat, goes mad and is imprisoned. The sombre tale of war and disintegration is interwoven with more optimistic strands involving human relationships which give her comfort, the thought of a better future for later generations and the effect on her of the telling of her own narrative bringing a release from fear.

Kassandra's struggle is hinted at early on. The opening words of her narrative, 'With this story I go to my death' (p. 5), immediately evoke the sense of confrontation with death which is indeed the essence of the story. The German text here ('Mit der Erzählung geh ich in den Tod') gives a sense of going *into* death, and hence into a distinct realm, of a metaphysical nature. It is worth noting that the theme of death figures prominently in Wolf's work and that it is a major source of tension within the individual. By the time the story has begun, Kassandra's process of self-discovery is in one sense over, her fate is sealed, she is soon to be slaughtered. Faced with a terminal situation, a hopeless predicament, she begins the work of reliving the past, working through the struggle of her life and reviewing it from different angles. Like other of Wolf's characters, Kassandra is engaged in a kind of *Trauerarbeit*, a work of mourning and a working through of her sorrow and of the problematic stages of her life which might otherwise be forgotten or suppressed (Greiner, 1985 p. 134f). She analyses her childhood and youth, her coming to maturity, and her reasons for wanting to become a priestess and seer. She is royal daughter and favourite child of King Priam and thus in a privileged position. She admits that a certain amount of pride and self-love are involved in her will to be different, and through her difference to prove herself as woman in a society of men. Not without a degree of arrogance and stubbornness, she is ambitious and jealous of her sister Polyxena's beauty. Consequently, she needs to assert herself in other ways. Had it not been for these traits, she would not have desired to be different. It also reveals the sources of guilt, the guilt which is one prime motive in her telling of her story. We see that insecurity is part of her character. Linked with this, however, is a sense of fear and uncertainty which cannot be entirely explained by her character alone. It derives in large measure from the society in which she lives. For this is a society which is dominated by men and the preparation for war and combat. Her decision to become a priestess and lead a solitary life which is also partly motivated by an aversion to men which is linked to the revulsion at being physically abused and the pain of rejection as a young woman. She submits in order to survive. The structure of society is depicted by Kassandra from her own subjective point of view (and indeed it is so viewed by Christa Wolf as well, as we see from the *Voraussetzungen*) as dominated by a materialistic male ethos which does not hesitate to deceive and dupe the very society it is supposedly protecting. Kassandra herself is protected in the royal environment where she has a close relationship with her father, but she is gradually forced to admit to herself that he too is deceived, relies on this deception, and is the pawn of forces beyond his control. Bit by bit we are presented, through Kassandra's eyes, with the picture of a society which degrades human relationships and women. Helen of Troy, for example, on whose account the war is ostensibly being fought, is in fact nothing but a phantom; Polyxena is used to bargain with and lure Achilles to his death; Kassandra herself is used by men, both sexually and in the power game by her father. We are given a picture of society then which presents women as the objects of history, exploited, downgraded, the losers. Kassandra is a product of this Society. As she says early in her story, there is something of everyone in her, and we may think of her as a kind of receptacle, a human sponge.

This corresponds to the picture presented to us in the *Voraussetzungen* and it is evidently one of the reasons behind the writing of the work. We are shown a society which has moved from being a matriarchal one (when goddesses were worshipped rather than Gods, and a Great Mother was thought to be the begetter of all) to a patriarchal one, shown here in its infancy, and surviving in its essentials to the present day. This may be a schematic and controversial reading of history and in itself partly a myth, but it is essential to the work's argument and structure.

This, then, is the society against which Kassandra rebels. As time passes and the community as a whole and the royal circle become more and more involved in preparation for war, she is able to perceive more accurately than anyone the motives for war, and particularly the fact that these are economic and political. (It is made quite explicit in the text that the control of the Dardanelles is the real reason behind the conflict.) The second expedition ('ship'), to recapture Priamos's sister, precipitates a split within her: her lover Aineias is involved. The Trojans fail to get the King's sister, and one of their number, Kalchas, defects. The court's hushing-up of this brings home to Kassandra the extent of deception involved. She is more and more a divided figure, still bound to the court by blood relationships, but impelled away from it by the truth of the situation. She hovers for a time, finding a delicate balance between her own desire for truth and the need to survive. But she cannot maintain this position indefinitely. The contradiction has become too deeply rooted in her own personality and it needs to be resolved. As the war progresses, so opposition to it grows. There is a group resisting the pull towards slaughter, which has its roots in the matriarchal culture associated with Kybele (Cybele, Eileithyia, or Rhea, 'the Mother of the Gods', and the personification of Nature's power of growth). Hers is a forbidden name in this society which has progressed from matriarchy to patriarchy. It is an idyllic community living in caves at the foot of the Ida mountains on the banks of the Scamander. Kassandra feels drawn towards this community. But it is not a simple matter of switching allegiances. She is regarded with suspicion by her own family. Moreover, there are limitations to the potential of this alternative community (which, in some respects, resembles a modern 'green' commune). It seems self-sufficient, peaceful, intellectually stimulating, led as it is by the enlightened androgynous intellectual Anchises, a sympathetic male figure who has been excepted from the process whereby men have come to dominate and who aspires to a utopia (see Haas, 1988, pp. 39, 40). But in the end this community is a dead end. It has been noted that the willow tree between whose roots the caves of the community lie is associated on the one hand with the womb, but on the other hand that it is also a symbol of sterility. This community in fact survives only by virtue of antithesis: opposition to the warring faction (Marx, 1985, p. 176). Its members would not be able to survive beyond that opposition.

Another alternative to the policy of the Trojan court is represented by the figure of Penthesilea, the leader of the Amazons, a group that is fighting with the Trojans against Greece. Penthesilea is the aggressive woman bent upon destruction and annihilation of the enemy. Kassandra is drawn to Penthesilea as a woman and it is a painful process for her to have to reject her, but the reasons are plain: such a path cannot further the individual's autonomy, it can only destroy itself. Christa Wolf is here rejecting the stance of aggressive feminist thinking of her own time.

It is this very *opposition* between different alternatives and the tension it creates within Kassandra which is the novel's main interest. The conflict between two sides of a community produces a crisis in an individual which leads to her destruction. (The philosophically aware reader may well discern here the Hegelian pattern of thesis, antithesis and synthesis.) As she moves away from life at the royal court, Kassandra becomes involved in discussions with Anchises. These discussions do not simply produce a new and better person in the way that intellectual discussions might idealistically be thought to do. What they help to produce is a crisis in her. As we have argued, she is the object of history, the gathering-point of tensions within a society. The ultimate expression of this crisis is her madness – the near destruction of her conscious self. This very insistence means, as she well knows, certain imprisonment, and is thus a form of conscious and willed self-destruction. But in undergoing this process of conscious unconscious decision-taking, she changes. She becomes in effect a new person, the subject of history.

The place of her imprisonment is symbolic; Kassandra is locked up in a 'hero's grave', a place of special significance in this society with its cult of heroism. Her presence there is thus profoundly ironical. She, who has pitted herself against this aggressive masculine society, now finds herself imprisoned by it and linked with its immortal symbols. The irony is crucial, for here Kassandra undergoes a regeneration. The stages by which she undergoes this regeneration and makes the transition from object to subject have been carefully analysed (Haas, 1988). She experiences shame and degradation at being buried alive and close to death. Gradually, her conscious voice and will-power begin to assert themselves. Consciousness of pain grows, the emotional pain of complete separation and rejection by her father. By struggling, she is able to remove a strip of willow from the door enclosing her, thus gaining contact with the outside world. The women of Troy she talks with, once beneath her, now despise her. This is yet further degradation, but a further key to the unlocking of her role in history. Achilles is dead, the greatest hero gone. What will the future bring? At this point she is able to recognise the rightness, the authenticity of her own decision, the fact that she said 'no' with her life, body, and soul. Her role in history has thus been consciously verbalised. In doing this she takes a vital step towards becoming the subject of history, recognising herself. By coming to terms with the pain of losing her father she has also overcome her submissive attitude to patriarchy. Self-confidence results from her incarceration, the exact opposite of what was intended.

Her release from prison is immediately followed by a *Berührungsfest* or festival of touch, celebrating the body, in the Scamander community, a sign that verbal realisation alone is not enough to achieve autonomy. A synthesis of body and mind is implied. But there is one further stage in Kassandra's progress towards the subject, and it is wrong to suggest that her return to the community outside the town represents the ultimate solution (*pace* Kuhn, 1988).

What is important about this regeneration is the recognition of the forces that have created her. She has learned to see herself in a new light, she has perceived the forces operating behind history and how they have made her. In recognising this, she has, in a sense, also conquered these forces within herself, and she will be able to stand as an example to posterity if she can, by some means, assert herself, her own personality, her very own name and existence. She has become an autonomous individual. How exactly does she do that, given that she has willed her own destruction? Here, the pessimistic strand of the novel, the nearness of death we referred to earlier, is inseparable, in Christa Wolf's way of thinking, from the more forward-looking, optimistic elements.

All creation implies destruction. This is a fundamental truth and a tenet of Christa Wolf's writing. By accepting her own destruction Kassandra wills the existence of something else, another entity which is the symbolic expression of her own personality. This other entity is her writing, her story. By reliving her past through the retelling of it, she has overcome her *fear* of death and in a sense triumphed. ('With this story I go to my death.') Here we pass to the second aspect mentioned at the outset, that of the work's 'subjectivity'. It is essential to realise that the subjective element, so much a part of Christa Wolf's writing (so much so, in fact, that the presence of her own person is often felt near the surface in her writings) is not mutually exclusive with the mimetic element and verisimilitude, as we shall see when we look at the novel's language. It is naturally a matter of emphasis, and 'objective' factors are surely involved, but the idea of 'subjective authenticity', it is argued by Wolf, is an underlying precept of her fiction (Wolf, 1968 and 1973). Partly, this idea evolved in opposition to the official literature of the GDR. We find her opposed to the notion that authors should hide behind their creations (Thomas Mann and Kafka come to mind here as examples of writers who do just that); rather, their own emotions and experience, which are vital prerequisites of literary creation, should come to the fore. There is also the refusal to take over any preordained way of thinking which might stifle free expression as well as the liberty to come to terms, through writing, with one's *own* life. Unable to write about anything which does not cause her anxiety, she sees writing as a process of overcoming (1973, pp. 318, 322) which leads to seeing reality in a new light (1973, p. 324). These notions of 'subjective authenticity' may well have their problems and they are not systematically developed by Wolf, but in the present context they help to explain the *emphasis on the subject*.

We shall return to the author's relation to her own work in due course, but for the moment we may note that these ideas have parallels with Kassandra's case. She writes in the first person, continually foregrounding her own emotions. Though she admits there are other points of view, she is not concerned with them; indeed, the necessity of coming to terms with her own personality means that she has to exclude other perspectives. She is concerned with her story and its telling and her process of *becoming* through analysis of her suffering, accentuated as this is in the face of death.

Writing, then, or the telling of one's own story, is a process of self-discovery.

This is particularly clear at the point in the story when Kassandra experiences a sense of elation at having *become* herself: 'The happiness of becoming "I", myself, and therefore being more use to others – this I was still able to experience' (p. 15). This process of becoming oneself is, as Kassandra says, experienced by few (*ibid.*). Most acutely, it is experienced by the writer. That the experience of writing, of self-discovery, the re-forming of experience and its transmission is vital to the novel's message, is shown in the passage where Kassandra, momentarily contemplating begging her captor Klytaimnestra for mercy, says to her:

> Give me just enough to live. But, I implore you: give me a scribe, or, better still, a young slave with a good memory and powerful voice. Decree that she passes on to her daughter by word of mouth what she hears from me. And that daughter to her daughter, and so on. So that beside the great river of heroic lays this little trickle would, with difficulty, reach those far-away, perhaps happier people who will one day live. (p. 93)

Naturally, this idea of emphasising the first person and a woman's own self-discovery raises questions which are at the heart of many feminist discussions of literature. There is undoubtedly in the text an opposition to a standard male way of writing, which at its worst is seen to be phallocentric. This is exemplified in the rejection of Homer's version of Achilles, presented as a brute. Critics have detected the influence of various influential feminists in Wolf's writing, and especially in *Kassandra*, with that of Irigaray (the idea of transcending the dualism of the sexes) being prominent (see Risse, 1986; Kuhn, 1988). This is reflected in the role of touch (*Berührung*) in her relationship with Aineias, or in the body language of the Scamander community (the emphasis on the dance). But it needs to be emphasised that Christa Wolf's presentation of the struggle for autonomy has a more generalised significance than is implied by the linking with any one particular theory of feminism. As we can see when we look at the novel's structure, Christa Wolf has her own *fictional* response to the problems of women's writing.

Writing, of course, can never be totally subjective, and Christa Wolf has been attacked on philosophical grounds for her emphasis, in theory, on subjective experience (1973, p. 325f). It is here that we must see that the author's creation is also a conscious construct, a reconstruction of an ancient mythological character from a modern perspective conscious of its own existence, which will always remain part of that imagination and is, in another sense, always the *object* of that imagination. The opening section of the novel alludes to this: the first paragraph describes Kassandra's situation as that of another person, centuries ago. 'Here it *was*. There *she* stood. These stone lions, now headless, looked at her (p. 5, emphasis mine). The final section of the novel echoes these words. 'Here it is. These stone lions looked at her. In the changing of the light they seem to move.' If these lines evoke an optical illusion and therefore the role of the senses, the echo also implies that this story is a conscious reconstruction, conceivably having taken place in the author's imagination. It is not the real Kassandra we find here, but one imagined by the author. The reader of the *Voraussetzungen* knows this to be the case. The Kassandra project began as the search for an 'objective correlative' to feelings experienced in the present. A trip to Greece followed. The journey is carefully described, sometimes in minute and seemingly trivial detail, in the *Voraussetzungen*. Several strands are woven together in this 'preamble': the travelogue itself, letters and diary entries, reflections on history, mythology, archaeology, contemporary world politics and the imminence of atomic war, and feminism. The arms race is directly paralleled in Kassandra's story, which can be read as a piece of anti-war propaganda, but that is only one aspect of it. The *Voraussetzungen* show us a writer who is very much aware of the present and of the tension between present and past. This tension, incidentally, in relation to Christa Wolf's own life, is also the theme of her novel *Kindheitsmuster* (A Model Childhood), where the depiction of the Fascist past is used as a means of access to the present. What began as a search for Kassandra, with an important degree of identification between modern writer and ancient seer, involves in the end an attempt at distancing. Thus Wolf notes in the *Voraussetzungen* (p. 38) how she gradually overcame this initial sense of identification with the 'first professional woman of literature' and something of a proto-feminist, later (p. 119) coming to see the figure of Kassandra with an increasing sense of irony and detachment.

This consciousness of her distance from the figure of Kassandra has important consequences for us. We are forced to view it as the conscious *rewriting* of a myth by a modern woman, a counter-mythology, anti-myth, or anti-*received-myth*, for it presents a rereading of mythology and a controversial rewriting of one of the greatest works of world literature, Homer's *Iliad*. The very close focus on Kassandra is in itself a new and striking aspect, for she was a figure marginalised in ancient history, and even in Schiller's poem on her ('Kassandra', 1797) she is seen one-dimensionally as prophetess of gloom. Another provocative aspect of this rewriting is the portrayal of Achilles, the hero of Homer's *Iliad*, here seen as a weakling, incapable of love, whose thirst for blood is linked with homosexuality and necrophilia. Such a view coincides with the author's view of history as presented in the *Voraussetzungen* and it is contentious, but that in itself proves the point that there is no ultimately correct version of a myth, only constructions and reconstructions from different points of view. The element of conscious reconstruction we noted is also part of an emphasis on the Kassandra story as aesthetic entity, as the artifact shaped by a writer.

The three aspects we have been discussing are prime thematic elements. In order to consolidate our view of their importance we must turn to the novel's structure. In *Kindheitsmuster* there are three distinct time levels which are used and interwoven in the novel: the period of Nelly Jordan's childhood stretching from the beginnings of the Third Reich up to just after the War; a second time level located in 1971, when the narrator goes on a two-day visit with her daughter and husband to the scenes of her childhood; thirdly, there is the more recent past, closer to the reader's perspective and the point at which the novel is written, from which the narrator looks back on the second level and reflects on the present state of the world and on the processes of memory. A perspective into the future is opened up at the end of the novel, when the heroine recovers from an illness and looks ahead with a new emphasis. The tension between these levels gives the novel its unique texture and power. In *Kassandra*, as we have seen, there are also different time levels. There is the narrator's present in the *Voraussetzungen*, which involves reflections on the recent past. In contrast to this level there is the manifest 'pastness' of Kassandra's story, emphasised by the narrator's framing of the story. That story is, however, told from the point of view of another present, looking back over a section of the past. Kassandra's narrative switches frequently from the present to the past and back again, without warning, following her moods and communicating a sense of tension and urgency. Like the narrator's perspective, however, it also looks forward to a future. As we have seen, the struggle for autonomy implies that this will be a better future. This is no simple optimism as the complex 'enveloping' of time levels surely illustrates. We may well say that we are dealing with a *Zeitroman* of a new type here, a novel about its times, but also a work of fiction which seems self-consciously aware of past, present and future.

It has already been seen that Kassandra's story is carefully and consciously 'framed' by a narrator. We should not confuse the use of this device with the framework technique so often used in the German *Novelle*, even though the length of the story might seem to suggest it. The subtitle, 'Erzählung' should not mislead us either, and it has been argued that the emphasis can easily be seen to be on the *telling* of Kassandra's story as oral process as opposed to a preconceived notion of literary form, which the short story might be said to have (Risse, 1986, p. 112). We are certainly dealing with a novel here, one with a dense and complex structure, with many of the hallmarks of Modernism. On the one hand the story seems to follow the ebb and flow of Kassandra's emotions without any rhyme or reason, closely akin to the stream of consciousness technique used by many modern writers. Characters come and go, time levels intermingle, the subconscious enters in the form of dreams. What Christa Wolf has evidently done is to move away from a variety of fiction (which we need not necessarily accept as masculine) with firm contours, rigid structures. She has the Greek epic in mind, though even this highly structured form of literature might be said to have its own deeper, hidden structures behind its surface conventions. She has attempted to create a kind of narrative web or network ('erzählerisches Netzwerk': *Voraussetzungen*, p. 117), an idea consciously borrowed from Virginia Woolf's fiction.

Nevertheless, despite the appearance of formlessness and the implication of entanglement which the web or net has, the novel has its own structure. If some novels treated in this volume can be likened to symphonies, *Kassandra* might well be likened to a work of chamber music in which the narrator Kassandra adopts different voices corresponding to different moods, always tense and compact. Some critics (e.g. Stephens and Wilson, 1987, p. 280) feel that a sense of linearity is evident, indeed too evident, and others have insisted on the 'closed-endedness' of Kassandra's story (Kuhn, 1988, p. 184), but it seems wrong to me to insist on this, for it is surely the tension between the seemingly formless, emotional elements and the other elements of structure which give the work its power. We have referred to its framework, but within the frame there is a structure too. It is suggested by the desire Kassandra voices to follow the *thread* of her life, which is of course the thread of her own subjective experience, but there is also a progression, as we have seen, towards self-realisation and towards the present, which is open-ended. It is a gathering in of experience, a pulling in of threads towards a centre. Some symmetry is given to the novel by the three 'ships' or expeditions to Greece, but these are not the crucial factor (and the second ship is mentioned before the first!). Structure is given to the novel principally by its symbolism which runs parallel to Kassandra's development and self-discovery.

The narrator's framework immediately suggests the importance of symbolism: a laconic voice presenting a visual image. As Kassandra herself states, 'The last thing will be an image. Words die before images' (p. 26). In the course of Kassandra's story we find certain symbols emerging and re-emerging, some gaining in importance as the story proceeds, emphasising its main theme of the struggle for autonomy. Two symbols may be singled out here: the willow tree, and the symbolism of light and darkness. We have already mentioned the willow tree as dual symbol of fertility and sterility. It is also a traditional symbol of mourning, hence its appropriateness to Kassandra's *Trauerarbeit*. Baskets are woven in the Scamander community, a symbol of its closeness to nature; piglets are sacrificed on willow branches to Cybele. Out of the willow Kassandra makes herself a bed, on the advice of Oinone (Oenone in Greek mythology was granted healing powers by Apollo). But the willow-branch bed of the Scamander community does not help her in the way it is intended to. Part of the door of her prison is also woven from willows, at once a symbol of her dissociation from the community and, as it becomes, a link with the outside world. For she works in order to find a hole through which may be perceived the light of day and to communicate with the women outside. A willow basket is also her last abode before she is killed by Klytaimnestra. There, too, she is able to see light. Throughout the novel, light is contrasted with darkness. The darkness of Kassandra's place of death is mentioned in the novel's opening paragraph. It is used not only in connection with death, but also with blindness, madness (the German word *Umnachtung* combines the two concepts of insanity and darkness), oblivion. Kassandra lives in fear of this darkness. The patriarchal society she inhabits is depicted as primitive and regressing to a darker age. Her friend Myrine is described as bright and bold, burning with passion, in contrast to the dark, self-destructive Penthesilea. Light eventually conquers darkness, corresponding to Kassandra's increasing inner awareness, her ability to see. It is also significant that the symbolism of light is used in the narrator's concluding remark: 'In the changing of the light they [the stone lions] seem to move.' This is clearly a message to the reader, a challenge to look within. In sum, the symbolism of light and dark reflects the novel's underlying themes: the constant friction between consciousness and unconsciousness, sanity and madness, acceptance and refusal. These two symbols, that of the willow and that of light, are interwoven, mutually complementing each other, developing in meaning and thereby creating tension. This use of symbols is typical of the novel.

Closely related to the novel's symbolism, its structure, and to the centrality of the subject, are dreams. To begin with Kassandra, unlike some others, places great importance on dreams and their interpretation. Dreams are scattered through her narrative. She interprets Priamos's and Polyxena's dreams, and there are her own dreams which she discloses to others. They reveal to her human weaknesses rather than strengths, closely connected as several of them are to feelings of guilt and sexuality. It is evident from attitudes to dreams in the novel that people understand them in different ways, interpreting them as it suits them and as the logic of the situation demands. Through Kassandra's story we are able to see that dreams do not necessarily yield all their meaning to the individual, but are related to deeper wishes and anxieties. In a dream she remembers Apollo giving her the gift of seeing, but the important part of that dream is that he appears to her first as man, then as wolf, to conquer her; she rejects him. Her mother Hekabe tells her she should have had no fear of submitting, and puts about another 'official' version of the origins of her prophetic powers, in which snakes licked the inside of her (and Polyxena's) ears while their nurse Parthena was sleeping. Thus a rift is seen between her version of the truth, with its implication of the fear of being sexually overpowered, and the court's version, implying punishment for another's neglect. Later she has a dream in which the sun-god Phoebus Apollo and the moon, Selene, are in contest in the sky to see who can shine brighter. Apollo's out-shining of Selene is seen by Kassandra as a judgement on herself, a guilty verdict. Marpessa tells her she has asked the wrong question, and who is right or wrong we do not know. Kassandra's need to interpret and see her own guilt is a constant feature of her story. Without it she is nothing.

There comes a point however, when Kassandra's dreams become less important. In one of the worst atrocities of the war, when the conflict is well advanced, Achilles burns the corpse of his lover Patroklus and kills twelve Trojan prisoners. 'From this day on I no longer dreamed' (p. 132). This marks an important stage in her progression towards the subject. As dreamer she is subject to outward forces within herself. As her self-consciousness grows her decisiveness and will-power develops, resulting in her ability to review her life;

the conscious element begins to overcome the irrational one. In a brief conversation with the charioteer before Klytaimnestra's palace, she shows her awareness of a dialectic of victory and defeat. She avers that victory is self-perpetuating. Only consciousness of defeat and the recognition that defeat and destruction (*Untergang*) are part of human nature bring ultimate insight into history. History must not be allowed to repeat itself; a vision of the future, beyond defeat, is required. This is Kassandra's position, and she says of the charioteer's remark that it is the 'question of all questions' (p. 132).

Questions are by their nature verbal, and this novel has a striking verbal texture. There is tension between words and images on the one hand (shown by the necessity of putting dreams into words) and there is tension between the different strands of language as well. Kassandra's struggle for autonomy is also a struggle with and for language. As she asks early on, 'Who will, and when, find (the) language again?' (p. 26). (The German text here, 'Wer wird, und wann, die Sprache wiederfinden', separates subject from object by a temporal phrase and uses the definite article to create ambiguity.) In this war, one of the greatest battles of history, there is also a war of language. This is one of Wolf's lasting insights. We have seen that this society is based on a hierarchical structure, with a small influential group at the top and the mass of people at the bottom. As the war progresses it is necessary to win the people for the cause even if they have to be deceived. (Parallels with recent history, to the Third Reich and to the Cold War, are intended here.) A key figure in the process of influencing the people is Eumelos, Priamos's chief of arms. He it is who sees that new terms are introduced, that language is 'regulated' as the situation demands. This official language sees things in black and white, in terms of friend or foe, victory or death. 'Functional innovations' (*zweckmäßige Neuerungen*) are made, words like *Feindbegünstigung* (favouring the enemy), and glib phrases like 'He who does not stick with us is working against us' are introduced. The word 'war' (*Krieg*) is obliterated and becomes replaced by *Überfall* (storming, p. 82). The word 'guest' (*Gastfreund*) is eliminated from the official vocabulary of the palace as the Greeks become the enemy. People are given tags (like Priamos, 'our mighty King', 'the very decisive one'). Phrases like 'special measures for the controlling body' (*Sonderbefugnisse für die Kontrollorgane*: p. 116) and the notion of the 'perfection of power' (*Machtvollkommenheit*: p. 117), which smack of bureaucratese and the levelling mechanisms of a totalitarian regime on the defensive, are part of the novel's powerful critique of language.

This rigid, divisive and destructive type of language stands in antithetical relationship to the authentic strand of language of Kassandra. Her aim, she says, is to speak with her own voice. That is the ultimate value, nothing else matters (p. 6). This involves feeling her way through the language of pain and suffering, fear and anxiety. Guided by her emotions on the one hand, she is determined to conquer them through language by giving an account of her story. We thus find hers to be the antithesis of the official language she hears insidiously taking a hold over the Trojan community. In creating an authentic language to reflect Kassandra's struggle for autonomy, Wolf has furnished a unique combination of the classical and the modern. Gnomic statements abound (e.g. 'Between killing and dying there is a third thing: life' p. 134); one often finds the archaic preposed genitive ('Groß vor mir stand der Klytaimnestra Rache' (Great before me stood Clytemnestra's revenge: p. 63); sometimes sentence structures seem inspired by classical diction: 'O über die furchtbare Fruchtbarkeit der Hekabe' (O alas for the frightful fertility of Hecuba: p. 91), or inspired by the metres of poetry ('Fähnchen, Winken, Jubel, blinkendes Wasser, blitzende Ruder': p. 42); stichomythia is used to break the flow of the first person narrative, for charged moments of dialogue, as in Kassandra's words with the charioteer.

All this adds variety to the language of a novel which, because it is a sustained first-person narrative, might otherwise run the risk of being monotonous. But it cannot be said that it makes an overall classical impression. In many ways Kassandra's narrative is close to modern everyday colloquial German, emphatically so for it is a spoken narrative. As distinct from much of classical literature, it follows completely the narrator's spontaneous account to an intimate listener of her own life. Many pithy statements (e.g., 'So war es immer, wird es immer sein' (That's the way it always was, the way it will always be: p. 89) are equally characteristic of modern German. Characteristic of the spoken idiom, direct and down-to-earth, is the frequent use of ellipsis ('Blieb Kalchas der Seher' ([There] remained Kalchas the seer: p. 44); 'Soll ich doch absteigen' (Should get down I suppose: p. 88); 'Kann ja nichts mehr verschieben ...' (Can't put off any more)) and of elision, especially in the final syllable of verbs (e.g., 'Sie lacht, hör ich die Weiber sagen, die nicht wissen, daß ich ihre Sprache sprech': p. 8 and *passim*). These are characteristically modern linguistic features, then, which help to produce the effect of urgency and spontaneity. This, combined with the more classical features, help to produce that tension which characterises her story. Those critics who feel that demands of the ancient myth clash in *Kassandra* with modern psychology (see Stephens and Wilson, 1987, p. 292) neglect the power of its language and its link with the struggle for autonomy. The struggle for autonomy, the search for a language to express the individual's feelings is as real now as it was then.

Kassandra's language has a descriptive power very different from the language of the ancient epic. It has some of the qualities of Büchner's prose, whose 'fantastic exactitude' (*phantastische Genauigkeit*) Wolf admires (Wolf, 1978, p. 32). There is certainly attention to detail and no attempt to reject mimesis, but which details are selected is determined by Kassandra's heightened state of emotion; she chooses details which become symbols in the descriptive process. Thus we find passages like the following, which bring action to life, stretching sentence structure to an extreme:

Ein Pulk von Griechen, dicht bei dicht sich haltend, gepanzert und die
Schilde um sich herum wie eine lückenlose Wand, stürmte, einem einzigen
Organismus gleich, mit Kopf und Gliedern, unter nie vernommenem
Geheul an Land.
A pack of Greeks, holding close as close together, clad in armour, and
their shields around them like a wall without a hole, stormed, like one
single living thing, with head and limbs, and a howling never before
heard, onto land. – p. 83)

We must remember too, that although Kassandra's story is a monologue, it
is in effect a conversation, a conversation with the self, at some points with
another character and all the time with the reader (see Hilzinger, 1986,
p. 146). To this it owes much of its spontaneity and directness. Without the
imagined counterpart of the reader or hearer everywhere implicit in the text,
this story would have no point. Symptomatic of this is the use of questions:
questions, however, which are often not posed in the standard form but, for
example, as emphatic statements or casual asides. One of the most important
questions Kassandra has to ask appears without a question mark and is all the
more arresting for that: 'When war begins, that we know, but when does the
build-up to war begin.' Kassandra's narrative could be called a series of
questions, and her story as a whole presents the reader with a question about
the future in the same way that a play by Brecht leaves questions open at its end.

Finally, it may be said that Kassandra's language lives from the combination of different elements. The net of her language is cast wide to include the
body and the senses. Hers is an intuitive and sensual perception of truth, as
the symbolism of the light and willow make clear. She knows the importance
of touch through her relationship with Aineias, and of sight ('Otherwise our
eyes spoke. That we loved each other' – p. 127). From the community she
learns the value of laughter, singing and dancing. This is all part of her
rebellion against restrictive forms of communication. But tension is never
absent from the senses, and it is only through her verbal recognition of the role
of other forms of perception that she is able to conclude her struggle.

In conclusion, we might return to the work's genesis and note how it was
written (appearing in 1983) against the background of the arms race and threat
of nuclear war on the one hand, and the growing peace movement and interest
in feminist theories on the other. Its topicality is manifest, and in so far as
none of these issues has disappeared, *Kassandra* is likely to be seen for some
time as a work of considerable *political* relevance. This is shown clearly by one
of the main strands of thought in the *Voraussetzungen*. But the lectures do not
offer an interpretation of the story; they are part of the work itself, showing
the origins of the search for a subject which continues into and is developed in
the story. Any programmatic element is secondary, and it has been shown in
detail here that this topicality is only one aspect of a novel with a deep and
intricate structure reflecting moral truths. By laying bare that structure with
its different time levels and its fluctuation between optimism and pessimism,

we have of necessity focused on the subject; we have seen the work's deepest theme to be that process of moving from being an object to being a subject, but the process does not end here: Kassandra becomes an object again, of the writer's imagination. This process touches on some of the most fundamental issues of literature: the relation of the individual to society and his position in history, the relationship between the sexes. But perhaps most importantly, it touches on the relation of the self to the self, that is, to different stages of the self and the maturation of the personality, as well as on the creative process.

REFERENCES

References by page number only relate respectively to the first edition of *Kassandra* and to the *Voraussetzungen einer Erzählung*, both published by Luchterhand, Darmstadt and Neuwied 1983. (The English translation, *Cassandra*, published by Virago Press, incorporates both texts in a single volume.)

GREINER, B. (1985), 'Mit der Erzählung geh ich in den Tod': Kontinuität und Wandel des Erzählens im Schaffen von Christa Wolf, in Mauser (ed.), 1985.

HASS, F. (1988), *Christa Wolfs 'Kassandra' als 'Modellfall politischer Erfahrung'*, Frankfurt: Peter Lang.

HILZINGER, S. (1986), *Christa Wolf*, Stuttgart: Metzler.

MARX, J. (1985), Die Perspektive des Verlierers – ein utopischer Entwurf, in Mauser (ed.), 1985.

KUHN, A. (1988), *Christa Wolf's Utopian Vision: From Marxism to Feminism*, Cambridge: Cambridge University Press.

MAUSER, W. (1985), *Erinnerte Zukunft: 11 Studien zum Werk Christa Wolfs*, Würzburg: Könighausen und Neumann.

RISSE, S. (1986), *Wahrnehmen und Erkennen in Christa Wolfs Erzählung 'Kassandra'*, Pfafenweiler: Centaurus-Verlagsgesellschaft.

STEPHAN, A. (1975), Die 'subjektive Authentizität' des Autors, in *Text und Kritik* 46, ed. H. L. Arnold, 2nd revised ed., Munich 1980.

STEPHENS, A. and WILSON, J. (1987), Christa Wolf, in K. Bullivant (ed.), *The Modern German Novel*, Leamington Spa, Hamburg, New York: Oswald Wolf Books, Berg Publishers.

WOLF, C. (1968), Lesen und Schreiben, in her *Die Dimension des Autors: Aufsätze, Essays, Gespräche, Reden, 1959–1985*, 2 vols, Berlin and Weimar: Aufbau 1986, vol. 2.

WOLF, C. (1973), Subjektive Authentizität: Gespräch mit Hans Kaufmann, in her *Die Dimension des Autors: Aufsätze, Essays, Gespräche, Reden 1959–1985*, 2 vols, Berlin and Weimar: Aufbau 1986, vol. 2.

A Guide to Further Reading

The English-speaking reader who is approaching the discussion of novels and narrative technique for the first time would do well to turn to E. M. FORSTER, *Aspects of the Novel*, originally published in 1927, and available as a Penguin paperback since 1962. Other general works in English which it is appropriate to mention here are PERCY LUBBOCK, *The Craft of Fiction*, London 1921, and WAYNE C. BOOTH, *The Rhetoric of Fiction*, Chicago 1961. A systematic typology of narrative writing is provided by FRANZ K. STANZEL, *A Theory of Narrative*, Cambridge 1984, and for readers of German, Stanzel's earlier *Typische Formen des Romans*, Göttingen 1964 is also instructive.

Turning to the theoretical and programmatic pronouncements of twentieth-century German novelists, a very useful short anthology of these is HARMUT STEINECKE (ed.), *Theorie und Technik des Romans im 20. Jahrhundert*, Tübingen 1972. Two publications give comprehensive surveys of German theories of the novel since the seventeenth century; these are REINHOLD GRIMM (ed.), *Deutsche Romantheorien* (2 vols), Frankfurt 1968 and BRUNO HILLEBRAND, *Theorie des Romans*, Munich 1972, volume two of which contains individual chapters on Thomas and Heinrich Mann, Kafka, Broch, Musil and Döblin, as well as a general assessment of thinking about the novel after 1945. Other volumes which document the development of theorising about the novel in the twentieth century are VOLKER KLOTZ (ed.), *Zur Poetik des Romans (Wege der Forschung)*, Darmstadt 1965 and EBERHARD LÄMMERT (ed.), *Romantheorie: Dokumentation ihrer Geschichte in Deutschland seit 1880*, Königstein 1984. DIETRICH SCHEUNEMANN, *Romankrise: Die Entstehungsgeschichte der modernen Romanpoetik in Deutschland*, Heidelberg 1978, gives a close account of the development of thinking about the novel in Germany from the impact of Zola in the 1890s to the contrasting programmes effected by Heinrich Mann and Alfred Döblin in the 1920s. Scheunemann's book is also valuable for its critique of the assumptions behind the discussion of a 'crisis of the novel', which was widespread in mid-century and was epitomised in the German context by WOLFGANG KAYSER, *Entstehung und Krise des modernen Romans*, Stuttgart 1955.

There are two books available in English (and German) which may be regarded as standard works on Realism in the broad context of European literature; both combine a sense of Realism as a 'perennial' possibility in literary expression with a subtle awareness of the specific features which characterise Realist fiction in particular historical periods. These are ERICH AUERBACH, *Mimesis*, New York 1953, and J. P. STERN, *On Realism*, London 1973. An important recent study of the Realist tradition in France is CHRISTOPHER PRENDERGAST, *The Order of Mimesis*, Cambridge 1986. For a comprehensive study of the significance of literary Realism in the context of nineteenth-century Germany, see FRITZ MARTINI, *Deutsche Literatur im bürgerlichen Realismus 1848–1898*, Stuttgart 1962. RICHARD BRINKMANN, *Wirklichkeit und Illusion*, 2nd edn., Tübingen 1966, is a painstakingly cautious attempt to define the meaning of literary Realism with reference to the German nineteenth century; and STEPHAN KOHL, *Realismus: Theorie und Geschichte*, Munich 1977, gives a clear and thorough account of theories of literary Realism down the ages, from Plato to the German theorists of the twentieth century. Two short essays in English provide counter-perspectives to the frequent tendency towards abstract theorisation in German publications: J. M. RITCHIE, 'The ambivalence of "Realism" in German literature 1830–1880', *Orbis Litterarum* XV (1961), pp. 200–17, gives a pragmatic view of the various historical tensions to which the use of the term Realism in nineteenth-century Germany must be related; and RENÉ WELLEK, 'The concept of Realism in literary scholarship', *Neophilologus* 45 (1961), pp. 1–20, argues for treating Realism as a 'regulative' concept to assist critical discussion rather than as something existing in any absolute sense. (Both essays are reprinted in German in R. Brinkmann (ed.), *Begriffsbestimmung des literarischen Realismus (Wege der Forschung)*, Darmstadt 1969.) An interesting discussion of the concept of Realism in the light of more recent theoretical developments is STEPHEN HEATH, 'Realism, modernism, and "language-consciousness"', in *Realism in European Literature: Essays in honour of J. P. Stern*, edited by N. Boyle and M. Swales, Cambridge 1986.

A good place to start reading about Modernism as a broad European cultural development is the section on the modernist novel in MALCOLM BRADBURY and JAMES MCFARLANE (eds), *Modernism* Pelican Guides to European Literature, Harmondsworth 1974, pp. 393–496. This section includes an essay by J. P. Stern on Thomas Mann, and one by Franz Kuna on Mann, Kafka and Musil (together with Joseph Conrad), as well as an early version of David Lodge's discussion of the relative significance of metaphor and metonymy as structuring features in Realist and Modernist fiction respectively. An interesting recent attempt to define the 'code' of Modernism, with its emphasis on hypothesis and uncertainty, and its tendency to fragmentariness, is D.

FOKKEMA and E. IBSCH, *Modernist Conjectures: A Mainstream in European Literature 1910–1940*, London 1987, which includes chapters on Thomas Mann and Musil, but curiously excludes Kafka from the Modernist canon because his works do not display the *intellectual* self-consciousness about epistemological problems which Fokkema and Ibsch see as essential to the Modernist code. A representative of the school of thought which would distinguish 'Modernism' as a more conservative stylistic trend from avant-garde experimentation in the early twentieth-century novel is HELMUT KOOPMANN, *Der klassisch-moderne Roman*, Stuttgart 1983. The most stimulating general book in English on the German novel in the twentieth century is probably still THEODORE ZIOLKOWSKI, *Dimensions of the Modern Novel*, Princeton 1969, which contains individual studies of the works by Rilke, Kafka and Döblin covered in the present volume, as well as *The Magic Mountain (Der Zauberberg)* by Thomas Mann and *The Sleepwalkers (Die Schlafwandler)* by Hermann Broch. An important recent supplement to Ziolkowski, which situates the transition from Realism to Modernism in the German novel within the general context of shifting social and cultural awareness, is RUSSELL A. BERMAN, *The Rise of the Modern German Novel: Crisis and Charisma*, Cambridge, Mass. 1986. STEPHEN D. DOWDEN, *Sympathy for the Abyss: A Study in the Novel of German Modernism*, Tübingen 1986, offers a rather widely-cast and cursory introduction to the subject of Modernism, but with plentiful references to relevant theoretical texts, as a preamble to close studies of works by Kafka, Broch, Musil and Thomas Mann. Two important recent German publications which explore the complex intellectual background to Modernist prose fiction are PETER BÜRGER and CHRISTA BÜRGER, *Prosa der Moderne*, Frankfurt 1988, and JÜRGEN H. PETERSEN, *Der deutsche Roman der Moderne: Grundlegung – Typologie – Entwicklung*, Stuttgart 1991.

Two works in English are particularly helpful on specific aspects of the development of narrative technique in the period covered by the present volume. These are ROY PASCAL, *The Dual Voice*, Manchester 1977, for a broad-based discussion of 'free indirect style' (*erlebte Rede*), and DORRIT COHN, *Transparent Minds*, Princeton 1978, for analysis of innovative techniques for depicting mental states. Still of interest for its close studies of prose writing since the late nineteenth century is FRITZ MARTINI, *Das Wagnis der Sprache: Interpretationen deutscher Prosa von Nietzsche bis Benn*, Stuttgart 1954.

Other collections of essays on German novels, which range more widely over the period covered by the present volume, are HENRY HATFIELD, *Crisis and Continuity in Modern German Fiction*, Ithaca, N.Y. 1969; M. BRAUNECK (ed.), *Der deutsche Roman im 20. Jahrhundert*, Bamburg 1976, and P. M. LÜTZER (ed.), *Deutsche Romane des 20. Jahrhunderts*, Königstein 1983. WERNER WELZIG, *Der deutsche Roman im 20, Jahrhundert*, Stuttgart 1970, presents short descriptions of individual novels under encyclopedia-style headings, such as the 'political' novel, the 'historical' novel, the 'utopian' novel, etc. For broader coverage of the German novel since 1945 see MANFRED DURZAK, *Der deutsche Roman der*

Gegenwart, 3rd edn., Stuttgart 1979; KEITH BULLIVANT, *Realism Today*, Leamington Spa 1987, and KEITH BULLIVANT (ed.), *The Modern German Novel*, Leamington Spa 1987.

For further reading on the individual texts and authors presented in this volume, the reader should consult the reference lists given at the end of each chapter.

Index